NO PLACE FOR A WOMAN

NO PLACE FOR A WOMAN

Marie Christine Ridgway

To Jess

with best wishes

Marie Christine Ridgway

November 1991

LONDON

VICTOR GOLLANCZ LTD

1991

First published in Great Britain 1991
by Victor Gollancz Ltd
14 Henrietta Street, London WC2E 8QJ

A CIP catalogue record for this book is available from the British Library.

ISBN 0 575 05205 8

Typeset at The Spartan Press Ltd,
Lymington, Hants
and printed in Great Britain by
St Edmundsbury Press Ltd, Bury St Edmunds, Suffolk
Illustrations printed in Great Britain by
WBC Print Ltd, Bridgend

Contents

Illustrations

DEDICATION

'Once upon a time there was a little girl called . . .'

'What name, Mamalita?' my companion butted in impatiently.

'Elizabeth . . . Elizabeth Berg Huaman, and she lived with her granny and grandpa on an emerald green mountain. Beside her village was a river, where waters rushed down from snowy glaciers, and hurried to join the mighty Amazon. In the day the hot sun shone from a deep blue sky . . .'

Our shoulders hunched into a north-west wind coming straight from Greenland, as we battled our way home after the school bus had dropped this small pupil at the end of the tarmac. Three miles of rough path, morning and evening, gave plenty of time for storytelling, and this tale was often requested. I fear my companion understood only part of the story; part was born away by the wind, and part was yet to unfold.

You were my companion then, Elizabeth – then and now. So I am writing this for you, before our memories fade. It is a story about your new family and about your new home. It is also about you and how we came together, about your family in Norway and in Peru. It is a story which maybe one day you will want to tell to your children, for there are many different threads that are woven into its pattern: it was not brought together in any haphazard fashion. Writing it down has helped me see that what has happened was meant to happen – it was our destiny, and yours.

PART ONE

Marie Christine

Chapter One

FORTUNES

In the poorly lit caravan sat two figures, one old and hunched, the other a girl of barely sixteen, nervously twisting a thin silver ring on her right hand.

'Well then, let's have a look,' the old woman barked impatiently.

The girl placed her hands on the scarlet-clothed table between them.

'Open them up so as I can see.' The old woman picked them up in her own hands, dark and worn with age.

'Oh, yes,' she muttered. 'Oh, yes.'

'What can you see?' the girl asked timorously.

'You'll fall in love and marry your man. You'll travel plenty – yes, I can see that quite clearly.' She squinted into the creases of the young soft hands. 'Two children, both daughters, that's what you'll have, dearie.' She paused. 'And that'll be one shilling.'

The girl handed over two sixpenny bits and stepped out into a night bright with the flashing lights of the fairground. Her friend rushed up and shouted over the noise, 'What did she say, Bobby? Tell me.'

'Oh, that I'll marry a millionaire, and have ten children, and become a star before I'm twenty-one.'

'Oh, is that all? I am going to have six husbands and play at the Albert Hall, and be very, very rich.'

They laughed their way to where the rest of their friends stood beside the Lightning Skid, waiting for the green-faced passengers to get out so that they too could be shaken up and scared stiff. Elvis took over from Connie Francis as the monster slowed down and they rushed to the vacating seats. The two girls clung to the shiny bar, which held them in tighter and tighter while the monster hurled them up and down, swooping and diving as they screamed. Would life ever again be as exciting as this moment?

★

I had been a tomboy as a child but at seventeen I was impatient to grow up; I wanted above all else to be as beautiful as my two older sisters and for life to be exciting. I felt fiercely that it was time for the swan within me to emerge.

I was sent from my strict boarding school for the daughters of naval officers to a finishing school in Arosa in the Swiss Alps, and then on to the south of France to learn to speak French and walk with poise. We practised balancing books on our heads for hours – I presumed it would be important one day.

Once back from France I hurled myself on an unsuspecting world in the early summer of 1962. I did not make much impact, but I felt that all my efforts had been leading to this point in my life where the adventure must begin. It was a time of parties and boyfriends, of swimming, tennis, fancy dress, cocktails, rock 'n' roll, balls, birthdays, more parties and yet more boyfriends – and then there was one special party.

I had read my horoscope: *You may meet someone this weekend who will alter the course of your life.* 'Oh yes?' I thought. 'A rather extravagant prediction.' But the words would come back to haunt me.

That evening was long ago; now I am a very different person, yet I can remember it all quite clearly. The party was at Burnham Beeches, half an hour's drive from Beaconsfield, where we lived. I wore a black velvet dress which I hoped would make me look older and more sophisticated, and mask how shy and uncertain I felt. My brother James, whom I adored, was down from Oxford, and we drove to the party together in his old car. Turning off the ignition, we could hear the music flooding out of the brilliantly lit house. We went in, my heart thumping with excitement. Would I know anybody? Would anybody talk to me? This kind of gathering was a ritual devised by families to try to make sure that their offspring were introduced to suitable partners; guest lists were carefully checked through; it was a marriage market. Despite this, I would sally forth to these parties with romantic hopes in my heart, longing to be swept off my feet by somebody different. The prospect of marrying and settling down in the Home Counties filled me with a sense of despair: the predictability of it all horrified me. I liked to think I was different – but, for heaven's sake, different from what?

The people throwing this party were rich; the house was big and extravagantly furnished. Leaving our coats with a maid, we made

our way into a large drawing room. Set up in the centre was a
roulette table, the wheel spinning, people crowded round to see
where the silver ball would fall. James and I stood side by side. We
were handed glasses of champagne, and some chips to start playing
with.

This was fun: it seemed to me to have all the ingredients for a
good evening. We started to play.

'*Faites vos jeux*,' the Buckinghamshire croupier drawled. Carefully, I risked just two chips – one on Five and one on Red. Five was
my lucky number, and red was more daring than black.

Across the table, standing alone in the crush, was a tall fair-haired
man. He also went for Red. Our eyes met. His were blue; they
never flickered. He gazed long and hard, no smile to soften a look
that burned with intensity. I looked away. I was not in control of
this: my romantic heart was like the silver ball now spinning wildly
out of control in the wheel of fortune.

The wheel slowed and the silver ball rattled to a halt. '*Cinq, impair
et rouge.*' The stranger and I had both won.

When I plucked up courage to look again at him he was talking to
somebody else. What despair! Would he come over and talk to me?
Would he think James was my boyfriend and leave us alone? But he
did come, and he introduced himself; we danced. We hardly spoke.
My mind was in a turmoil. Who was he, what was he, would we see
each other again?

By the end of the evening I had decided he must be a spy. He was
with the parachute regiment ostensibly, but he had come with a
powerfully built American who could not be anything but a CIA
agent. My mind was racing: I might get drawn into some net. How
would I cope under interrogation? Would I have to be dropped by
parachute at night into enemy country? I felt I could do anything
with this man by my side.

He drove me home in his white MG. He parked a short distance
away up the tree-lined avenue, and kissed me. My whole body
somersaulted with desire.

'I'll call you,' he said. Then there was a roar, and he was off. I
hardly slept that night. I was in love.

We married in 1964 on 21 March, the first day of spring. Bobby was
laid to rest – John preferred my real name, Marie Christine. It was a
wonderful windy day: photographs show my petal-scattered veil

nearly touching the tree tops. Our parachute regiment guard of honour performed a mock battle outside the church during the wedding ceremony, and all but ran through the photographer with their swords.

This was to be John's last official engagement in uniform: he had decided to resign his commission, and our plan was to head north. We fervently hoped to make a life for ourselves somewhere remote by the sea in Sutherland. We had no very clear idea of how we would support ourselves. John thought he could get a job with a fishing boat, and I naively thought I could make some money keeping bees and producing honey.

His white MG had been exchanged for a green minivan which we stacked up with our wedding presents, the top tier of our wedding cake, and John's fishing rods. The journey took forever, but I did not care. I was with my husband whom I loved to distraction and would follow to the ends of the earth. What faith one has at twenty! How possible everything seems!

Our initial objective was to find somewhere to stay. In a totally exhausted state, after having knocked on many croft house doors in the area of Lochinver, we met Dolly. Grey-haired and with a comfortable figure, from what her layers of woollies permitted us to see, she had the beautiful smooth skin of a woman who lived with soft rain.

'Aye, you can have the caravan in the field over there,' she announced in her loud Highland singsong voice. She pointed to a green square bordered by a monumental dry stone wall, with an iron bedstead for a makeshift gate. 'We're very busy in the summer with the Beddy Breakfast, you understand, and the caravan is popular with the tourists, but if it's just a week or two you'll be wanting it for, and so long as you really are man and wife . . .' she looked sternly at us both – I am sure she thought we had run off together: I did not look particularly married, just a bit silly in my high heel shoes and flimsy clothes – 'I can't see the harm.' Her strong features broke into a smile, she pulled her home knit cardi tight across her ample chest and shut the door.

We unloaded the van and set up our first home. Sitting staring out at the grey hills all around us, I knew John was completely happy. Down from the field, and across the quiet single track road with grass growing up the centre, was a small freshwater loch; in the still evening light we could see tantalising circles dimple the dark water. Soon the hunter was out with his tackle casting his lure, setting the pattern of our days. We were always hungry, and we fed off the delicious nutty-tasting brown trout that John managed to catch, winding up our feast with a small cube of dwindling rich wedding cake. There was no spare cash to splash on food until we could get jobs.

We searched all around for somewhere to live. 'The MacPhersons at Ardmore are keen to go,' we were told. Where was Ardmore?

We found the beautiful rocky peninsula, fifteen miles south of Cape Wrath and three miles from the road, and even to my less restless spirit, this place beckoned. We could see in the distance, encompassed by barren hills, the curve of a green hill that is Ardmore, running down to the sheltered bay like a mother's soft arm protecting her sleeping child.

We first walked out on a soft spring day, when the trees on the sheltered side were bursting into leaf and loud with birds. The narrow uneven path, which led on from the metalled road to Ardmore, skirted the sheltered sea loch, Loch a' Chad-Fi. Up and down the rocky hills the path trailed with ever-nearing glimpses of a green welcoming place. Ardmore has the last most northerly wood on the west coast of the mainland of Britain. Half-way along the path at the top of Gentle's Brae you can see the ocean to the north-west; facing south you can see where Loch a' Chad-Fi flows into Loch Laxford which in turn leads out into the ocean. A narrow strip of boggy ground anchors Ardmore to Sutherland. Passing through a rickety gate at the bottom of the last long hill you are faced with the waterfall. It is hardly more than a trickle in summer to keep moist the ferns and bright the butter yellow kingcups. In deep winter, we were to learn, the rocks are covered with treacherous ice; but other times when it rains it is worthy of its name, as water cascades down and spills rushing on its way to the sea. Out of the trees and at the top of the waterfall is Upper Ardmore, two houses: the first one stone, Number 79, and three minutes on up the now grassy path, the second house made of corrugated iron, Number 80. This was the house the MacPhersons wanted to leave.

We enquired as politely as we could what were the MacPhersons' intentions. Johnny MacPherson was in his eighties and had had a stroke; he needed regular medical care, and his remaining two pretty daughters welcomed the thought of a brighter life. I was shocked to hear how Joey, all dressed in her finery, had once walked the three miles of rocky track to the road for a dance only to find she had gone on the wrong night. We managed to buy the small tin house and croft for £180.

A croft is the name for the ground, 'the in-bye land', which is usually fenced carefully to keep the sheep in for lambing, and fenced even more carefully to keep the sheep out from the potatoes and oats – crops that can survive late bitter springs, long growing days of endless light in June, spells of drought in early summer, and rain and more rain. Ardmore land yielded little, but just enough to sustain those that had lived here: two families at Upper Ardmore, and three families through the wood at Lower Ardmore in the stone crofts Numbers 76, 78 and 77. They were numbered as part of the Parish of Eddrachilles in the sequence of when they were built, not of where they stand. In the early summer of 1964 only two of the five families remained and no children.

Anxiety, however, surrounded our uncertain future, and soon marred the idyll. This anxiety was to be the spectre that has haunted our lives ever since, appearing with greatest insistence in the dark hours of the night. We needed work. The retired lieutenant and his new recruit searched in vain for jobs up and down the rocky convoluted coast. Most of our friends had poured scorn on our plans. 'You'll soon be back,' they had said. And sadly, within six months, we were. The great dream had become a nightmare, a dark trap into which we had fallen.

John had hoped to get on a fishing boat, and eventually to save enough money to buy one of his own. We talked of me being crew, but I wondered if I could handle it. We soon discovered this was a closed shop, any free places on boats were taken by relatives, certainly not a raw paratroop officer just up from the soft south. We did, however, manage to find jobs of a sort. I worked for the fish salesman on the pier at the small fishing village of Kinlochbervie, a good ten miles north of Ardmore and too far to walk in and out along the track each day. John got two jobs: lifting fish boxes on to lorries for a pound a night and, in the day, assisting the crew of a salmon coble, setting and lifting the bag nets twice daily. This went well until he suggested a more efficient way of operating the scheme which meant losing one of the team; he was the one who was dropped. The only job now left for him in the day time was that of mending fish boxes on the pier. John knew he should better justify the expense and time spent on his education and Sandhurst training.

At night we would go back to our caravan close to the old wooden pier on the rocky shore of Loch Clash. We shared our cramped home with a sporting border terrier called Tottie cursed with terrible bad breath, and also one of John's army friends. The set-up did not fit with my romantic idea of married life. But how to get rid of him? I could not confide in John, who enjoyed his friend's company. Tottie's breath, and prunes for supper most nights, sent him on his way eventually.

Above all else, John wanted to live at Ardmore, but we knew that crofting was no real alternative, it would have been like retiring, certainly not the challenge John was seeking. I felt miserable as John became more wretched for, ironically, the very thing he had trained for during his time in the army was now happening: his battalion was seeing action out in the Yemen. I knew he would have loved the excitement of being out there with his friends, and here he was stuck with me in a caravan in the north of Scotland thinking his life was over, and that he had missed his one great chance.

So we headed south. John got a job counting traffic in London, and I worked as a temp at Kilburn Town Council. I felt the great dream was over, and I was now just an encumbrance. In the autumn John was lucky to be taken back into his regiment, and I got a well-paid job in Farnham close to Aldershot where we bought a small terrace house on a huge mortgage which we vowed to pay off in three years.

The croft at Ardmore was still ours, but how could we live there? Whenever we could we would dash north, driving all night and day in the minivan. Sometimes it was a long weekend, sometimes a brief holiday but always to work on the croft house; to boat over and carry up the steep hill a cast iron bath, roofing material to patch the leaky roof. The jobs were endless if this small house clinging to the hillside was not to become a ruin, and I knew it meant much to John. As for me, I was not yet sure.

Disappointment firms the resolve. 'We're not finished yet,' John would mutter frequently, and his chance did come. Spurred on by failure and the wish to do something extraordinary in his life, he set off in the early summer of 1966 to row the North Atlantic.

John had been restless ever since returning to the army. While we were at Ardmore the previous summer we heard on our battery-powered wireless a Farnham man, David Johnstone, being interviewed. He was talking about his proposed trip to row the Atlantic the following summer. I thought it sounded preposterous, highly dangerous and probably impossible; I was getting to know a bit about boat trips going up and down the loch to our tin house. But not John; the idea totally captured his imagination and straight away he tried to make contact with Johnstone to ask if he could go with him. We hurriedly returned to Farnham so that they could meet, but it was obvious they were not compatible. John went into overdrive, completely obsessed with the idea. He decided on a plan to race Johnstone's boat, the *Puffin*, across the North Atlantic the next summer, and started searching around for a partner. One early choice was dropped because of his chronic seasickness, I was painfully aware that if no one else came forward maybe I should offer myself. Then Chay Blyth, a sergeant in John's platoon, said he would be keen to accompany John. We knew he was the right man from the start. Tough and resourceful, Chay had been a champion swimmer, both in his youth and in the army, and John knew him well from long-distance canoe races they had done together. We had both thought of him as a possible partner but John did not think it fair to ask him because he was married. I found that Maureen, his wife, felt much the same as I did; this was the great adventure our husbands craved for and who were we to stop them. Peacetime soldiering can be frustrating for a certain type of man, both John and Chay were of that kind.

The trip was mounted on a shoe-string. We borrowed money from the bank on our house and life insurance to finance it, and I had to keep working to pay off the loan. The army allowed the two men unpaid leave for the summer. It was totally crazy but I knew John had to do this for himself. People could not understand why I was actually helping rather than discouraging him.

The night before they left for America we danced for hours together, the following morning John's foot was swollen, when he landed in America he had to be hospitalised: he had a badly poisoned toe. It was not an encouraging start. The rowing boat which had been built in Britain arrived and Chay had to row it round the dock for a few curious American pressmen. He had only rowed Maureen round the Serpentine before and had difficulty manoeuvring it. The press were sceptical about the two lunatic British paratroopers' chances.

Final phone calls were all too brief and unsatisfactory. They set off from Cape Cod on 4 June 1966, several days after Johnstone and Hoare. Maureen and I were desperate for any news of our husbands, we could not help but worry. We had read a quote from the Cape Cod Coastguard: 'This attempt has a ninety-nine per cent chance of suicide.' We had no radio contact with them and relied only on sightings from ships, we got three messages during the entire trip.

Contrary to all predictions, John and Chay achieved their almost impossible goal. After ninety-two days at sea in an open rowing boat twenty feet long, with no cabin or shelter, and having encountered two hurricanes, they made landfall on Aran off Galway in Southern Ireland. They had talked of making a reverse charge call to my uncle in Dublin to ask him for money to buy tickets back to England. They were amazed to find the world press waiting for them, fighting for their extraordinary story, and to see Maureen and I, for we had been rushed to Galway by a Sunday paper for the reunion, it was all wonderfully exciting.

Later on in September the chilling news came through that Johnstone and Hoare had perished. Their abandoned upturned boat was found in the middle of the Atlantic.

Almost nine months later to the day of our husbands' return two babies were born: first to come into the world was Rebecca Ridgway, shortly followed by Samantha Blyth.

Bec was just three weeks old when I caught my first sea trout on Loch Dionnard. Again we were spending our summer leave at Ardmore not far away, in the leaky tin house that now meant home to John – perhaps more to him than me. I liked our old terraced cottage overlooking the graveyard in Farnham, where we had electricity, running water, and a flush lavatory, small luxuries not to be found at Ardmore.

We had had to walk over the hills to get to this remotest of lochs, the tiny baby carried in John's rucksack. 'She's the first bairn that's been up there for at least fifty years,' the keeper told us the following day on our return. The ruined croft house along the shore had long since been abandoned, but once there had been children, bringing this ancient valley alive with their laughter. The Highlands were full of ruins and deserted straths, and Ardmore with its gentle green sward of grass running down to the shore – perhaps because it looked so welcoming – seemed emptier than anywhere else. But we were to change that, for two years later, we were there again – to stay.

The rowing trip had dramatically changed the lives of both John and Chay. Suddenly they were no longer viewed as foolhardy and reckless but as national heroes, the army who had generously allowed them the three summer months of unpaid leave was now quick to cash in on their endeavour, by sending them off on a lengthy lecture tour to most of the major public schools around the country. In between, they were invited to many glamorous events, but it was disorientating, they had returned humbled by their experience. Why were they spared and not Johnstone and Hoare? More than ever, John wanted to return and live simply at Ardmore.

At last it almost seemed a possibility. But first John had two more ambitions, one was to get into the SAS and the other was to sail single-handed non-stop around the world. The first ambition was soon achieved, but the second was more difficult.

Some money had come from the book of their trip, most of it went in tax but at least now we were no longer in debt. Chichester and Rose had just circumnavigated the globe with a stop at Australia, John wanted to go the whole way without stopping. Once again we scraped around and with a bit of sponsorship we bought a thirty foot twin bilge keel sloop. It seemed huge and wonderful. John was not the only one with this idea, soon a race had been set up by the *Sunday Times*. Again with unpaid leave from the army John set off first, from the point where he and Chay had landed on the Aran Islands off Galway. There was much press interest this time, and a trawler which had been hired by a television news company got too close and hit John's fragile craft. The damage was not obvious but once he got south of the Equator he noticed the shroud plates on deck were lifting, these held the stays which supported the mast. Bitterly disappointed, he put into Recife, Brazil and managed to come home on a military flight.

I filled our small terrace house in Farnham with white lilies to welcome him home and tell him about an offer of another boat. 'No thanks, Marie Christine – I've had this plan, but we are going to need all our cash,' he gazed rather disapprovingly at my extravagant floral gesture.

'I've thought of a way we can live *and* work at Ardmore.'

John had dreamed up the idea whilst on the single-handed sailing trip. We would try and run courses for children, during the summer at Ardmore, where they could climb and sail; in the spring and

autumn we would run courses for adults. Nobody took us seriously until we went ahead and printed a simple brochure. In it
John wrote, 'I decided to create a small enclave, a corner of the
world where people could experience the same direct confronta-
tion with the elements which I found so satisfying.'

The place with its awesome beauty lifted any jaded soul and we
were happy to share it with others. Once again we were about to
try and survive on our own in the Highlands. In October 1968 we
packed our belongings and took North what would be useful –
leaving behind our few precious electrical items. Bec was one,
blonde and fragile-looking. I was now a twenty-four-year-old
mother and wife who believed she could be pioneering and
resourceful. John was a twice-retired army officer of thirty. This
time we could surely make our living here.

We were a curious pair John and I: he a restless soul, ever
seeking greater challenges, feeling only truly alive when testing
his own mortality; and me – who on earth was I and what was I
doing about to embark on this desperate struggle? I am sure my
family had expected me to make a reasonable marriage, to live in
comfort in the Home Counties, to bring up my 2.4 children well-
mannered and accomplished, and to create a charming home for a
man who would protect me from the harsh realities of life. Yet
here I was living at Ardmore standing sometimes very still,
thieving time that should have been spent on the daily tasks,
gazing beyond the green pasture of our croft, across Loch a'
Chad-Fi, loch of the spindrift, linked to the oceans of the world,
towards Foinaven, Arkle, Ben Stack, and Cran Stackie and southerly towards Ben More Assynt and Quinag – great rocky spurs of
gneiss and granite thrust up three thousand feet from the sea bed
long before man was born. This was certainly enough to fulfill all
my romantic longings, but there was a harshness too, for which
John was far better prepared than me.

I had been so sheltered all my life. My father was an Air Marshal.
He had held many key posts abroad during the Second World
War. My mother chose to be at his side; so my two sisters,
Yvonne and Susan, and my brother James spent the war years
with my Irish grandmother in County Wicklow. I was born seven
years after Susan, at the end of the war, not long after my mother
had survived from being in a torpedoed ship and feared dead. My

father was then fifty and had taken over the peacetime job of setting up and running London Airport.

We lived in an old village called Longford. In our rambling garden there was a hollow tree where Dick Turpin, the infamous highwayman, would hide before holding up the London to Bath stagecoach. It was a happy time for my mother and father: we were all together as a family at last. We did all the things families did. We went off on summer holidays to Ireland to see the Irish relations, and on trips to Aldeburgh where my father had spent his youth.

On one of the frequent picnics, my elder sister took a photo; then in white ink the names and place were written on the stiff black paper of her bulging photo album. 'Mummy, Daddy and Bob aged 5 – Datchet – Summer 1949.' There are my parents stretched out on the grass, probably on the banks of the Thames where we would go and swim when it was hot. The small girl sitting between them, peaky and thin, her mousy hair tied up with two butterfly bows, her pale face furrowed in consternation, is probably cross, I do not remember. But it is the look of love on the face of her two parents, my mother and father, that has haunted me over the years. They loved each other, and they loved me; they loved all of us.

I grew up secure in this knowledge, but as I grew older I searched for challenge and excitement which I recognised in John the moment we met. He lived in Datchet. Maybe the day of that photo he had been a short way upriver, rowing his precious green wooden boat *Chinook* to secret fishing spots. When fate brought us together, thirteen years later, he would hold me spellbound with stories of how we would sail around the world, of the mountains we would climb, of the faraway place we would make our home.

I was young and naive, and very struck by the dashing parachute officer who would whisk me off to London in his white sports car. I did not really understand why he married me. He used to say it was because I could make a fish pie for two shillings. It was hardly an explanation to satisfy my doubts, when I needed reassurance, but it was true I could make a passable fish pie for not much, and fish pie after fish pie I did make that first season at Ardmore.

We were lucky the school ever got off the ground. Before we started many said, 'People will never go all that way for a holiday.' Yet, one of John's favourite maxims, 'Luck favours the bold', came true: February 1969 was bitterly cold and because of cancelled sports fixtures, the *Sunday Express* ran a half-page story on our proposed school. It resulted in Willie the Post's worn post-office bag spilling out bundle after bundle of letters on to our kitchen table. It was a mixed blessing because, on top of all the other jobs piling up, all of the letters had to be answered. Each day Willie laughed as he undid his postbag, proud as if they had been a catch of silver herring, and each night my old manual typewriter clicked away till very late. I was getting exhausted and irrational and we had not even started, and when was this daily flow of letters going to cease? Eventually it stopped, we got the brochures sent out, and then, the excitement to cap all excitements, the bookings started to arrive. From a paltry ten reservations before the article we managed to fill nearly all of the 250 places we had available.

Our clients, children and adults, came for one or two week courses. Some slept under canvas, others in a ninety-foot building we had bought from a bankrupt company. Their days were filled with hill-walking, canoeing, dinghy sailing, yachting down to Handa Island, orienteering, rock climbing. People seemed to like the formula, for it was a good way to forget the preoccupations of work and home. After all, if you are abseiling over a cliff with a fifty-foot drop to the water below, or battling to keep your sailing dinghy upright, it can put normal worries into perspective. Above all else, it seemed to be fun, and normally rather grave men and women would fall about laughing, forgetting themselves in the thrill of the moment.

'Yes, I can do the secretarial side,' I had said. I had worked at the Arts Council in the Drama Department before marrying, in elegant but shabby offices in St James's Square, off Piccadilly. I had taken down shorthand and typed letters regarding the increase and decrease of grants to provincial theatres around the country; I had made tea for Harold Pinter, and Peter Ustinov had complimented me on my pink skirt; on special occasions we would join the Director for a glass of Madeira, and shortbread would be handed round on a doyley covered plate. Handling the office at Ardmore was not the same at all. The work to be done was unending, typing letters at night with the Tilley lamp wobbling beside the clattering Underwood on the shaky kitchen table. During the day I was cooking, another task I had undertaken. It was not something we had really considered. I think we had half assumed those coming would cook their own food, but we knew that would not work for long. We never asked them to. 'I'll do it,' I confidently volunteered. John expected one hundred and one per cent effort from his team: me.

By now we had moved our few possessions out of the MacPhersons' house down through the birch wood to Lower Ardmore, to a fine, if leaky, stone croft house which we had been able to acquire, somebody wanted to sell it in a hurry, and we were just able to afford it.

We advertised letting the tin house in the *Sunday Times* and got eighty replies. Part of that first summer was exceptionally dry and hot, one irate tenant complained bitterly that the well had run dry and what was I going to do about it. I refunded him most of his rent and, as an afterthought, to cheer him I said what a good suntan he had acquired: 'This is dirt!' he shouted angrily back at me.

In the small pantry at the back of the croft house I set up my kitchen and got very fit carrying up provisions from the shore, a hundred feet below. We managed to lay water on from a freshwater loch above Ardmore and piped it down a long alkathene black snake. This was luxury: I now had a tap coming through the window with precious water. Bec played in the small wild garden whilst I cooked dish after dish of food on the two domestic cookers we had not very successfully converted to calor gas. Occasionally they blackened everything in the oven; too late to start again, I would try to salvage meringue-topped lemon pies by scraping away the worst and liberally sprinkling on white icing sugar.

We would feed everyone in two sittings in one of the two main rooms: it was a squash with benches round the wall of the twenty-five-foot-square room. One of the young men who came to help instruct that first summer played the pipes, and after supper we would go and sit in the stillness of the evening and watch the dipping sun colour the rocks across the loch crimson, while bewitched by the haunting melodies of 'Morag of Dunvegan' and the 'Skye Boat Song'. Bec would jump up and dance like a sprite, her yellow plaits flying as she spun around.

I wanted to help John achieve his dream but the effort required was considerable. Exhaustion would sweep over me at the end of a day when I had cooked for up to fifty people, typed countless letters, collected provisions from the mail box five miles away, boated them across and manhandled them up the rocky shore, close to tears from the struggle. But there were other days that first

summer when we managed to find that elusive satisfaction of
achievement, of having been able to make our own mistakes and
successes, made all the sweeter from the knowledge of that first
failure to support ourselves.

Our work that year was shared by Rod and Jean Liddon, who had
come up with us from Hereford, John and Rod had been seconded
into the SAS based here from the parachute regiment in Aldershot.
Before John's attempted circumnavigation we had shared an army
hiring, and had got to know each other very well. Jean and I were
both young mothers, Jamie Liddon nearly the same age as Bec.
They had an old Land Rover which Jean drove with great panache,
and when going down steep Quarry Hill into the town it was hard
to decide whether it was safer to push Bec in the rickety pram which
was almost impossible to control, or to go with Jean who seemed to
have difficulty judging the distance from the lamp posts. We
laughed a lot and had great dreams for our future and for Bec and
Jamie.

We all put immense effort into our first season, with me in the
kitchen and the office at Ardmore, and Jean over on the southern
shore of the loch where we had put up the main school building.
John took the course members sailing on his boat, *English Rose IV*,
down to Handa Island, ten miles south along the rocky coast. (This
was the boat he had sailed to Brazil in his attempt to be the first man
to sail single-handed non-stop around the world, a race won by
Robin Knox-Johnston.) The boat was our flagship, it looked very
fine in the bay below Ardmore. When not at sea they would be
climbing the mountains and tackling the tricky cliff faces nearer
home, with Rod. In any spare moments Rod continued with the
building, there was still much to be done. Sometimes at night when
we had wearily dropped into our bed, the sound of Rod's hammer
would still be echoing around the loch. He exhausted himself with
the effort.

Also that first summer, the British Tourist Authority organised a
visit from the press, we hoped they would put us on the map with a
few good articles. It rained solidly for ten days before their visit;
there was mud everywhere. We were coping with our first-ever
course, which was going well, in spite of the poor weather, as the
young people were lively and giving it a go, but I felt close to panic
at the thought of seven journalists descending on us. We did not
have enough bedding, or, come to that, beds. Where could they

sleep? On top of everything else I would have to feed them for at least twenty-four hours, and how would it fit in with the forty course members and extra helpers?

The first car arrived at the end of the loch just as the sun started to shine. Several cases of wine and spirits were carefully unloaded from the boot and carried over the slippery seaweed to the waiting boat. Then came our visitors. They were an illustrious mob – well, perhaps it was more correct to say they came from illustrious papers: the *Times*, *Observer*, *Telegraph*, to mention a few. Food was of secondary importance. In fact, everything bar the contents of the bottles seemed of secondary importance. A wonderful party was to follow. Once they had dumped their kit at Ardmore, John took them to watch the course rock climbing. As I rushed round in a last-minute frenzy I could see in the distance the climbers like red ants climbing up a stone, across at Ardbeg. Ardmore is Gaelic for big hill, Ardbeg a diminutive echo across the loch, little hill, but its sheer face big enough and challenging for the rock climbing. The tour was soon over, our guests were keen to get back to our croft house and the booze. The party began. Bottles were opened, lobsters cracked, chairs broken, cream and blackcurrant mousse devoured with fingers of buttery shortbread.

The rain had left an intense clarity, and as the sun slowly dropped behind Cnoc na Suil into the Minch beyond the rocky Ardmore peninsula, an ever-deepening rose hue touched the mountains. These men from the city who had seen and done everything stopped to gaze at the beauty before them. God's hand touched us at that moment.

The journalists left the following morning, and shortly afterwards good articles appeared in the press. It was invaluable. Once again, letters of enquiry poured in from all over, and as they began to build up I wondered when interest would abate – at its height we received over five hundred enquiries in one week. They took some dealing with, though we knew how vital they were to us.

John's nightmare was that things might not work out and we might be forced back to the south of England once again. He hated the thought of having to return to Surrey, or Hampshire, or Sussex, of having to live in a stifling dormitory town and commute into London each day. The idea of having to conform filled him with a strange terror. He had gambled with his life on the rowing, and solo sailing, and now he wanted to live under the wide open skies, facing the physical challenge of existence at Ardmore, however precarious it might be. He needed space to feel his own identity.

John's needs and feelings were so strong they rather eclipsed mine: I just worried about him being so anguished. The last few years had shown me that I could adapt to just about anything. When we had first of all moved to Ardmore, there were times when I was totally dismayed by the isolation: the primitive living conditions; no chance to go out and buy something pretty to wear. Sometimes I used to think, 'This phase in our lives will end and we'll return again to the south, and start living in an easier place with kinder weather, in a house with electricity and water laid on, a house which doesn't leak when it rains, a house that you can drive up to and not have to carry in your shopping three miles along a hilly track, or battle up the loch in a wooden boat with an outboard engine that won't start.'

Sometimes I used to feel Ardmore was no place for a woman. Had I stepped out of life? Had I, by marrying John, become, in his words, 'a fugitive from society'? I missed my family very much and, even though my mother came up to visit us from time to time, I felt there was a big hole in my life. These thoughts crowded in on the black days, the days when the struggle seemed too great; the odds loaded against us. But most days I felt inspired by John's great enthusiasm, his dream for us to stand free and to live our days and years on this rocky peninsula on the outermost edge of the world. So many people doubted we would be successful in running the school, John and I were determined to show them they were wrong. Perhaps this one common aim over the good and not so good years has united us more than anything else.

The winter was a little easier for us all, but the fury of the weather shocked me. Our season ended in September, we knew that the weather would start to deteriorate around the time of the Equinox and great storms would blow in from the south-west. Overnight the bracken turned from green to brown, and soon the trees sheltered by Cnoc na Suil were stripped bare. The leaves of the rowan, silver birch, hazel, and alder, were torn from their branches and thrown to the mossy ground to lie in drifts amongst the tumble of rocks. Arrows of geese passed overhead, alerting us with their honking cry and beating wings. They were heading south to softer climes – a sound and sight profoundly sad, as they signalled the end of the brief northern summer and, for us, time to bid farewell to friends whom we had worked alongside. Now we had to secure and tie down anything that might be picked up and thrown about: roofs, boats, buildings – nothing was safe. Daylight hours shrank away fast, from the glory of our northern June when at midnight it is bright enough to read a book outside, to deep December when the daylight was cut to five hours. During these quieter months, we repaired our weary selves and continued with the improvements to the school.

Halfway through the next summer John heard from John Cowie, a distant friend in the parachute regiment. He too had left the army. He was now farming but wanted to pursue a career in photography, and had thought up a scheme to make a name for himself.

'How would you feel about leading an expedition down the Amazon, from its furthest source in Peru to the mouth at Belem in Brazil?'

'Well, I wouldn't be free until the autumn when our season here finishes,' John replied hesitantly.

I could tell he was keen, but was wondering how I would react. Running courses at Ardmore was certainly challenging but I knew John was greatly tempted – it was the life-and-death excitement that he seemed to thirst for. It was obvious we could not both go: the office had to be manned, and three-year-old Bec could not be left. I felt guilty anyway. She had been rather neglected during the two busy summers and I wanted to give her more of my time.

The Amazon plan proceeded in fits and starts. I knew I must let John go, but I was not very happy about it. We had survived two summers of gargantuan effort, but there was still lots to be done in the way of improvements at Ardmore. I realised it was sort of sour grapes on my part. I was not keen for him to go if I could not go myself. Yet I knew I could not possibly cope with such a trip. I just did not want him to be away from me. John reasoned, 'How can we pretend to be adventurous if we just stay at home?'

Of course he must go, and I just hoped I would manage to stop the whole show blowing away. Then I heard that John Cowie, the mastermind of the expedition, had met a glamorous Spanish-speaking, third-fastest-in-the-world downhill skiing lady whom he thought they should take along. Anna would be the only Spanish speaker of the team of four, John, Mac – an army medic sergeant mad about moths and butterflies – and Cowie. Although I had not yet met her, the legendary Anna seemed to possess all the qualities which I knew John would admire. I was in a turmoil of unreason-

able jealousy but I felt I had to keep quiet. To add to my distress, a
'friend' had sent me a newspaper cutting with a short note to say
how sorry she was to hear things were not going so well for John
and me. It was a report from the *News of the World* saying that John
Ridgway was planning to row across the Pacific with his girlfriend
who would be wearing only suntan oil – it should have read Fairfax
not Ridgway. Its rival paper, the *People*, had agreed to run a series of
articles from John on the expedition of, in their words, 'Three men
and a girl'.

The four left for Lima, Peru, on 3 October 1970. Their plan was
to go high into the Andes to find the furthest source of the Amazon
and then follow it on its four thousand mile journey to where it
spills out into the South Atlantic in Brazil. It would at times be a
treacherous journey. In his initial approach to John, John Cowie
had written: 'It has been described as probably the last of the
world's great river navigations. A lot of people have been killed
trying to navigate parts of the rapid- and whirlpool-infested stretch
where it is known as the Apurimac and plunges through five
thousand-foot gorges between densely forested mountains.' We
knew there were hostile tribes of Indians, the chance of illness and
altitude sickness.

I waved goodbye with a heavy heart as we watched the Inca
Imperial DC-8 jet take off. Sadly Bec and I could not stay long in
the south with my mother – there was so much to do at Ardmore –
so we set off on the seven hundred-mile drive home in the now
empty Land Rover.

Chapter Two

AMAZON

Bec and I plodded along the familiar winding track into Ardmore after our mammoth drive home. The late autumn day was warm, and the low October sun shed a deep colour upon our wild land. Bec clutched her favourite toy, her grey woolly lamb. I carried what I could manage. Tomorrow we would fetch the rest in the boat, if it stayed calm. Wearily we clambered down the path through the wood. The leaves had blown off the trees in a gale while we had been gone: the wood was diminished and shrivelled to its winter status of scrub.

Round the corner we went, and there stood our croft house, limed white and patchy roofed. We hurried to open the gate and take the few steps past my flowerbed, now a wither of summer blooms, and on into the rickety porch which had been built on to the house, as vital as an escape hatch is to a submarine, keeping the savage winter out of our refuge of a home. The geraniums lining the windowsills would soon need cutting down and protecting from the frosts, but their pungent smell welcomed us as I heaved off my rucksack and dropped the two heavy bags that had my arms singing with pain. We were home safe within the three-foot-thick stone walls.

Memories rushed at me of the summer just past: the many people who had filled the house, the dramas of each day, the laughter and despair – and now there was only Bec and me. And somewhere on the other side of the world John was battling forward to find the furthest source of the Amazon and follow this mighty river to the sea.

Bec was exhausted. Though she was only three few allowances were made for her, she just had to fit in with whatever was going on around her. I loved her for her valiant spirit: she was always with us in our struggles, and I used to wonder what she would turn into.

'She needs a brother or sister,' the friendly local doctor would say.

'Oh, I haven't time.' How could I ever manage with two small children and trying to run the school?

'It only takes a few minutes,' came the cheeky reply.

The fortune-teller's prediction would echo in my mind: 'Two children' – yes, but when? John delighted in Bec, but he wanted no more. He had seen too many of his friends get tied down with a wife, two kids, a mortgage and a black labrador.

Thumb in mouth, Bec collapsed on the small sofa which had been brought over with odds and ends of furniture from my late grandmother's house in Ireland. The last leg of the journey had nearly finished off an old oak chest which had always stood in the hall of her house in County Wicklow. It was very heavy, and the team who were lifting it out of the boat had lost their grip and it had fallen into the loch. We eventually hauled it up the nearly vertical hill and settled it into its final resting place in the small wood-panelled sitting room. I reached for the old paraffin Tilley lamp, which stood on the chest's polished surface, and took it into the kitchen to light it. Soon it would be dark. Striking a match, I lit the meths-impregnated wick and clamped it around the stalk of the lamp. The sweet meths smell filled the darkening room, and as the blue flames began to die I tightened the filler cap and gently started pumping the shiny round brass base, forcing the paraffin up the hot stalk where it would vaporise, filling the room with a brilliant light from the delicate globe mantle. I held my breath. Pumping too soon resulted in yellowy black flames leaping dangerously out of the top. Then you had to start all over again by undoing the cap to release the pressure and beginning once more with the meths.

Wonderful: it worked first go, and by its bright light I filled my kettle and placed it on the battered gas cooker. What sweet delight, what a rare pleasure, we had the place to ourselves. For the first time in what seemed like a lifetime, I was making tea for just my daughter and myself.

That autumn the gales were late in arriving. Sometimes on really good days Bec and I would set off in the old red and blue painted wooden boat with a basket containing a small gas stove and sausages. It was a treat to row to a nearby island, run up to the highest point screaming at the top of our voices, 'I'm the King of the Castle; get down you dirty rascal,' as Bec tried to push her mum off the high rock, and then to find a sunny sheltered spot to cook our lunch. What a paradise we had found! Gazing out on the peaceful islands in Loch Laxford and to the horizon's sharp edge with all the world beyond, I knew it was worth struggling for.

Now the days fitted into a more measured pattern than the hectic summer season. During the day, Bec would be beside me, playing and helping – sort of – with a multitude of jobs such as house painting and sorting through stores after the rush of the summer. In the evening when she had gone to her small bed under the eaves, I would answer the post which came in like a remorseless tide. Willie the trusty postie walked the hilly three-mile track each day in all weathers. He never failed. As old Mrs Fraser, the Rhiconich postmistress, would say, 'You can set your watch by Willie.' At four in the afternoon, in his smart navy blue uniform with red piping, cap at a jaunty angle, Willie would lay his canvas postbag down on the kitchen table, peering through his fast misting pebble glasses as he unpacked the mail, our link with the world beyond the loch and the mountains.

We had been home for little more than a month when one afternoon Willie announced in his singsong voice: 'Here's a telegram for you.' He pulled it from the top of the pile of letters, done up tightly with rubberbands, which were to be taken back to the small post office at Rhiconich. My shaky hands pulled open the envelope. Willie kindly stood by, just in case, his square frame blotting out most of the light from the one small kitchen window.

Raft wrecked. Lost most kit. All four still alive. Join me Iquitos. Love JOHN. I was stunned.

A short week, and several more telegrams later, I was queuing at the Inca Imperial desk at Heathrow to fly to Lima. I had spent seven busy days shutting up the house at Ardmore, taking the Royal Highlander overnight train with Bec to London, racing around to get replacements for the stuff John had lost, and visiting the Millbank Hospital for the necessary innoculations.

My mother had very kindly offered to look after her grand-daughter while I was away. She was far from happy at the prospect of me going out to South America as she had known one of my brother's friends from Oxford, who had gone on an expedition to the Amazon a year or two before and been killed by Indians. She tried very hard to dissuade me, but I was adamant. I knew I was being selfish, giving her cause to worry about me and leaving Bec with her, but I felt that unless I accepted John's invitation to join him on this remaining part of the journey I might not get the chance again, and in the future would always be the one left at home. But most of all I wanted to be with him again, more than anything else in the world, and I sensed he was missing me and needed me.

'Your luggage is way overweight.' The needle swung round the scale dial and I swallowed. Luckily there was no one behind me in the queue. Feeling foolishly melodramatic, I explained that the British Amazon Expedition had lost most of their vital equipment in a raft wreck and I had to get replacements out to them. My baggage contained more cameras, film, medical supplies and clothing. I had kept my own possessions to an absolute minimum. The check-in man at Heathrow took a lenient view, as it was not an overcrowded route.

I waved goodbye to two of the three most precious people in my world, and felt terribly alone.

Just before leaving I had a phone call from Anna's brother, Nick Asheshov, a journalist in Lima, following a letter he had received from his sister. The plan was that Nick would meet me at Lima and somehow I would get over the Andes and meet John in the Peruvian jungle town of Iquitos. The flight took forever. After a night stop at Caracas there seemed to be no one left on the plane who spoke English. On filling in the landing card I was just able to make out that I should declare any gold bars I was carrying in my luggage, an exciting thought for the ex-secretary from the Arts Council, St James's Square, London SW1. On arrival, panic seized me. How would I find Nick? How would I recognise him? Home seemed very far away as I made my way through customs, not understanding a word anyone said to me. A slim fair-haired man waved wildly at me from the barrier, startlingly different from the sea of dark Spanish Indian faces.

'I'm Nick. I'd hoped you could spend a few days in Lima, and try out the Pacific surf, but I've managed to get us two tickets on a flight to Iquitos in a few hours.' His enthusiasm was infectious. As we stopped outside his home, his children rushed out and I was introduced to his wife, Consuela. Waves of exhaustion were knocking me over as Nick showed me Anna's letter. 'Nicky, let her rest,' Consuela's soft voice urged.

Then it was time to get going again. The rickety old Dakota lumbered along the runway and heaved itself into the air. The crowded cabin smelt of the sweat of fear mixed with the reek of aviation fuel. We craned to look out on to the misty Pacific and desert. Soon we were climbing and passing the foothills of the *cordillera*, then up high, looking out on sharp snow peaks, every bump echoed by a gasp of fear from the passengers. Over the divide we went, down into the forest and across a flat sea of jungle trees stretching three and a half thousand miles to the Atlantic. Somewhere below, on a muddy ribbon of a river, John and his team had passed.

At first I thought it was heat from the aircraft engines that hit me as I stepped off the plane, but it was the midday equatorial sun beating down on the cement runway. It was like a constant blast from a furnace. I followed Nick to the customs hut. Temporary bamboo walls and roof gave relief from the piercing sun, a brilliantly coloured macaw screeched, and all around there were cages of sad-eyed squirrel monkeys waiting to be shipped to America for medical research. It seemed inconceivable that a day and a night ago I had been in England.

'Hello, Marie Christine,' I turned in the direction of the familiar voice, and that typically British greeting. John's head and shoulders showed above the crowd of dark South Americans. 'Come over here.'

Nick and I struggled through the throng. John was much thinner than when we had said goodbye in London, and tanned. He could also speak Spanish which impressed me greatly. After brief greetings Nick went off to find his sister, and we headed for our hotel. It turned out to be a pretty shaky place with bed bugs and foul latrines, but I did not care, I was just so delighted to be with John again.

Exhausted, I soon fell asleep under the mosquito netting. Some time later I was awoken by a deafening crash. Where was I? It sounded as though someone was trying to kick the door to our room down. *Crash* – someone *was* trying to kick the door to our room down. John leapt up. Pulling on his trousers, he hopped to the door. As he opened it I could see through the chink a white-skinned man of medium height, with thick, light brown hair streaked paler by the sun, his whole body hunched up in rage. It was one of the other expedition members. After a short exchange of angry words, John wearily shut the door again.

'What's going on?' I asked, shocked by our shattering awakening.

'We've had a tough time. Maybe a few days' break from each other, and things will seem better.'

John's few words worried me. I was dismayed to find my idyll shattered. I might be reunited with John, but was apparently right in the centre of a hornet's nest. On future expeditions I was to find that such strife is common, and frequently brought on by physical hardship. Living at close quarters, normally reasonable people can behave quite irrationally towards each other. Frequently it is the single-minded type of person who chooses to go on expeditions. He expects much of himself and feels let down if misfortune befalls another of the team, often blaming him for being careless – after all, the weaker person is jeopardising the aims of the expedition. The unfortunate weaker one will probably be feeling overcome with self-pity, and his low morale can take him on a downward spiral and split the loyalties of the group. It requires wisdom from the leader to be firm and compassionate and sometimes ruthless if the objective is to be achieved.

From what I could gather, this team was still together, but only just. But though not much camaraderie remained, they still shared an aim – to follow the Amazon four thousand miles from its furthest source to the sea. Even if the most challenging part of the voyage was over, there was still much journeying to be done before they achieved their goal; they had to stick together.

I was dismayed by this new experience of coming into a group of four who hardly communicated with each other, and, later, to find that they also resented me. Still, as I was there, and totally enthralled by all that was exotic and new, I resolved to ignore the atmosphere and not get drawn in.

I spent the next few days wandering around, dazzled by all there was to see. We were trying to fix our passage downriver, 2,300 miles to where the mighty river pours out into the Atlantic. The river mouth is so wide that if London were on the north bank then Paris would be on the south bank, and water flows out at the rate of seven and a half million cubic feet per second, a discharge more than twenty-five times greater than the Nile, its nearest rival in length.

The facts about the river Amazon were mind boggling, and so too, I found, were those about the rubber boom. 'An orgy of opulence and a frenzy of fear and madness virtually unparalleled in the history of the New World,' was how the Schreiders described it in *Exploring the Amazon*. It was the rubber boom which had spawned Iquitos. This island city set in a sea of deep green jungle, started as a small fishing settlement, but grew rapidly to a city of 15,000 inhabitants during the twenty-five years from 1890 to 1915. We could see faded, elegant buildings from that period, now mostly shabby shops, but still faced with brilliant Portuguese *azulejos*, glazed tiles; an old iron bandstand with its stained glass cornice; bronze statues set in now neglected squares.

Less important than its big sister, Manaus, further downriver in Brazil, Iquitos was nevertheless an important centre then for the collection and shipping out of rubber. Indians, mostly from the Huitoto tribe, were captured and forced into labour to collect latex, the milky sap that flows from the *Hevea brasiliensis* tree. The French word for rubber *caoutchouc*, is derived from the Indian word *cahuchu* – 'the tree that weeps', tears of terror for the atrocities that were committed by those in charge against the enslaved Indians if they did not collect their quota. Before rubber gathering started, there was a native population of fifty thousand living in the Putumayo area, lying between Iquitos and Manaus; six years on it was thought to be down to ten thousand, most of this decrease caused by murder and starvation.

Two young American travellers discovered what was going on by chance and came to London to publicise the facts. Eventually Sir Roger Casement was sent out by the British Government to investigate. Casement returned with first-hand accounts of the horrors to which the Indians were being subjected, but those whose exploitation he was trying to expose wasted no time in discrediting his reports, and their counter-campaign was greatly aided when, during the First World War, Casement was charged and executed for treason.

The ill-treatment of the Indians finally ended in an unexpected way: before the Amazon rubber boom had even started, an Englishman, Sir Henry Wickham, had collected seeds, packed them in banana skins and had them shipped from Manaus to London. Two thousand seeds germinated in the orchid house at Kew, and were then sent out the East, mostly to Ceylon and Malaya. By 1911, 1,500,000 acres of cultivated rubber trees were being tapped in the East, where the cultivated trees grew faster and yielded more than the Amazon wild trees. The prices then dropped so dramatically that the Amazon rubber millionaires were practically ruined overnight.

My first three days in Iquitos passed in a blur of heat. I was slowly acclimatising to the stifling temperature. Apart from trying to fix up our journey on down the river we also had to draw some more money. Arrangements carefully made in London counted for nothing out here, but after many cables and phone calls we managed to get what we needed. I did not mind about the hours spent waiting in the bank, for at least here it was cool. I would stare past the fierce looking armed guard at the door, out into the white-hot light of the main plaza and study the buildings lining it. Many had fine *azulejos*-decorated balconies. There was even a bizarre two-storey metal relic, now a grocery store but originally designed by Alexandre Gustave Eiffel for the Paris Exposition. It must have been a disappointment to the rich man who had had it shipped out bit by bit from France to impress his neighbours. It could not be lived in, because, being made of iron, it heated up like an oven in the day and was noisy with rain at night.

A cold shower taken several times a day helped to revive us as did stops at the many juice bars dotted around the main square. The favourite was the Apollo, which had just room enough for two people to stand inside. One wall was covered with a graphic picture of an Apollo space launch. Here breakfast was *huevos fritas*, the eggs always broken deliberately, *tostadas con mermelade*, and then wonderful tropical juices whizzed up in a liquidiser. There were so many different kinds of fruit that we had to call again and again to try them all. *Vitamina* was one of the best. It was a meal in itself, a syrupy textured drink made of avocado, orange, banana and other fruits which I had never seen before, with sometimes an egg thrown in. It was nectar.

In our search for a passage downriver we called first at the Booth Line Office and met Pat Nicholls, who was also the honorary British consul. He invited us round to his home, an old colonial-style bungalow, where his wife kindly gave us tea. Pat loved the tropics and enthusiastically told us many hair-raising stories, one in particular about a French explorer who had spent some time with the headhunters of Borneo. Named 'Viva la France' by the Europeans he fraternised with in the bars in Iquitos, he duly headed off into the jungle to try to find the Jivaro Indians who were well-known for killing visitors and then shrinking their heads. Predictably, he never came back. A year or two later one of his old friends was sold a shrunken head. It had been shrunk to the size of a fist and the mouth sewn together with string, but the eyebrows and wispy beard were instantly recognised as those of Viva la France. Pat showed us the gruesome object.

Pat also showed us his collection of deadly Jivaro Indian blowpipes, the largest of which were for human prey, and his many beautiful and varied orchids. His garden was like a zoo, with tame parakeets flying on to our shoulders, and a huge boa constrictor which he kept under the house and fed on pig. Here too we met the largest rodent in the world, the capybara, a docile creature, in appearance part bristly pig, part chunky dog. John took a photo of me scratching its nose which later featured in his slide show on the Ardmore courses. At every lecture, and much to my annoyance, he would say 'And here is a picture of the largest rodent in the world,' with his pointer wavering in my direction.

Pat had to leave the next day, and Nick had taken Anna back to Lima temporarily, so we were without our good contact and our fluent Spanish speaker. This made finding a passage that much more difficult. Up until a year before, Iquitos had been a busy free port, and people would fly up from Lima for weekends to buy duty-free goods which had been brought in by river. Stopping this facility, coupled with a severe attitude towards smuggling by the military on both the Colombian and Brazilian stretches of the river, had considerably lessened the amount of river traffic. Still, after knocking on many doors and much wrangling we finally found a boat going downriver. Then Anna returned and was able to secure the deal in her fluent Spanish.

It was late afternoon when we boarded our boat, the B/M *Addelita*. It was made up of a couple of ancient sixty-foot barges, one of them topped with a rather rickety wood–and–tin super-structure and both pushed by a tug. The fat bearlike captain was drunk and we were told he was an unlucky man by one of his friends seeing him off. His girlfriend clung to his side while he rang the empty cartridge case that served as a bell and signalled the engineer to start up; patches of sweat were already darkening his clean white shirt. As the setting sun coloured the sky and river red, all that was left of Iquitos was a silhouette of shabby grand buildings and stately palms. By now we were midstream, going along with the flood. The sound of the engine did not inspire much confidence: it would cut out then choke back into life, belching clouds of smoke. Suddenly we lost steerage: the rudder had broken. We realised then, in the dark velvet tropical night, that the rest of the crew were also drunk.

Eventually we limped into the bank a mile or so downstream from our starting point. The captain's pretty girlfriend was extremely angry about something, probably his continued drinking and the predicament we all found ourselves in, and after hitting him about his crewcut head and knocking his heavy rimmed spectacles askew she leapt for the bank and scrambled into the dark, her screams of abuse getting fainter as she disappeared from sight into the jungle.

It was clear that this was where we would spend the night. By the morning the captain and crew would, we hoped, be sober enough to repair the rudder and engine. We got on with hanging up our hammocks and mosquito nets. I had never done this before and, anxious not to appear as the limp wife just out from home unable to do anything for herself, I set about unravelling the confusing tangle of lines. I did not have much confidence in my knots, but John checked them and seemed to think they would hold.

Feeling nervous of the drunken crew, I then made my way cautiously to the stinking latrine hidden behind a dirty curtain aft. Somebody had left the hatch off the main hold, and before I knew it I had tumbled in. Terror seized me. What was in this filthy hole – rats? Floundering ten feet down in the stinking darkness, I could hear close by the engine running roughly, left on to keep the pumps going to keep us afloat. Where was it, and would I get mangled in its mawlike pistons? Somehow I struggled back on deck, hauling myself up on sacks and boxes. Feeling shocked but relieved to be alive, I went with greater caution towards the stern and the latrine, which was as revolting as I feared.

'All well?' John asked from under his mosquito net as I tried to clamber into my hammock and then tie the strings beneath the hammock to make the net mosquito-proof.

'Yes. Fine,' I lied, as I nursed my bruised body and tried to get comfortable in this unaccustomed angle. How people slept, made love, gave birth and died in hammocks I could not imagine.

The next little test for me were the cockroaches. Feeling quite secure at last in my hammock, with the mosquito net tied around it, I lay thinking on the day and wondering what was to come. Before long I noticed large black cockroaches landing on the net around my hammock. They must have been attracted by the single light on our crippled boat and had flown out from the thick jungle riverbank. At all costs I must not panic, but were these huge beetles on the outside of the net or – terror of terrors – trapped on the inside, ready to fall on my defenceless body? I woke John, who rather gruffly told me not to be silly.

In the darkness, trying to quell my fears, I reflected on my weaknesses. I had severe doubts about myself. It was obvious I had not had the military training of the three chaps, nor the discipline and determination that Anna undoubtedly possessed to achieve what she had on the downhill skiing. Yet I knew that if I was not self-reliant and cheerful I would be a burden, and the fears of the other three would be confirmed. Most of all I wanted to impress John. Plenty of chances would come my way.

At dawn I awoke to the screaming of jungle birds. The sun was creeping up above the thick green trees into a pale blue sky, and wreaths of mist steamed up from the milky brown water. It was going to be another scorcher. The cockroaches of the previous night had not eaten me, but we all found we had been quite badly bitten by mosquitoes. Efforts were made by the hungover crew to get the boat going again, and we lurched forward – this time to the other bank. There they found the damage to the engine more extensive, dismantled the gearbox and sent it upriver back to Iquitos for repair.

I felt a bit like Katharine Hepburn stuck on the *African Queen*. However, the day passed quite pleasantly, as I learned to play bridge with a young Italian from Milan, called Stephano, and Mac. Poor John lay in his hammock with a bad stomach, probably caused by eating the tomatoes we had found growing on the bank in a yucca plantation where we were moored. Mac, the fount of all medical knowledge, told us the Indians peed on them to make them grow better.

In the late afternoon the captain told us they had not been able to fix the gearbox, and that he would try to go upstream to find a *mechanico* at a Canadian mission between where we were and Iquitos. In the end, the captain left us on board for another night, and the following morning we flagged down a palm-roofed dugout canoe heading back to Iquitos with a top-heavy cargo of bananas.

Still unused to the exotic surroundings, I found this a thrilling trip, but my main concern was how to pee. The Indian women on board wore ponchos; they could just sit on the side of the boat in these large cloak-like garments and no one could see what was happening underneath, but I was in trouble. I was wearing trousers. Eventually the boat put into the bank where I had to leap out and get up the crumbly red cliff so I would be out of sight and into jungle. Imagining jaguars and giant anacondas, I did not linger long. I was thrilled to hear a bird's call which exactly mimicked the sound that introduces the song, 'The good, the bad and the ugly,' but without wasting too much time looking around for Brynner and Bronson I hopped back down the bank to the boat, thankful I had not eaten the tomatoes of yesterday.

Late in the afternoon, two days and nights since our departure, we arrived back at Iquitos. Because we were one of the last of the small traders in for the night we had to tie up some distance from the bank and cross the many boats moored there. We formed a chain to offload our luggage and the bananas, the last section being another test for me: we had to walk along a single shaky plank to the shore. It was balanced above stinking grey slime, and our torches picked out huge grey rats which were scampering around below. The rotten smell was sickening, and once ashore we found the cause of it: we were just beside the municipal slaughter house and all useless bits of beasts were just chucked into the river, supporting a colony of monster rats. This time I did not lose my footing. I was learning fast.

Since my joining the expedition five days earlier we had made absolutely no progress down the Amazon, but it had been a good grounding for me, and I was acclimatising to the exhausting heat. Our search for another boat to take us on, however, was becoming increasingly difficult, because there was now a fuel shortage. Stories also abounded of a huge drug trade to America, so the authorities were highly suspicious of us. Still, we had to get on down the river so we paid the high fee of fifty pounds to a canoe captain to take us on the two-day trip to the Colombian border. He had a dugout canoe with a palm leaf thatched roof and a twelve-horse-power outboard.

We made good progress during the day, and the first night tied up to the bank in a big thunderstorm. John and I made the mistake of not hanging our individual hammocks; instead we lay wrapped close together in a poncho on the floorboards up in the bow. We suffered for our night of covert love. Mosquitoes attacked through the densely woven material of our blanket, our shirts and trousers;

added to these bites were those of the fleas from the captain's dog; then the continuous downpour of rain soon filled the boat, and bilge water stinking of dog and human urine and rotting vegetables gradually crept up and soaked our clothes. At first light, as the engine started up and we pulled away from the bank and the mosquitoes to continue our journey downriver, John and I smiled wanly at each other through swollen eyelids puffy with bites.

It was a lesson to take more care, but our misery was nothing compared to the early explorers: we would not catch malaria; we were not frightened of attack from hostile Indians; we were not short of food. With my body on fire from the bites I thought of the Jesuit Priest, Father Samuel Fritz, who, on his death in 1723 as his body was prepared for burial, was found to be deeply ulcerated by insect bites. He was content to accept any punishment God might send and had never brushed any insect off his body, and in an age when mortification of the flesh was taken as a sign of piety, he was considered holier as a result.

We reached the Colombian river port Leticia two days and two nights after having started out from Iquitos. Here were bizarre contrasts: the smart hotel which boasted the only swimming pool on the Amazon – and this heart-shaped – faced a dilapidated main square dominated by a huge statue of Colombia's liberator and streets lined with tin stalls leading nowhere except to the edge of dense jungle. I took my bites to a chemist for some balm, and there, kept in a cage, was a giant python which the crinkly walnut-faced owner would take out and feed with live rats and chickens. I wondered about his cures if this was what he had to do to attract custom.

Once again we were having problems with getting more cash. The head office of the Bank of London and South America in Queen Victoria Street, London, was far away and no one here seemed to know or care about our banking arrangements. Having shelled out so much for our canoe trip we were now very short, and on Christmas Day we had to decide which meal was the most important, as we could only afford one. After much debate and increasing hunger we decided on breakfast, which turned out lucky, as the kindly manager of the hotel bumped into us and asked us round for a free dinner.

With a bit of persistence our banking facilities were finally agreed to, and we managed to find another boat to take us on down the river. This time it was a much bigger craft, the ocean-going *Montenegro*. She had been up with a cargo of Russian cement which had come via the Black Sea and was being unloaded at Tabatinga, a mile downstream and just over the border in Brazil. There seemed to be a building race between the two river ports. The unloading of hundreds of tons of cement was not being helped by the heavy rains – paper sacks were tearing and the trucks were bogging down once loaded – but eventually on 28 December we set off downriver.

Our fare was ten pounds each. The trip of two thousand miles would take ten days, and it included our food: generous helpings of rice covered with an overripe yellow-coloured stew containing the feet of various creatures. It was dusted with farina, a rather gritty type of semolina flour which enabled people to eat their whole meal with their fingers. We soon came to recognise the trotter of a turtle from that of a tortoise by its webbing, and I got quite thin.

Our quarters were on a crowded deck measuring about twelve by twenty yards. We hung our hammocks in tiers from metal posts which supported a similar deck above, and shared our space with another seventy-one brightly coloured woven hammocks, families of Indians travelling downriver with their belongings and animals, tortoises, chickens and ducks confined to small baskets, dogs, one small grey monkey with sad eyes, a frightened black pig, and lots of babies. The children amused themselves for hours with ginger rhino-horned dung beetles, collected in numbers from the wash area next to our deck (which was used more as a lavatory). Their owners would tie twine to the beetles' legs and then race them up and down on the grey metal deck, shouting them on.

The river now had become so wide the far bank was just a shimmer on the horizon, and the days were punctuated with stops at villages and towns along this inland sea. Sao Paulo de Olivenca. Santo Antonio do Iça. Our ship's hooter boomed out our impending arrival to settlements whose history had seen the horrors of their people being rounded up and taken away as slaves; the coming of the Jesuit fathers, bringing Christianity and a different order; those who came feverishly searching for gold and rubber; and now the logging and destruction of the rainforest. The faces of these people attested to their history, you could see, mingled with their Indian blood, the races of their oppressors – Carib, Spanish, Portuguese.

We went ashore at Tefe. Here the river level varies forty-five feet according to the time of year. We were now into the humid rainy season and the river was swollen with flood and earth, while trees and rafts of lilac-blue wild hyacinth swirled on down towards the Atlantic. Once elegant and ornate buildings from the rubber period lined the main square. Here two of the great naturalists of the nineteenth century, Bates and Wallace, spent some time collecting and studying the vast and varied insect, animal and bird life. Vivid descriptions of what they found are recorded in their respective accounts: *A Naturalist on the River Amazon 1863* and *A Narrative of Travels on the Amazon and Rio Negro 1853*. In particular Bates describes camping on a sandbar off Tefe when a large alligator crept ashore and ate the poodle belonging to one of his friends. Bates awoke to find the alligator just below his hammock. The water was full of them, but in spite of this the explorers swam in the river to cool themselves, the trick being to keep your 'eyes fixed on that of the monster, which stares with a disgusting leer along the surface of the water'.

We did not swim. It was hot and the cool water was tempting, but it was of an opaque coffee colour, and it was hard not to imagine falling victim to packs of piranha, electric eels, anacondas and the leering alligators.

We saw turtles, but in not the teeming numbers that had been reported by these two naturalists over a century before. A female turtle will lay over a hundred eggs, and at that time eight thousand jars of turtle oil a year were produced from the Amazon Valley. It required six thousand eggs to produce one jar, which meant one season's production took the fruitless effort of forty-eight thousand turtles.

For the others, the journey had really ended at Iquitos where the river is big enough to take ocean-going ships, and John in particular found it difficult to adjust to the inactivity of this leisurely progress. An air of anti-climax settled about him, but for me, straight from Britain, it was the most exciting and enthralling event of my life. Even if considerably depleted from the previous century by man's plunder, there seemed to be still an abundance of everything: animals, birds, fish, trees, vivid people always smiling and laughing. Our rather bare peninsula on the north-west coast of Scotland felt like a distant memory on some far off planet.

I was a little more at ease now with the other three. In Iquitos I had felt an intruder and miserably awkward, young and naive with nothing to offer except a cheerful disposition, and even that seemed out of place. Now, a few weeks on, physically and mentally I had adjusted to this different life. My body was tanned and spare, I felt wonderfully well and strong, and I was quite entranced by my surroundings. Anna I held in great awe, the fact that she remained somewhat aloof adding even more to my feelings of respect. However, I learnt that I need not have worried about her and John. I had felt that two such courageous beings must be matched in heaven, but this turned out to be not at all the case. I chuckled to myself at what John told me Anna had said to him high up in the mountains after a day of increasing stress: 'You not only look like an ox, you think like one too!'

Mac and Cowie were friendly enough, but I felt they were talking not to me but to John's wife, and too much had happened to them all high up in the Andes for me to be anything but a rather annoying intruder. Four strong-minded individuals, with John as the elected leader, and all with widely varying personalities, they had kept together as a group but not I felt as friends. And here was I, the leader's wife, joining John and thereby strengthening his hand. To counteract this John was resolutely impartial towards me. I inwardly begged for reassurance and help, but he could not be seen to give me preferential treatment. Two years of living at Ardmore had taught me much about self-reliance and resourcefulness, but there I was on my own territory and could anticipate what was to come. Out here it was altogether different, and my only way forward was to get good at the challenges that came along, small challenges to the four experienced travellers, but big to me.

Hour after hour I would lean on the rail, gazing out at the passing riverbank of uninterrupted dense green jungle, surprised by noisy bursts of green parakeets and the brilliance of the blue morpho butterflies, listening to the story of the expedition.

John told me their aim was to be the first expedition to follow the Amazon from its furthest source to the sea. By luck they had met a mining engineer who was running an ancient but still workable silver mine. He took them beyond the normally accepted source, Lake Vilafro, to where the Apurimac rose out of the Chila Mountain Range on the Continental Divide. There on the 17,875-foot-high slopes of Minaspata was the true furthest source of the Amazon. Suffering from altitude sickness they had to

descend quickly or die. So started the long journey following the
Apurimac, 'the great speaker', as it tumbled and fought its way
through gorges torn and worn from the torrents of water gushing
down to join the greatest of mighty rivers.

The race against the expected heavy rains kept pushing the team
on. If the rains came early, they would have to abandon any
prospect of rafting or canoeing which could cause them to abandon
their attempt. Sometimes they walked, sometimes they rode, and
travelling as far as they could each day they gradually descended,
their journey taking them from the vast empty Altiplano down into
warmer climes, revealing different vegetation and fruits with each
day's progress. They would sleep in the small villages along the
way, often on the beaten earth floor of the mud-walled school-
house.

One of these stops was at a village called Lucmahuayco, deep in
the valley bottom of one of the racing mountain tributaries. The
team had walked for ten hours, and were exhausted, when they saw
grey woodsmoke curling up from a cluster of thatched huts, half
hidden by the mantle of green forest. They were welcomed, and a
stout Quechua Indian wife bade them sit down on ponchos outside
a simple hut. They were offered sweet lemons, and bought bananas
and eggs, which they cooked, and then they fell into an exhausted
sleep. They left the next day early. It was just another village along
the way, but in the years to come something would happen here
that would dramatically affect John's and my life.

A six-hour walk on from Lucmahuayco they came to what was
called the 'German's' farm at Osambre. Imagination working
overtime, John expected to be greeted by a high-ranking Nazi,
maybe even Hitler himself in this jungle hideout.

The German turned out to be Abel Berg, a Norwegian Peruvian.
With his wife and their family of five sons and one daughter, he
lived a simple, industrious life in harmony with a couple of Campa
Indian families. John liked them instantly, and their Swiss Family
Robinson style of life. It was a paradise where they could grow all
the food they needed, while their annual coffee crop raised
sufficient money to buy them books and clothes.

The Bergs insisted that John and his team stay at Osambre,
resting and eating until they had regained some of the strength lost
on the earlier stage of the journey. Señor Berg considered the
Campa Indians to be the most tranquil people on earth, and those

living the sophisticated life of Northern Europe the most un-tranquil. John was greatly taken with his philosophy of life. He wrote in his diary, 'My own feeling is that at the end of my life there will still be Bergs at Osambre – just as there will be Ridgways at Ardmore.' Both were pursuing a dream to stand apart.

Elvin Berg, the eldest son, then twenty-two – whom John described as looking like a young Elvis Presley – decided to accompany the team down the next section of the river, covering a hundred miles a day in a forty-foot dugout, shooting through the rapids. This young man was the pride of his father, the embodi-ment of his teachings of self-sufficiency. It seemed that with Elvin as the head of the next generation of Bergs, the future of Osambre was assured.

John's encounter with Elvin was a delicate gossamer thread of fate which drifted into our lives, and one day the weaving would begin. But we knew nothing of the future then, and talked about the present and immediate past. Elvin had been as stalwart as expected, and led them to safety, shooting the rapids in the crude dugout canoe. Many people had lost their lives on this perilous stretch, Elvin's skill and judgement had undoubtedly kept John and his team alive. They bade Elvin a sad goodbye at the Benedictine Mission of Granja Sivia, and John gave him his watch as a keepsake – he felt he owed him much.

From the Mission they would have to go by balsa raft, the rapids being too dangerous for canoe travel. Within four days a raft was built with balsa logs and tied together with bark by two Quechua Indians who swore they knew the river well. In fact, it turned out they had never been down it before.

A couple of days on, it finally happened – the raft wreck mentioned in John's telegram to me. Trying to avoid one obstacle in the fast river, they missed seeing a partly submerged slab of rock and hit it with terrible force. Anna was thrown off, but, miracu-lously, Mac managed to catch one of her ankles before she was carried away in the raging torrent and pulled her back on to the raft, which was now at a precarious angle, half-pinned under by the rushing water.

Mac then heroically offered to swim to the shore to try to find help. He was an army champion swimmer and he did manage to swim the perilous sixty yards. It was doubtful that any of the others would have managed to make their way to the shore – certainly not the crippled Campa Indian child they were taking to Atalaya for medical treatment. The main worry was that if they did not get help before nightfall, six hours away, there was a very good chance the raft would break up in the night and they would then all be swept away in the dark. There was also a very good chance Mac would not find help, that he would get eaten mercilessly by mosquitoes and black fly, and that his feet would be cut to ribbons.

These thoughts occupied the minds of all of those still stuck in the middle of the raging river. However they were lucky. Mac found a Campa hut a couple of miles downriver, attracted their attention from the other bank, and soon they were paddling big dugouts up to John and his team. With great relief they abandoned their crashed raft and were taken to the Campa village, and probably because they had been trying to help the young crippled Campa boy they were made welcome. They spent the night in a hut on stilts in the Campa village and the following day were taken by a skilled Indian in his dugout canoe through ten more miles of rapids described as '*mucho peligroso*'. They finally emerged from the mountains into a new land where the river flowed strongly and gently towards the Atlantic. In the first six hundred miles the river they had followed dropped sixteen thousand feet, but here where it was flowing more gently on its journey of 3,500 miles to the sea, it drops only seven hundred feet. They said goodbye to their Campa Indian friends at Atalaya, a small frontier settlement. They were now back in the *civilised* world and only a day or two of river-boating away from Iquitos.

The throbbing twin six-cylinder Sulzer engines pushed us ahead of the flood water. The scorching brilliance of the days now ended suddenly but dramatically with crimson and gold sunsets. Blowing and gasping, freshwater porpoises leapt and played in our bow wave, graceful arcs of pink and silver. Birds screeched from the jungle bank as they settled for the night. On such an evening we docked at Manaus at the confluence of the Rio Negro whose truly black waters streaked and mingled with the coffee Amazon. It was the last evening of 1970, and after a good meal we joined the throngs of garlanded people who were dancing through the streets to a samba rhythm. At midnight the velvety black tropical sky was bright and loud with showers of exploding fireworks, the church bells tolled, and every horn in the southern hemisphere sounded with true Latin verve. We had a day and half to explore this fabled city, another island in this vast ocean of a jungle, accessible then only by river or light aircraft.

The rubber boom had transformed Manaus from a settlement of a few shacks in one of the poorest areas of the Amazon into a boomtown of immense wealth. This area has no stone or rock, so stone was shipped in from Europe to pave the streets and build the opulent houses and palaces for the rich. A magnificent opera house, Teatro Amazonas, was built to seat two thousand people. To overcome the problems of a sixty-foot rise and fall in the level of the Rio Negro, a floating dock was built by an English firm, and Manaus boasted the first tramcar system, ahead even of Manchester or Boston.

The cost of living was considered to be four times higher than New York, but money kept pouring into this new city. Every luxury could be bought: champagne at fifty dollars a bottle; diamonds; the finest linens from Ireland which were then sent back to Lisbon to be laundered. At one point police reckoned two out of every three of the fine houses were brothels. All of this came from the sale of rubber. Rubber had been used for centuries: Cortes' men in Mexico had used it for waterproofing their garments, and, before that, Columbus found Indians playing with rubber balls in Haiti. Its commercial development began when in 1823 Mackintosh started using it for his raincoats. Then in 1839 Charles Goodyear found that, mixed with sulphur and heated, it became more elastic and stronger. But it really got going when a Scottish veterinary surgeon by the name of John Boyd Dunlop took out a patent for 'a hollow tyre or tube made of Indian-rubber and cloth, or other suitable materials, said tube or tyre to contain air under pressure or otherwise and to be attached to the wheel or wheels in such method as may be found most suitable.' Bicycles and the motor car industry were burgeoning at the turn of the twentieth century, and the market was insatiable – but at a dreadful cost to the wretched gatherers of the latex.

And now sixty years on from the slump, when the rubber barons' fortunes were wiped out overnight, we wandered round the streets of this once dazzling city, marvelling at the wide paved streets, gardens filled with fountains and statues. To try to keep it alive Brazil had made it a free port. There were twenty-seven different banks. People flew in from all over Brazil to buy modern luxuries: watches, cameras, radios.

We managed to persuade a caretaker to let us into the opera house. Its gilded opulence would not have been out of place in any of the capitals of Europe. Its dusty velvet curtains were now home to bats and giant moths which fluttered around, stirred by our voices, as ghosts of over half a century before filled our heads with visions of glittering, flamboyant nights loud with the sound of operas popular of that day. Did Caruso really sing here on its opening night? We wondered what would become of this extraordinary building, now long silent and decaying. Its dazzling life had been so fleeting – like the wealth of the rubber barons themselves. (I was told that one of the rubber barons was still living here, impoverished and old, he now sold newspapers and chewing gum on a street corner.)

Tired from our wanderings, John and I sat for a while in the main square shaded by huge trees. After a while we got up to go, and continued to wander round the city. Suddenly John noticed the wad of low-denomination cruzeiro notes he had been carrying around, enough to last us the rest of the trip, was missing. Panic! The most likely explanation was that he had been robbed. We hurried back to the square in the scorching heat, cursing ourselves, just on the off-chance that the bank roll could be lying beneath the ornate bench on which we had been resting. We searched but the roll of notes had gone.

'Let's try the main hotel. It might have been handed in,' I weakly suggested, knowing there was no chance. A city full of beggars would see this as a gift from on high – why hand it in to the hotel staff who would probably pocket it themselves anyway.

Feeling stupid, we nevertheless hurried to the hotel, and in our poor Portuguese put our ridiculous question to the young man with an El Greco face who commanded the reception desk. His pale features broadened into a smile. We could not believe it as he unlocked the safe and brought out our wad of notes. Yes, they had been handed in earlier. No, he did not know who it was who had brought them. Yes, he would thank the person on our behalf. Rather humbly we left a small reward. We were astonished that this could have happened in a city where there was so much poverty.

Back on the boat we travelled on towards our destination, Belem, the big modern city on the southern bank. Our days were fast running out. The others were making plans: Anna would fly back to Lima via Manaus to be with Nick; Mac was planning to take a bus to Brasilia and then on to Rio de Janeiro with Stephano, my Italian bridge teacher; Cowie was heading back up into the Amazon to take more photos.

John could not wait to get back home to Scotland, but I was sorry my journey was so nearly over.

'Don't worry, I'm sure we'll come back one day, Marie Christine, and I'll take you to see the Bergs in their Garden of Eden,' John reassured me.

I fervently hoped he was right.

Chapter Three

ARDMORE

'You did all right, Marie Christine – three out of ten.' Nobody ever got higher than three from John. I sat very still, pleased I had not let the side down. We were travelling very fast now, in a DC8 high up in the deep blue sky. Through the small window I could see far below the pale muddy Amazon water pushing far out into the blue-grey Atlantic, freshening the salt of the sea to a distance of one hundred and fifty miles. John looked relaxed beside me. He had accomplished what he had set out to do.

The six weeks away had seemed like a lifetime. I had jumped at the chance to go out and join John. Now on the way home I could only think of seeing Bec and my mother. The flight took forever, it seemed. Eventually we touched down at Heathrow, and there they were.

We hugged and kissed, and little Bec smiled all the time and kept very close to us. We took the crowded train to Brighton, Bec sitting with the stuffed crocodile we had bought in Iquitos on her lap. Then, as we talked of our trip to my mother in her elegant Regency house on the sea front in Brighton, it all began to seem like a dream.

We had been away for long enough and had to get back home. There would be much to do. As we boarded the night train at Euston for Inverness the tall silver-haired lady bent to give her blonde fragile grandchild a final kiss and then waved goodbye. They had become firm friends.

In the early dawn we stood in the narrow, lurching corridor looking out on the wintry Grampian and Cairngorm mountains, the asthmatic engine needing all its power as it wheezed up to Drumochter summit and then gathered speed as it raced on down past Dalwhinnie, Kingussie, Aviemore.

'It's just like the Altiplano,' John commented as we gazed out at the empty land, patched with rags of snow.

'I'm glad I don't have to get out and search for any river sources,' I muttered to Bec. We were both feeling chilled. It was a few degrees colder still, as we climbed down from the train on to the icy platform at Inverness, and the sounds of seagulls calling in the cold morning air mingled with the slamming shut of the train doors.

Breakfast of porridge and kippers at the Station Hotel was the last comfort allowed before we changed into wellies and rough clothes to do a final tour of the town for essentials. We then took the A9 to the north, the road dwindling to single track with grass growing in its centre. The journey took us three hours and we arrived at the loch just as dusk was falling, to be met by our new colleague, Lance Bell. Sadly Rod and Jean Liddon had left us in the autumn to follow their dreams elsewhere. They had both worked very hard at setting up the school with us and running the first two seasons, but after a while our views and interests began to conflict. John's wish to succeed pushed aside any chance of days or weekends off; Jean felt, probably quite rightly, she wanted more time for her family to be together; Rod was torn between his family and his friend and business partner's obsession. I could see both sides' point of view, but I suspected the school would not succeed unless we were prepared to work all hours, every day of the week. Perhaps we were better motivated. People came to see John, after all, and it was not so easy for Rod who was in the background – doing every bit as much and maybe more – to feel so much part of the dream. 'Partnerships are harder to maintain than marriages,' our sage solicitor commented.

In their place had come another couple who were to play a major role at Ardmore in the years to come, Lance and Ada Bell. Lance had been a foreman in an iron foundry on Teesside, and possessed great knowledge and the practical ability to make almost anything. Ada was equally talented. She could sew, cook and knit to such a high standard that the term 'home-made' was almost an insult. Lance and Ada had moved into the first house we had bought – now called the Blue House, as we had painted the rusty black tin walls blue-green to cheer us on grey days. Straight away Ada had started helping out with some of the baking. Her cakes and pastries would be carefully carried down through the wood from the Blue House by a terrified instructor, and brought to me to put out for the course. My only criticism was that they always looked so professional that people did not realise that these individual masterpieces, decorated with angelica and cherries or perfectly iced, had been created in the small tin croft they had panted past earlier that day coming back from the climbing.

Ada's hair was snowy white, cut short by Lance and always neat, her complexion smooth and pale. She was slim, made most of her own clothes, had an overriding obsession for knitting and was rapid at the tasks she undertook. Never had I seen anybody peel potatoes as fast as Ada. Lance had first spotted her sitting high up in a crane when he was working at the foundry. 'She was one of the best operators I ever saw,' he would remark romantically. When they were married, Lance continued in the foundry, becoming foreman, while Ada ran a perfect home. Crane driving was replaced by child-rearing and home-making. They had two children: one achieved a Ph.D. in Chemistry, and the other was so talented a cook that within a year of opening a restaurant she was recognised by Egon Ronay and Les Routiers.

From the moment they came I knew that Ada and Bec would become good friends. Apart from the Liddons' son, Jamie, who was a bit tough for Bec – he once buried her favourite toy lamb – she had not met many other people of her size. She was rather quaint and serious. Ada welcomed her into the small neat house, and would teach her how to knit, bake bread and biscuits, how to stamp on sheets in the bath to get them clean. Together they would bottle the home-made beer Ada brewed in a bucket beside the stove, always referred to as 'Lance's beer'; they would go fishing with worms and bring back trout; they would search for old screw-top bottles in the ancient rubbish dumps left by another generation of people who lived long ago at Ardmore.

Now, shouting over the roar of the Seagull outboard, Lance told us that Ada was expecting us for supper, which cheered us. We could see the single light of their Tilley lamp beckoning from high on the hill across the darkening loch. Bec's hand was tight in mine as we climbed the familiar path from the foot of the croft through the trees to the tin house where we had lived two summers and winters.

The tantalising smell of Ada's supper greeted us as she opened the door to let us in. Boots, hats, coats, gloves were shed in a rush and soon we were seated round the table, Bec on several plumped up cushions so she could reach the glass of orange Ada had poured specially for her. She was the most important guest as far as Ada was concerned and Ada wanted to hear all her news.

Once Lance had opened the first of the quart bottles of home-brew beer he was avid for details of the Amazon trip. Lance had read copiously on every subject and, blessed with a remarkable memory, liked nothing better than to exchange ideas and facts. Soon the talk grew louder, filling the small and very tidy kitchen, while the polished brass Tilley hissed out its fierce light. Ada produced from the oven her special Yorkshire puddings, crisped round the edges and with centres like soft creamy custard, served with lots of gravy made from the delicious meaty juices from the roasted lamb. Had anything ever tasted so good?

After supper, Bec's head began to droop and her yellow plaits fell into a curl on the table top. It had been a fine home-coming party. We were soon out in the bitter air. The night was bright, a half-moon hung high in the deep sky, all of heaven's stars shone intensely and, as we turned to wave goodbye to our two friends framed in the doorway, we could see the aurora borealis sweeping the northern sky with shafts of shifting light. We tottered cautiously along the path through the wood, and underfoot the frosted leaves crunched with every step. Through the gate we went, and at last were home.

John opened the porch door, then the hall door. We stopped, holding our breath. Did we hear a sound? I sensed we were not alone. I lit a candle and went with Bec into the small pantry to put a kettle on for our hot-water bottles. In the arc of light I could see mouse droppings, everywhere.

Too exhausted to care, I filled the bottles and we clambered up the stairs to our damp bed – I knew chilblains would soon take the place of mosquito bites. John did a quick tour of the house by torch-light, then joined Bec and me, and we all curled up together for warmth. I lay beside my husband and small child, chilled and sorry for myself: the house was as cold as a mortuary, the mice had come in while we had been away; the exciting trip was just a memory. Worries twisted inside my head like snakes: would anybody come on the courses? how many letters would I have to write to reach out to them? would we survive? was this life fair to Bec? Normally John was the worrier and I the optimist. Maybe I was just exhausted.

We woke early to find a fine mist of dew covering our bed and felt very reluctant to get out of the warmth of the covers. There was a great deal to do, but with a new day I felt a resurgence of my fighting spirit. It would not really be light until after ten, so we lit the lamp. (Some days deep into our northern winter, it never seemed to get light at all, and the lamp would be left on all day.) The bright fierce equator sun of only a week ago was like a faint dream.

Unfortunately, the mouse droppings of the night had not been a dream. I had packed up in a hurry and had foolishly neglected to put into tins some of the dried food we had been using. I would know not to do it again. Warehouses will frequently refuse to store dehydrated food, because it is such an attraction to rodents – they had been into everything. I even discovered nests in my chest of drawers, made from my favourite lambswool and cashmere jerseys; they had spurned the ones made from artificial fibres, of course. John did not seem too concerned until he found that the cork handles on his precious fishing rods had been nibbled. After that, he searched out the mousetraps and set them, savagely muttering death threats to the timorous beasties.

There was also other work to do. The black alkathene water pipe that poked through the pantry window was frozen solid. With buckets, Bec and I went to draw water from the well next door, sweet clear water that welled up from the side of the hill filtered through sparkling quartz and granite.

I met Hughie, our friend and neighbour, as we came through with the second load. 'I'm just coming in to continue with the cupboards,' he said as he took my buckets from me. Whilst we were away, Hughie, in between bouts of lobster fishing, was making a bathroom in the tiny pantry where last summer I had been cooking for forty. He was also making cupboards in one of the two rooms downstairs which had been the dining room and was now to be the kitchen. It was chaos, but what luxury it would be to be able to put everything away and have clear surfaces and order – a dream that I still cherish but have never yet realised.

'Have you seen the new patch I had to put on the wall above the skirting in the kitchen, Marie Christine?'

'No, Hughie,' I replied, and went in to examine the piece of new boarding twelve inches by nine.

'I was sawing away in the pantry, and when I had stopped I realised the sawing noise continued.' He grinned mischievously at me. 'I think it was rats. They have terrible sharp teeth you know, and they cut right through the boards in no time.'

'Oh no, Hughie,' my new-found image of myself as a tough Amazon traveller was evaporating with every quake of my voice.

Mice I could cope with, but rats – I had heard somewhere that a
breeding pair can, in three years, provide a population of two
million.

That was it. There was no question now of Bec going back into
her tiny room under the eaves where the low wall was just a jumble
of loose rocks, and where the raw roof sloped up over her narrow
bed to a gap where the ceiling started: rats could easily run in and
out of there. She would sleep with us until we had the problem
solved and the rats were gone. Our bed had belonged to my parents
and had been brought up from the south. We had shortened the
legs, taken the headboard away and replaced it with the footboard.
It was not interior sprung nor ultra-comfortable – indeed the base
was made up of rather curious tensioned chain-mail – but we were
always ready to drop when we went to bed and could have slept on
a bed of nails.

In the evening now as we sat around the kitchen table, we would
hear a scuffle from behind the matchboard lining. The walls to our
stone croft house are three foot thick and made of two piles of
roughly matching rocks resting on top of one another and held
together with loose sand, shells and just a little mortar. The outside
is rendered and whitened with lime: inside it is lined with pine
matchboard. There are deep recesses where the small windows are
set, and it was over the kitchen window that the rats would run.
First there would be a scratching patter of their feet, then loose sand
would fall in a trail on to the windowsill through a crack in the
wooden boarding, and finally you could hear their heavy tails as
they were dragged along behind their bodies. How was their
breeding cycle progressing?

We were lent a rat trap, a wire cage a bit like a lobster creel.
Baited, the rat would be attracted, and would clamber in through
the opening. Once it was inside, the entrance would be triggered
shut and there you had your captive rat. Then you had to kill it.
Drowning was supposedly most effective, but the prospect of
having cold-bloodedly to kill a creature into whose eyes I had
looked appalled me. However, SAS-trained John said there was
nothing to it.

I also consulted my much-thumbed *TRY THIS: Useful House
Hints and Economies*, fourth edition, printed in 1925. It provided
these hints on the subject: 'RATS, TO CATCH. Get a barrel
without a lid. Stand a brick on end at the bottom of the barrel. Fill

the barrel with water to the height of the brick. Cover the top of the barrel with strong paper or parchment, tie it down very firmly so as to completely cover the barrel for the rats to get up by. Sprinkle the paper on the top freely with bread and cheese, scraps of meat, corn, or any other food. Repeat this feeding for three nights. On the fourth, cut very carefully a large cross in the paper cover, and through it the rats will speedily fall in, having gained perfect confidence in their three nights of happy experience. The screaming of the vanguard will induce all the others to follow. The brick makes a standing-ground for the first rat; the next comers fight for possession of this place of vantage, and the noise they make attracts the others.'

I was only half-hearted over the trap, and we did not attempt to try the barrel method; so we will never know what it was that sent the rats scuttling away eventually to find another tumble of rocks. Perhaps they did not care for my music, and on their own accord left for somewhere more peaceful. There had been a dearth of music on the Amazon, and now I could enjoy Mozart to Mahler to Bach to Brahms, for as much time as we had batteries to power the portable record player. Bec loved the Beatles' *Abbey Road* and the Corries, and we would dance wildly around the kitchen, knowing there would never be anyone peeping in. And sometimes on clear nights, when the moon struck a path of beaten silver across the dark ripples of the loch, John and I would listen to Sibelius, the sound filling our veins with liquid gold.

I missed the concerts I had so enjoyed when I lived in London, and now had to content myself with the radio and records. I always felt – though could never say why – there was more magic in listening to the poorly received sound of a concert being broadcast live than in the perfect sound of the same music on record. But there was a lot of magic around that I did not understand.

There was certainly a magical aura surrounding John; he held me entirely in his sway. Born out of his time, to me he was the hero who, in another age, would have rescued maidens from dragons, drawn swords from rocks, led nations to victory against impossible odds. Enthralled, I was anxious to win his approval, and help in any way I could. I felt my Amazon performance had almost promoted me to being considered for another trip, but I dared not mention this.

John expected a great deal of Bec and me, and me in particular. It was fortunate in some respects that my mother lived at the other end of the country, for although she was very fond of John she would often tell me I had quite enough to do already.

'You work far too hard. You'll wear yourself out, and lose your looks and then what will happen to you?'

Looks? What were they to do with anything up here at Ardmore? Yet sometimes, when John was caught up in a new plan and all his energy and force were concentrated on it, I did feel neglected. Had he taken me to this outpost to keep me to himself and hide me from the world?

As girls, if my father had ever caught me or my two sisters gazing at our reflections in the mirror, he would say, 'Vanity is one of the greatest sins.' We were brought up as dutiful daughters to be dutiful wives, and not encouraged to have too high an opinion of ourselves. Yet programmed to be dutiful as I was, I still struggled as though in a straitjacket. My problem came in the form of other people. We had many visitors who came in droves to see us – no, not us, John. I could not blame them. Of course they wanted to meet and talk to the man who had rowed across the Atlantic, who had sailed single-handed to Brazil, but the more they wanted to listen to John and not to me as well, the more unsure of myself I became. Perhaps I had married too young, before I had the chance to achieve much on my own. Poor John, it was hardly his fault. I do not think he really understood my rages of despair, but perhaps that is why he gave me the chance to join him on the Amazon. I knew that the only way I could maintain my self-esteem was to try very hard at whatever I tackled, to try to excel, to try to be self-reliant and strong. The challenges would present themselves in the years to come, and I would be ready.

It was sad in a way that a gulf had widened between me and my old London friends. 'Bobby, when are you coming down to see us?' they would ask. 'Are there lots of parties up there?' 'Do you live in a lovely house, and is it fun?' They were sweet and kind, but how could they understand my life. A small croft house three miles from the road, one hundred miles from the nearest town, no electricity or running water. They would just feel sorry for me because they would not share my dream, or understand John. Their hopes were for other things.

John and I were happiest when it was just the three of us.

Early in 1971, after our return from the Amazon, we started again on preparations for another season, our third. We were now feeling quite experienced – experienced, that is, in facing the unexpected. It was better to expect supplies and people not to arrive on time than be counting on them, better always to have a contingency plan. John reckoned it was more interesting. It certainly got us working on being resourceful; we were becoming less naive; there was no time for complacency. Judging from the previous year, we found that most people make their holiday arrangements after Christmas. As the plum pudding sits heavily on their stomachs, the idea of an active week in the bracing air of the west coast of Scotland becomes quite appealing – at least we hoped so. I was therefore all set for a deluge of enquiries in January. We had not considered there might be a mail strike.

The strike bit deep into our plans. There was no post, no enquiries, no bookings. Even the telephone started to play up. Each day at lunchtime we would await the next instalment from William Hardcastle on *The World at One*. His delivery was dramatic even over the milder news items, but he fired our fears that the postal strike might ruin us. Willie, our friend and postman, was quite embarrassed about the whole affair.

At least, during the strike, the table in the new kitchen was not a constant clutter of typewriter, paper and carbon, envelopes, files and brochures. Instead it held a wonderful black pudding, which we had just discovered. If fried fast, the lumps of fat and grains of oats within it crisped perfectly, and it tasted just delicious. A slice or two of this and a few Kerr's Pink floury potatoes helped lift our gloom at lunchtime.

On 9 March the seven-week strike finally ended, with a rather unsatisfactory compromise. It must have been terrible for the families of the postal workers, and we feared it might prove to have been the same for us. Would we ever pick up the lost business? We had sunk everything we had into the school and, most of all, our pride.

Now the work started in earnest. We had made up lots of brochures; it was just a question of writing letters to accompany them. We also advertised expensively in the national dailies and Sunday papers, hoping to jog people's memories. John insisted that the advertisement must be eye-catching. It started: 'Atlantic Rower, Lone Sailor, Amazon Explorer offers . . .' It was a while before we learnt that one paper had been using the words 'Atlantic *Raver* . . .'

Still, our expensive gamble at advertising did bring results, and the bookings started to come in again. For me it was a kind of Catch-22 situation. John and I were united by a strong common aim – to keep the courses going, but once the hurdle of getting the bookings was overcome, the struggle for me started in earnest, for I had to handle the paperwork concerning the travel arrangements and enrolment. Then, once our guests were at Ardmore, I had to feed them. In our five-month season there was not a day's break between one course ending and the next starting. It was challenging just living at Ardmore with no electricity and so far from sources of supply, but added to that was this huge workload. I could probably have got help if we had been by the road and if we could have afforded it, but our situation did not allow for that.

I could not have managed if it had not been for Ada. She was like a second mother to Bec. Sadly for me, there was not a lot of space or time for a lively four-year-old in the hubbub of my daily life. Bec loved to help, but I was usually in such a rush that I did not have time to show her how to do things, so she preferred the more orderly pace of the Blue House.

I worried about her growing up as an only child, and often wanted desperately to have more babies, but I could not see how we would ever manage and keep the school going. I was fully extended as it was. In any case, John was not keen: he felt most of the problems in the modern world sprang from over-population, and I could not help but agree.

Woman magazine came and did a piece about me, Bec and the part Ada now began to play in the first two years of her schooling. When the article appeared it was entitled: 'The Loneliest Little Girl in Britain'. This heading was like a slap in the face. I felt responsible and guilty, but caught in a dilemma between the needs of my husband and those of my child. It was true she did not have many friends of her own age, but she was never short of company. The young instructors were like older brothers to her and she loved to bask in their attention. There were always favourites, for whom she would bake little cakes, or pick flowers or draw pictures. There was Lance, too, who made her stilts and a swing which hung from one of the telephone poles. He showed her how to plant beans and weed the vegetables and how to pick up a hen and collect the eggs.

Bec knew how to work the situation to her advantage, and she would enquire what was planned for supper down our end and then ask Ada what they were having at the Blue House. She would then choose her favourite. She would also often go in next door as well, with a posy of flowers, to visit our dear friend Granny Ross, now in her eighties and confined to a chair beside the smoky stove. Granny Ross was completely round, and laughed a lot in a kindly way. She had wide apart brown eyes, and hair tucked neatly under a fine net. Winter and summer she would wear a brightly patterned overall, with layers of cardigans on top, the number depending on the weather. Her worn feet would be cosy in chequered soft slippers – feet that had walked many, many miles supporting heavy loads of food for her large family to eat.

It was the women at Ardmore and similar places in the Highlands who did the really hard work. The men would be away fishing, either on the east coast catching herring, or racing the lobster boats out to Ardmore Point, or setting the long lines which the women had baited the night before with mussels. Meanwhile, the women and children would be carrying in the water, the food, the peat. On hot days in summer the women and children would carry the blankets and heavy clothes up over the hill at the back of the crofts to one of the freshwater lochs for washing. There, they would light a peat fire and heat up the water in a big cauldron, which also had to be carried up. It must have been a bit like a picnic, and I am sure the children loved the fun of it, but I wonder if the women, who must have been worn down by their hard labours, could ever feel easy and forget the ever-present anxiety of their children's vulnerability. There was hardly a family that had not lost a member to tuberculosis; many winters they were hungry; there was very little money. It was a harsh life in the Highlands, and it was the fruits of these women's efforts that kept the family alive.

Granny Ross had lived nearly all her life at Ardmore. As Robina McLeod she had grown up in the house where we now lived, Number 76. She told us it was good and right we had gone to live in that house, as it had always been full of music. Two of her older brothers played the fiddle and accordion, and people would walk out to Ardmore from all around for ceilidhs.

She had married Hector Ross who lived next door, and had moved into Number 77 in the parish of Eddrachilles. Courteous and gentle, old Hector's shy face would crinkle into a smile whenever we met. The good shepherd to his flock of sheep, he spent his days tending his animals. He died in his eighties not long after we moved to Ardmore. Granny Ross took his death with fortitude: life must continue for Heckie her adored eldest son, the heir to the croft.

Heckie was in his fifties when his father died. With his brooding good looks he could have been Gregory Peck's brother: he had his mother's deep-set dark eyes and hair. He said very little except when he had had a few drams and then he would recite poem after poem in a passionate mournful voice.

Sometimes on hot days in the summer Bec would go in next door and ask if Heckie and Mona his dog needed help with the hay-making. Year after year, the cutting of the hay had fitted into the crofting calendar. The meadowsweet grass would be allowed to grow to a certain length, then Heckie, slowly swinging his scythe in a rhythmic arc, would cut line after line, working his way up the hill of the croft. It would be raked over to dry and then gathered and carried to stacks where the summer breeze would turn it to sweet smelling hay, to be stored away for the winter in the stone byre with the black tarred roof. There had once been nine young Rosses to help, but now, apart from Hughie, they had grown up and left this rocky peninsula, and I sensed Heckie felt it right for Bec to be there, helping, whilst Mona his dog would sit not far from his master, sniffing the air, one ear cocked, waiting for the mid-morning whistle from Granny Ross at the top of the hill, calling them in for food.

Molly and Bessie, two of Heckie's younger sisters, took it in turns to stay at home and help. A year away and a year back at Ardmore was how they agreed to share the task of looking after their mother and eldest brother. Like Heckie, they both had their mother's deep-set eyes ringed with long lashes and dark hair, which they wore coiled into knots at the nape of their necks. I thought it sad that their gentle beauty was seen by so few, since half their lives was to be spent hidden away at Ardmore. But they had been brought up with a very different view of life and its expectations.

The whole family were devout members of the Free Presbyterian Church. Its teachings guided them in all they did. Sunday was a hallowed day for them: no work of any kind was permitted; it was a day given over entirely to the teachings of Christ. It was not possible for Granny Ross to get to church in Kinlochbervie, but the rest of the family would walk out separately along the path, Heckie in a smart dark suit and tie, Molly or Bessie always with a hat, gloves and coat and Hughie in his best too, if he was at home. They would incline their heads towards us if we met, but we would not converse.

In contrast, I thought of Sunday as any other day, one to make the most of, if the weather was fine. Potatoes got planted, bonfires lit, washing hung out – or they did until we realised what an insult this was to the Rosses' beliefs. One day in particular in our first spring, we were digging the ground in readiness for the planting of the first potatoes. Bessie stopped on her way back from church, for a chat, we thought.

'Please don't labour on the Sabbath,' she admonished us quietly but firmly. I admired her greatly for speaking out, for she was rather shy, and I could see it required all her courage to say this to us.

We did not feel we could stop for a minute, let alone a whole day, but we tried to be discreet and respect their ways. A superstition hovered over us, for locals would say: 'A job started on the Sabbath will come to no good,' and it was uncanny how all the disasters that hit us in the early years seemed to happen on this day. So much so that in the end we decided it was safer not to tackle anything major on a Sunday.

Becoming friends with the Rosses gave my life a very different perspective. Their quiet faith and gentle humility were an inspiration. Their unselfish devotion towards each other was an example for us to follow. Their unfailing kindnesses and acceptance of us were encouraging and heart warming. Granny Ross's face would beam a welcome when we called to see her, and she was always particularly delighted to see Bec. 'Oh you're very wise,' she would chuckle as she looked deep into Bec's small grave face, holding her hands firmly together.

'Where are the sweeties?' Granny Ross would call to Molly or Bessie, whichever daughter was at home at the time, and she would fetch the tin off the dresser, where it helped prop up the ever increasing number of photographs of grandchildren and relations around the world. Bec's pale fingers would fish out an orange pandrop or sometimes an extra strong mint.

Having brought nine children into the world, she must have been rather sad that they were grown up and mostly gone, and that there were no grandchildren living on at Ardmore. It was bleak to be left as one of the last survivors in a place that had seen so much life and laughter and tears.

I could not hear enough stories of how it had been in the old days when there were at least five families living at Ardmore. She responded warmly to my questions, her gentle singsong voice telling stories of people long gone. Listening to her tales of a time when the place was alive with people made the present seem pale and faded. Could we ever change that and breathe life into this beautiful isolated place?

The story was typical of so many places on the remote west coast: gradually over the past forty-odd years, those living around our sea loch had dwindled to only elderly or single people. Someone had commented 'It's a form of genocide. The Highlander is doing away with himself and his kind: the men just sew up their trousers and grow old and lonely, and the women turn away.' The two wars must have disrupted the traditional pattern of their lives, taking young people away, many never to return. Of those that survived, some did not want the isolated hard existence they had been brought up to, and escaped to the cities and towns, but judging by the letters Granny Ross received from her relations it seemed they still yearned for the tranquillity of the place.

When we had put in potatoes when we first arrived at Upper Ardmore, we had planted them too close together and they came up like marbles, much to the mirth of Granny Ross who could not disguise her amusement. There was nothing she did not know about growing potatoes at Ardmore. As a young girl she had dug over the entire ground, stretching one hundred feet to the shore from below the house where we now lived at Lower Ardmore. She then carried creels of seaweed to fertilise the earth, then planted, hoed, weeded and heaped up the potato crop before finally harvesting it. The family depended on these potatoes to see them through the winter, to add substance to their salt-herring and mutton. Nobody got fat in those days.

Our first autumn I got a pick and loosened the hard-packed earth in front of the house either side of the porch, and at the south-facing gable end, for three small flowerbeds. They would be enough to start with. I dug deep and came across pieces of charcoal which Granny Ross told me had come from the house when it burnt down at the end of the last century. I carried up buckets of rotting seaweed, dross from the bottom of the peat stack, good red earth from the seam that runs along our side of the wood to the shore, and finally a few handfuls of bone meal. Bec and I then carefully planted our first bulbs. So far north, spring is long in coming and we waited impatiently to see the green blue spears of daffodil leaves and the shiny green cones of hyacinths, pushing up through the cold earth. I longed for the days to lengthen, for our frozen land to come alive again with the song of birds. The spring bulbs would look lovely, if the sheep did not get in and eat them. They would not touch the daffs but would devour the delicious juicy hyacinths.

We mended the gate and kept out the sheep. Encouraged, I planted pansies, marigolds, stocks and some mesembryanthemums, whose pink and purple faces only open to the sun. That summer was warm and my tightly planted garden bright and gay. When there was a moment's break in the round of cooking and letters, Bec and I would rush to be out in the sun. We would sit on a rug, half-drugged by the heady scent of the flowers, squinting in the clear bright light to where, beyond the currant bushes, gooseberries and plum trees of the summer jungle in front of the house, grey mountains stood guard over the sparkling sea loch and over us.

On the kitchen gable end I had planted a whole bed of *lilium regale*. As they came into bloom I picked a few and brought them into the house. I placed them in a stone jar on the old chest; at either side stood John's silver candelabra, a present on the occasion of our wedding from 3 Para, and on the wall above hung an icon of a sad-faced virgin Mary holding up her baby. The waxy flowers scented the whole house, and hiding in the depth of each pale trumpet were clusters of pollen-rich stamens and sepals dripping with sticky nectar. 'You're making the place look just like a church, Marie Christine,' John moaned.

These flowers lent a stillness to the room whilst all about was rush and noise. When I was alone and frantic with my tasks I would play the music that was balm to my soul: Elgar's musical setting of Cardinal Newman's poem, *The Dream of Gerontius* – the struggle of a man, a sinner, about to die and helped by his guardian angel – to me an exquisitely beautiful musical representation of the culminating drama of every human soul.

Then, when my back was turned and the gate had been left open for a second, a sheep furtively crept in and made a bee-line for my lilies. It left nothing except trampled stems and me in a rage, screaming and throwing rocks as it panicked at the fence in its rush to escape my wrath.

Apart from the lambs, which were a joy to watch as they leapt and played, I felt that sheep were best dished up on a plate with mint sauce. Our diet had been rather paltry for some time. We had potatoes, onions, carrots, white cabbage, pulses and spices and a little in the way of tinned meat. Ada had got me going on making bread and I could really have lived on bread and potatoes, but John and Bec needed to get their teeth into something. Lance suggested we should salt some meat down.

When the weather got a little milder, we set off for Inverness, and on the way back stopped at Balnafettack Farm where we joined the queue of lumpy people picking up bulk meat supplies for their freezers. Our order was for one sheep. We picked up the headless corpse and drove home with it. The following day Lance came down with his saw, wearing his usual Chairman Mao navy cotton jacket over his submariner's woollen jumper. (We all had one – they lasted for years – and mine even had the name and number of its previous owner, who did not have bumps where I did.) Lance's trousers were a hard-wearing navy serge which he got in lots from a mill in Lancashire. His saw was reverently wrapped in cloth to keep it dry, and the sharpened teeth were protected by a wooden guard. Most of Lance's tools had been made by his grandfather, and he knew just how to take care of them. Everything that should be sharp was kept that way, even the spade he dug the garden with was polished and put to dry in the kitchen after use.

Lance set to sawing the carcase whilst I made up the brine. I half-filled a plastic dustbin with water and then dissolved sufficient salt to make a potato float. We then put all the meat in, making sure it was covered by the brine. The lot was held under the buoyant brine by two smooth rocks. Over the next few days we stirred it around to make sure that all the meat was absorbing the salt, which would keep it fresh. The end result tasted quite good, if rinsed thoroughly. I would leave it in a bowl overnight with the tap just running allowing a trickle of water to cause the bowl to overflow.

As time went on we managed to find a paraffin fridge in which to keep our meat. It was quite tall, and had a lock and key, and was mainly for the export market. I imagined them in farms dotted around the Highlands of Kenya, keeping stores of chilled beer safe from the natives. The fuel tank was filled with paraffin, the trimmed Valor wick lit so there was just a blue circle of flame, a glass chimney placed over this and then the whole contraption pushed into position so the glass chimney connected with the pipe which went up the back of the fridge, heating the cooling agent as the heat rose. In principle it was a sound idea but in practice it very often burnt yellow then sooted up black and choked and stopped. Delicate adjustment meant I would have to lie on a cold cement floor for hours, turning and watching the flame until it was just right.

After this we got hold of a gas fridge which was made in Finland. It worked well, but was hard to regulate. We alternately found everything frozen solid or not cold enough; also we never knew exactly when it was going to run out. After being away one time, and finding it difficult to get it working again, I telephoned Calor Gas in Inverness. The helpful engineer said, 'Turn it upside down and hit it with a hammer.' I did just what he said, and it worked. Revolving it shifted air bubbles that had formed, blocking the movement of the cooling gas, and hitting the bends of the pipes loosened the liquid. It was amazing – and I thought he was pulling my leg.

He was the only person we ever met who had seen the Loch Ness Monster. I do not believe that was a leg-pull either. He had the air of a man almost tired of telling a story that always received the same sceptical reception. On one of his many visits to outlying districts to visit customers, he told us, he was driving back to Inverness when he glanced to his right and there on the loch was the unmistakable shape of something large and dark moving fast on the surface.

I understood all too well why the engineer did not relish telling his secret to sceptics, for many years before, when I was quite small, I had seen fairies.

I must have been about four years old. I had not been very well for quite a while and there was talk of taking out my tonsils. My bed had been moved into my father's dressing-room so that if I was ill in the night my mother was close at hand. I was very pleased. I had been worried that I would be put in charge of Gwen, my nanny, at the other end of the house. Gwen was very kind, but not as kind as my mummy or my dad.

The room was small, panelled in a light wood polished with beeswax. It had a small window and two doors, one to the passage and one to my parents' bedroom. There was a large dark wardrobe taking up one corner, and a mahogany chest of drawers against the wall opposite my small bed. I loved to examine all the items on the top of the chest: a small box with studs, cufflinks and collar stiffeners; a glass dish with the odd shirt button, razor blade and coloured golf tees, loose change from trouser pockets; two ebony-backed hair brushes; a jar of sweet-smelling Brylcream; and, to one side of the small mirror, a framed faded photograph of my grandmother who had died long before I was born. Her face particularly fascinated me: caught in that long forgotten moment, she wore a half smile and looked as though she was about to say something. I thought she was lovely, and it irked me slightly to know that I did not look anything like her but that Susan, my middle sister, did.

One night, when everyone was asleep, I lay in my bed, watching the moon-shadowed branches gently shifting on the panelled wall. One by one, small creatures crept through the open window to sit upon these shadows; they were bright like fireflies; they followed each other to find space to sit all around the window; they garlanded the pelmet; they jumped down on to the chest of drawers; they floated down to the foot of my bed. They had small sharp faces, wore coloured clothes, and each one had a musical instrument, the like of which I had never seen. They chattered amongst themselves and then they started to play soft percussion music.

I sat up in my bed. I do not remember feeling at all afraid, but watched in total fascination. 'I must wake Mummy and Daddy so they can see them too,' I thought. Pushing down the eiderdown and swinging my thin legs out of the sheets on to the floor, I crept in to my parents' bedroom. Standing at their door, I called, 'Daddy, Mummy, come and look at the fairies.'

The moment I spoke, the spell was broken and the fairies flew out of the dark window, their tiny frames linked together with garlands held by thin hands.

'Yes, darling, of course you saw fairies.' My mother tucked me back into my bed, but a sadness overwhelmed me as I knew she did not believe me. Night after night I waited in vain for another visit. I got tired, and black rings formed under my eyes, but they never came back. To have seen them just once was a privilege that not many share. I gave up telling people about what I had seen. There was no point.

Chapter Four

CHILE

'Come with me to Chile, Marie Christine.'

To *Chile*? *Me*? 'Hold on,' I thought. 'I must say yes. This is what I always hoped I would hear. I am being invited to join an expedition and right from the start. I can't be such a wimp, after all.'

John had talked much of Chile as we made our slow way down the Amazon. The southern tip of that mighty continent, its wildness and empty spaces, beckoned John. He had read Eric Shipton's books, particularly the ones describing Patagonia, and had spent hours looking at inadequate maps of this legendary area.

'Going down to the southern hemisphere in winter will be like a summer holiday,' he told me, 'but we can expect it to be windy.'

'Windier than here?' I asked. I remembered being lifted off my feet and flung to the ground like a rag doll the year before at Ardmore. How would I cope in stronger winds? When the wind hits face-on, it almost suffocates with its choking pillows of air. How would I breathe?

'Oh, yes, . . . much,' John answered rather dismissively.

In 1972, we had two meetings with the legendary Eric Shipton to decide on a plan of where to go and what to do. First, he came to visit us at Ardmore. We picked him and his friend Phyllis up by boat from Skerricha just as darkness was falling. Eric was lean and hard from years of walking in high places; his blue eyes scanned the distance as we set off to make the journey across the loch. Phyllis was charming and droll; her gold bracelets jangled as she clambered aboard the boat, and I could not help but notice her beautifully manicured scarlet nails. What would she think of our simple home? She told me later she was more concerned about the journey across the loch. Not knowing our destination, she feared we were setting off on a long and hazardous trip in an open boat as darkness was falling with one man who had rowed across the Atlantic and another who had climbed most of the high mountains in the world. You do not start asking anxious questions about safety in that company.

As we talked during that weekend, a plan formed. Ours was to be the first expedition to cross an unexplored ice-cap, Gran Campo Nevado. 'There are some good spots for climbing out there,' said Eric. 'You could reach them by boat.'

A few weeks later, just before the start of our fourth season, we met Eric at the Royal Geographical Society in Kensington Gore. My mother was with us and we all sat down to tea in the drab Victorian tea-room. The high walls were lined with portraits of grave looking explorers who had spent their lives struggling in steamy parts of Africa. I sat on the edge of my chair hoping Eric would not frighten my mother with descriptions of hanging glaciers, icebergs, tidal waves, killer whales, or other terrors. She could not understand why I wanted to be part of the expedition, and I felt terrible when she talked of selling her home in Brighton and buying a cottage in the country with a garden if we did not come back and she had Rebecca to look after. I should not go, she said. I should stay at home and give Rebecca a brother or sister instead. Once again I was torn. Lit up by John's enormous enthusiasm, which made the whole trip seem so exciting, I could not bear to miss it and I did not want not to be with him.

'And the wind, what is it like down there?' my mother asked.

Eric understood how we did not want to cause alarm, and he made the williwaw winds sound almost friendly, then told us how the land around the Magellan Straits is covered in Nothofagus, a type of false beech native to the southern hemisphere. It was beginning to sound like some summer holiday. (Only later did he add that it was hard to find anywhere to pitch a tent above high tide as the trees were so distorted by wind they grew horizontal to the ground, while elsewhere the Sphagnum moss was so deep you could sink up to your waist in it.)

My mother had to go, so we said goodbye and headed for the map room. The maps were unfurled and we pored over the jigsaw of inlets down at the bottom of the twisted tail of South America. Eric pointed to a spot on the map which seemed to be surrounded by quite a lot of dotted lines containing a blank area.

'Here it is.' John and I peered closely at the map. 'Gran Campo Nevado or Big Snow Field. It's unexplored, just waiting for you.

There seem to be at least two glaciers where you could try and get on to the ice-cap. With your plan to travel by water in rubber inflatables you could probably reach them, but it won't be easy. The channels leading to the Magellan Straits are desperately wild, though I couldn't say much while your mother was with us.' Eric turned his pale blue eyes towards me, with a conspiratorial smile. 'Now I must go,' he said, glancing at his watch. 'You two stay and study this a bit longer. We'll try and get you some photo-copies.'

As we made our way to the grand exit John had that special glint in his eye, and his footsteps were light and springy. He was humming the first few bars of 'War at Sea', with not much tune but much verve. I could recognise this as the same tune I had heard him hum before at other times like this, when it really looked that the rowing trip was on, when the plans for the Amazon were falling into place. Battle was about to commence. It all sounded terribly exciting, and easy to feel confident after buttered crumpets and tea.

How many Victorian explorers I thought, their heads also filled with plans, must have come through these very doors on to a gaslit pavement, hoping to plant the British flag in unexplored territory, wondering if they would have the fortitude to face danger, discomfort and possible death. But now it was the early 1970s, and puddles reflected electric lights and the headlamps of heavy traffic as it roared by towards Knightsbridge. A chill of fear crept into my soul. Why on earth should I want to risk losing my life and – worse – leaving my child an orphan?

It did not seem more than yesterday when I had my job nearby at the Arts Council in St James's Square, and shared a basement flat with two girlfriends, when we had had such fun and laughs and schemes. Certainly the eight years since John and I had married had changed me greatly. But to what? Who was I? What was I? Did other women have this doubt about their identity? They too marry, take on a different name, become wives, become mothers. Undoubtedly John's strong personality had had its effect on me, and perhaps it was lucky for us that I wanted to share his life, which meant following his call. But standing here in the chill night air, looking back at the domed roof of this bastion of British endeavour and remembering a different Marie Christine, I won-dered very much at the wisdom of what I was doing.

'Come on, what's the matter with you,' John called over his shoulder, and off we marched into the night to enjoy a rare curry with some of John's friends.

Back at Ardmore we had to plan for the expedition to Chile in the autumn whilst running our busy season. Once more I was immersed in cooking and typing, but now I had some more help. Kay Price had joined us that summer from Plymouth, and became a dear friend.

Kay had just retired from the Blood Donors' Association and did not want to stop work. She helped type and answer the phone. Sometimes in a lapse of concentration she would answer the phone saying: 'Blood Donors' Association' – which could put callers into a mild panic if they were calling to find out how their child was getting on. They would then get their breath back only to be told they could not speak to the child because he was 'on the other side,' referring to the southern shore of Loch a' Chad-Fi where the summer school was situated. Kay would answer all the post in our absence in Chile, one or two classic letters going out saying, 'John and Marie Christine hope to cross an unexploded ice-cap.'

Kay spent the summers in a single-room wooden cabin on the shore at Ardmore. She kept it beautifully neat with blue and white curtains at the windows, and cushions and rugs to match on the sofa bed and rattan chairs. Many chief instructors took up residence there after Kay had left, and it is still called Kay's Cabin twenty years on. 'Who was Kay?' they ask from their jumble of a home, and as I explain I see Kay still, climbing the hill to our croft wearing her waterproof leggings to protect her smart trousers from any dew or pollen which might brush on to them as she made her way through the long grass of early summer. She was always very particular.

Plans for the trip went on apace. Lance made a big box, seven feet by three feet by two and a quarter feet. It looked uncannily like a coffin. Into it went all our equipment for shipping out to Punta Arenas, including two folded ten-foot rubber inflatables, two Seagull outboard engines, a rifle and ammunition, ice axes, crampons and a certain amount of climbing equipment (none of which I was particularly familiar with), limited clothing and dehydrated food which was carefully heat-sealed at the school. We planned to get the bulk of the rations out in Chile. Willie the storeman threatened to write notes to us on the loo paper (we were to be allowed four pieces a day), and sure enough his cheeky messages would turn up just when they were most welcome, in the rain a thousand miles away.

The plan was for three of us to go: John, me and Richard Shuff, our chief instructor, who was the climbing expert. This time we felt it would be safer if we all knew each other well beforehand. Then Krister Nylund, a friend from Sweden who had helped at the school the previous year, and who had spent a winter on a kibbutz harvesting bananas with Richard, turned up late in the summer. John and I both agreed he would be a great asset on this trip. Tall with a blond afro hairstyle, he was always cheerful and he would be excellent in the snow, having worked as a ski instructor. Richard was delighted by his last-minute inclusion. By then, we had sent the coffin ahead by sea, and the rations for four months were for only three, but we felt we would rather go a bit hungry and have Krister along. We felt sure we could live off the land. The Chilean Indian tribes were nomadic. If they managed to find food, surely we could.

During the summer John negotiated a contract to write a book about our journey – the small advance was a help towards purchasing our air tickets – and at the last minute *The People* agreed to run a couple of stories on our expedition. They labelled John 'Captain Courageous', and once again tantalisingly described it as a story about 'three men and a girl' – only this time I, not Anna, was the girl. It was a bit more cash to go into the kitty to help towards the increasing expense of it all.

Finally, we looked to see if there was anything scientifically useful we could do once out in this remote area. Just before we departed I was summoned to the British Museum, and they told me they would be pleased to receive samples of Sphagnum moss. I was shown how to dry it and fold it between paper. It looked a fairly easy task, and now we could say when people scoffed at our schemes that we were officially aiding and advancing science.

The summer raced by, and autumn arrived. The dreaded moment for us to say goodbye to Bec was upon us. Bec had decided she wanted to stay with Ada and Lance and they seemed pleased. I could not speak. I held her close, and John promised we would bring her back a penguin to keep the crocodile from the Amazon company.

'Don't worry, Mum. You'll be back soon,' her cheery voice piped at me as I handed her over to Ada. Then off they went chatting over plans for putting up the swing behind the Blue House that weekend. I wondered if I would see her again and my heart felt like breaking in two.

As we touched down at Punta Arenas on the northern shores of the Magellan Straits, I was shocked to see snow on the ground. The place had a desolate air. We were met by Señor Barrientos who, dark eyes flashing behind horn-rimmed specs, proudly told us how he had held the position of assistant to the British consul for fifty years. We followed his squarely built short frame as he bustled us through the customs, switching from Spanish to voluble English which he spoke through a mouth crammed with poorly cared-for teeth.

They had expected us to stay at the best hotel in town, Cabo do Hornos, while John would have been happy if we could have got our tents out and camped in the tree-lined garden. In the event, we based ourselves at the more modest Plaza Hotel down a few windy corners from the centre.

We had a lot to buy before we could set off. The few shops had long queues outside them, and the shelves inside were bare except for Cussons Imperial Leather soap and dusty strings of dried mussels. But Señor Barrientos took us to a Yugoslav shopkeeper, who managed to find us from the back of his empty shop 168 packets of wine biscuits, a hundred pounds of sugar and seventy pounds of oats, to supplement the rations we had shipped out in the coffin. We would have to do without rice: there was none to be had. The country was going through a period of great uncertainty. President Allende had been democratically voted in at the last election to represent the Communist Party, so sanctions from the capitalist world had resulted in shortages from raw materials to medicine, to basic food. What price idealism!

On our last day the British consul, Denley King, a dapper man in his late sixties, invited us to have tea with him and his wife. We listened to their stories of how the English settlers now had either died or gone, while we drank tea out of fine bone-china cups and tried not to be too eager to demolish the spread of scones, pilchard-and-egg sandwiches and iced sponge cakes. Looking out of the drawing room window of their town house, past the topiaried trees, we could see right across the Magellan Straits to Tierra del Fuego. I could not help but think that soon the tea party and scones would be over and I would be out in that bleak landscape for a long time.

While we had been taking tea, Richard had met some personnel off the American Research ship *Hero*. 'They've invited you down to look at their charts this evening,' he reported. This was good news. We made our way down to the dock stepping through slushy puddles and muffling ourselves from the skinning wind that shrieked round every corner. On board it was warm and bright, and we were ushered into the compact chart-room and introduced ourselves to Captain Lenie. We explained our planned route, pointing to the narrows between the mountains at the southern end of the ice-cap. He looked aghast.

'You wanna go up here, in ten-foot rubber boats? Why this ship is a goddamn icebreaker, and I had to turn back. These glaciers on the sides of the mountains – they're just stuck on, waiting to come crashing thousands of feet down into the sea.

'Out here on the Pacific coast there's a terrific swell and here there's a tide race.' He stabbed the precise positions on the chart with his stubby finger as he emphasised each point. 'With the onset of spring that ice is pretty unstable, the glaciers will be calving. In these narrows there are rapids, and the icebergs get grounded by the tide.'

The list of horrors continued. Richard, who was keener on climbing than boating, looked as appalled as I. John simply jotted down some notes.

As Captain Lenie showed us to the gangplank, he urged us strongly against taking this route, the only one possible. 'We sure hate to lose good men,' he said, shaking his head in disbelief. Then he looked at me standing there defiantly, and added: 'Women too.'

The next day we took a lift in a truck the 120 bumpy miles to the start of our expedition, a sheep station situated on the shores of Seno Skyring, a large inland sea with narrow channels at the western and eastern ends which took the tidal water in from the Pacific and let it out to the Atlantic. Our aim was to make our way to the western end where we hoped we could pass through the narrows of Canal Gajardo, and out into the Pacific end of the Magellan Straits, to reach our ice-cap.

It was a cold drive. The four of us sat with the driver in the cab. Being the lightest I had to sit on the others' knees, changing every half hour. It kept me warm, but the low roof of the cab forced my head on to my chest. My view from the window was distorted but I saw rheas (the South American ostrich), ibis, many kinds of duck and geese and long-legged sheep. It helped to keep my mind off the discomfort. No way could I start this trip by complaining.

Gradually the grey-green of the pampas gave way to scrub and the sheep station's undulating country. We had been given permission to stay here for a day or two by one of the most powerful men in the government, a man zealous in fulfilling the promises for which the Communist Party was elected. We were told that Fidel Castro had been one of the last visitors to this model *estancia*, and that the workers who were now running the place were thrilled at the honour. The previous owner had moved over to Argentina.

We had mixed feelings. The well-off had had it their own way for too long and it was time for change, but those that had taken over did not appear to have the administrative skills to keep the system working. Here, at this *estancia*, the workers in their joint ownership of the place sat about instead of working, prime breeding stock was slaughtered for eating, and the buildings were falling into disrepair.

We spent the time at Skyring unpacking the coffin and sorting out the kit. Our plan was to inflate the dinghies and set off along Seno Skyring towards the narrows, hugging the coast of this stormy waterway for a distance of approximately fifty miles, but on our last day, three men called into the *estancia*, said they were heading the way we planned, and would give us a lift in their two home-made wooden boats.

Francisco was the leader. Stocky, with dark hair and a friendly smile, he was from Chiloe, an island to the north-west. His wife and seven children now lived at the woodmill at Las Colas along the shore, but Francisco spent his life travelling in his boat around the islands and extensive shoreline of Skyring to chop wood with his mighty five-foot axe. Along with him was Calisto. A dark bearded piratical figure with a wide flashing smile and high pitched laugh, he lived along the coast beneath the jagged white-toothed mountain, Cerro Dynover. The third, Alexandro, lived twenty miles to the west on the tiny island of Unicornio with his sister, Fresia, two of the last forty-six surviving Alacalufe Indians. He hardly ever smiled and just spoke in bitter bursts. It seemed the Agrarian Reforms had come too late for Alexandro. We would never know of his past, but his poverty of spirit struck me like an accusation.

We set off on 19 October. It was a startlingly clear morning, the glassy calm of this inland sea reflecting the mountains that were drawing us on, but it was too good to last. After three hours Francisco's ancient Archimedes outboard engine stopped.

We spent our first night in a hut belonging to a painfully shy solitary bachelor, called Sergeo. He must have been dismayed at his unbidden guests, Francisco insisted we should sleep in Sergeo's home. We would have been happier to pitch our tents, but we did not want to offend anyone. John and I were put in the *matrimonio* room, sleeping between Sergeo's grey sheets. I crept out early the first morning to relieve myself, putting on my orange waterproof jacket and rubber boots. Thinking I was safely out of sight from the seven men, I squatted, wondering as I undid Willie's package of lavatory paper if he had kept his promise and written me a note. Suddenly there was a savage commotion of barking and growling. Sergeo's dogs had seen me. They seemed to leap at me from nowhere, only to stop short, rearing and yelping in frustrated rage: the ropes which tied them to stakes held them just out of reach. I vowed to be more careful in the future. I had had a narrow escape.

For two days we were marooned there, while the weather showed its venom. Vicious williwaws shrieked down from the four-thousand-foot snow-covered mountain behind us.

We spent much of the waiting time zeroing the rifle. Luckily I could shoot. John had taught me in true military style back at Ardmore, as sadly there are times when it is necessary to use a rifle. Once at a fairground stall in Madeira I surprised a group of Portuguese soldiers by beating them all and winning the top prize. I think they thought I would just shut my eyes and pull the trigger.

John managed to shoot a goose and I watched closely as Francisco deftly plucked and eviscerated this lovely bird. (Later on I would do this, trying to remember exactly Francisco's method, but on my first attempt, as I cut through the bird's neck, it let out a loud quack. I dropped the carcase and ran off screaming. I realised afterwards it was only air being forced up through its voice box.)

When the weather calmed, we unpacked our Seagull outboards and mounted these on Francisco's and Alexandro's boats. We wanted to get on with our journey down Skyring. The sea at first was an oily calm, but once we were round the point the surface changed. The waves were steep and short, and our two heavily laden boats were thrown about, up and down and side to side. It

Left: Never look back – my wedding day, 21 March 1964

Above: John, the penniless paratroop officer I fell in love with

Below: Maureen and I join John and Chay Blyth aboard *English Rose III* after their epic voyage across the Atlantic, 5 September 1966

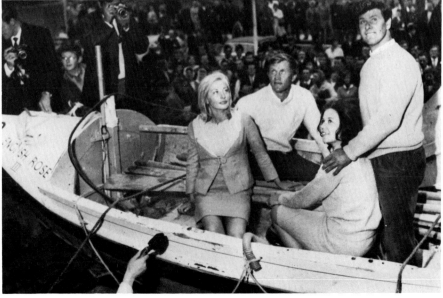

Left: Together again after 92 days, September 1966

Right: In 1970 *Woman* magazine called Rebecca 'The loneliest little girl in Britain'.

Below right: Crofting at Ardmore. John, Bec and me, 1970

Below: 'Twenty-six miles is a very long way.' Bec and me before the New York Marathon, October 1980

Chile, 1972. We travelled in rubber dinghies
into the Magellan Straits.

was not long before both engines stopped. Francisco's normally smiling face was now grim as he and the others reached for the oars to keep the boats heading for the safety of Calisto's home, Chinchorro. Stormbound we were pinned here for a further three days, and as soon as the weather eased we said a sad goodbye to our dashing friend Calisto. He was to die not long after in a knife fight over a sheep dispute.

On we headed along Skyring to Isla Unicornio, where Alexandro lived. As our boat scrunched on to the pebbly shore in the sheltered bay, his nine dogs came bounding up to greet us. I was dismayed to see they were covered in sores. The whole island had a forlorn air about it. Francisco shaking his head sadly told us Fresia and Alexandro had nothing but the boat we had arrived in, and a second one that lay half finished lashed down high above the water's edge: work had stopped as they had run out of copper nails.

Fresia, her heavy dark hair held off her strong face with a white nylon hair band, smiled a lot and welcomed us to their home. It was made of corrugated iron but so rusty that in many places the rain poured in. Inside it was filthy and stank of dog and cat excrement. They insisted we stay with them rather than put up our tents. Once again John and I were expected to sleep in the only bed. This time it was in a cupboard off the one room. As it got dark Fresia lit the lamp, the wick a grubby rag which lay in a tin of congealed mutton fat, and long-legged black spiders crawled out of the cracks in the wall of our cupboard. Richard and Krister carefully laid their sleeping bags down on the floor in the main room, Fresia blew out the flame, and I sobbed, silently engulfed in self-pity at the squalor.

We were all relieved when the damp day dawned, and we packed up quickly. But I was sad to say goodbye to Fresia as she hugged me. She did not see many other women – nor would I for the next six weeks.

We loaded everything now into Francisco's boat and continued on our journey. I greatly admired our quiet friend Francisco. His whole lifestyle was one of total self-reliance and simplicity. We must have seemed ridiculous to him with our latest equipment, and in our brightly coloured clothing. His clothes were all patches; he travelled in a boat that he had built from trees which he had selected and felled, fashioned and formed. His patched sail doubled as a shelter: he draped it round a tree and cutting a few whippy branches turned it into a teepee.

He carried in his boat a tinder box. With this each evening he lit a fire and fed it with dark green Nothofagus branches which blazed hot and bright. In a box he kneaded nuts of dough adding the fermenting yeast which he stored dry, most carefully, in an airtight tin. He placed his blackened cooking pot filled with solid mutton fat to heat on the fire. The swelling dough of the tortas was dropped into the smoking hot fat, cooked for a few minutes and fished out for us to devour greedily, along with giant mussels gathered from the shallow water. They were delicious. Then there was *pocito café* made in a battered kettle, and finally a special suck on the slender bronze tube that poked into the gourd containing the bitter *yerbe mate* brew considered by all those living in these deep southern areas as *mucho bueno por los organ*.

Each day now I felt stronger and more able to cope. I knew I could manage the practical aspects of surviving; I was just anxious about the rough sea conditions and wondered how I would cope with difficult climbs. We all wanted to get on with what we had come to do, and had not anticipated these long stops in our progress to the ice-cap. Too much time to think about what was to come did not help our nerves. We were all thinking of the hanging glaciers ahead.

The wind had dropped but once out of the shelter of the creek the old see-sawing motion started up, causing our engine to race and splutter; so Francisco took us to his home on Isla Chandler. He had built it strongly to last, to keep his family safe from the storms, but they had left; his wife and seven children were days away to the east of the *estancia* where we had stayed. There were reminders which must have saddened Francisco. Poking around the ground outside, I came across one small shoe, and in an attempt to keep out the draughts some of the cracks in the walls were filled with old brightly coloured cotton material, maybe from a dress his wife once wore. I felt I could have lived in this rather beautiful stormy place – in some ways it was very like Ardmore – but John was getting anxious. When would the wind ever abate?

It was late afternoon on 7 November, after ten days of waiting for calm, that we finally set off. Francisco would take us to the mouth of Canal Gajardo, but he could *not* be persuaded to go any further with us. Talk about the narrows and the Golfo Xaultegua beyond would reduce him to a rolling of eyes and shaking his head muttering, '*Golfo, malo,*' which did not do much for my confidence. Early the following morning we waved a sad goodbye to Francisco. His final grave instructions were issued to us in severe Castiliano: 'Light two fires on the southern shore of Skyring if I am to come with the boat. Three fires will mean I am to come immediately, if it's life or death.'

Now we had to get on. We had been going for nearly a month and up to now achieved very little, except for studying and practising survival, which I felt could almost be raised to the status of an art form. We must now get through the narrows, the first challenge in our Odyssey, which was to test our courage and resolve at every turn. Fortunately this day was the best one yet, with virtually no wind and the sun shining from a bright blue sky. But was this warmth good for calving ice and avalanching hanging glaciers?

In our ten-foot rubber dinghies we motored on down the channel. On both banks were steep cliffs with occasional trees clinging to their sides and traces of recent land and snow slides. On one side was the dazzling blue and white wall of the ice-cap towering five thousand feet above us.

Our plan was to head into the narrow part separately. John and I would go first, then Richard and Krister. The narrowest section was only about three hundred yards long, and no more than fifteen yards across. As our two boats approached the narrows, we suddenly noticed Richard and Krister waving their arms wildly to attract us. What on earth was it? What we saw turned my blood to ice. Between the two boats circled three sinister killer whales, their black triangular fins like menacing flags, and as they turned we could see the tell-tale white slashes on their sides. Were these sinister creatures guardians of the narrows?

Both boats made sharply for the shallows, expecting to be tossed into the air at any second, but they never came. They just disappeared. We waited for fifteen minutes and during that time we also watched, mesmerised, as stately icebergs were propelled by the racing current towards a giant ice whirlpool and once in its pull swung round and round in a macabre dance.

We refuelled, as we could easily need the maximum one hour of full throttle motoring time. Then as I paddled out into the deeper water and John primed the engine, he shouted to the boys: 'You wait until you're sure we are right through before you start. If anything happens to us let us drift clear of the ice, upside down or otherwise, before you come out to pick us up – and keep taking photographs.' I felt this last comment to be in very poor taste, but I was far too nervous to make a fuss.

We motored out into the full stream to where a line of small green whirlpools marked the edge of the racing current. Immediately we were swung violently to one side, our flank exposed to the full weight of the tide which was about to push us into the huge whirlpool of clinking crunching ice blocks which would crush us or at best just sink us.

We could feel the icy breath of Charybdis. John's instant reaction of pushing the steering arm away from himself saved us, altering our course and heading us up into the current. The two-stroke engine roared and our wake boiled white. We felt we were racing along but when I dared to look up briefly at the towering cliffs I could see we had hardly moved. One falter in the engine, one speck of dirt in the fuel and we would be swept back into the ice crush.

'Stand up and watch for rocks and ice.' Although I was sitting next to John, he had to shout to be heard. We were inching forward and had reached the narrowest part of the channel where the tide roared through two slabs of rock. Our only hope was to edge to the left and try to find a way through in shallower water, but this ran the risk of breaking a sheer pin if the propeller so much as touched a rock. It was our only chance, and I would have to judge if there was sufficient depth.

I waved to left and right as I nervously crouched on top of our cargo to get a better view. Then suddenly it was all over. The cliffs opened up on either side to a wider expanse of water. My navigation and John's steady hand had got us through. We had made it.

Feeling euphoric, we motored on into calmer milky waters of the icemelt to examine a glacier up a quiet channel. It was filled with blocks of ice, some so huge that we feared if they were unstable they might suddenly roll over and capsize us.

'The others should be through by now.' John was looking anxiously at his watch, and an awful sinking feeling began to overwhelm us. We had been larking about sightseeing amongst the icebergs while they were probably fighting for their lives. Then suddenly from around the corner came the small grey boat with its red dodger, and Richard and Krister grinning hugely at us.

'The big iceberg that came through just as you left turned over

and caused a bit of commotion in the whirlpool,' they shouted.
'Then the three killers came back, with fins like bloody guillotines –
we weren't going while they were around.'

It was with blithe hearts we set off. The narrows crossed off the
list, surely we could manage the other challenges.

It would have been nice to stop and have a brew, but we knew
this sort of weather did not come very often, and we had to make
the most of it. All afternoon we motored smoothly along the fiord
leading to the point where we would turn into the Pacific end of the
Magellan Straits, Golfo Xaultegua, the name of which had sent
Francisco's eyes rolling around in horror. But surely today was the
day to cross it. John's courage drew us onward: he never showed
any sign of fear or nervousness. I felt this was a power bestowed on
him by the gods and I hoped it would touch me whilst I was with
him.

By late afternoon we entered the widening bay of Golfo
Xaultegua. It was like a huge sea and once round the headland Punta
Quidora we would feel the ocean swell, which would have built up
on its way right round the world without any hindrance of land.
The breeze was strengthening and the slight chop was slopping
water into the two heavily laden boats. Krister and Richard were
keen to stop for a brew, as we had been going virtually all day; so
we headed across the bay to a small pebble beach, where we quickly
boiled water for tea and cooked a dozen or so enormous four-inch
mussels which we found nearby. Out in the bay we had all seen the
white surf breaking on the far shore. If this was a calm day what
would it be like when it was rough? John voiced our thoughts: 'We
must get along this exposed ten miles of coast while the weather is
good,' he said. 'We can camp at Portaluppi fiord tonight, and if the
weather holds then make a dash for the next stretch.'

Quickly we got back into our boats, refuelled and set off
together. All was going well, and the golden evening sun was
shedding a pearly light on the long slow swell we were confidently
riding. But once around the point it changed dramatically.
Suddenly we were tossed about in the short steep sea, with white-
crested waves over-falling themselves into deep troughs, breaking
white on the nearby shore, which was girdled in long strands of
yellow kelp. If we got into that we would never get out. Then the
sea hit the carburettor, and our engine stuttered and stopped.

'Paddle, Marie Christine. Paddle for all you're worth,' John yelled at me, as I was reaching for a dinghy paddle. I scrambled up on to our bulky cargo and dug the blade deep into the choppy water while John tried to re-start the soaked engine. The other two circled us to see if we wanted a tow, but John feared theirs would stop if they manoeuvred around too much; so he waved them to go back to the sheltered waters behind the point. I paddled hard one side, then the other. We were just about keeping our position but no more, and John was having no luck with the engine. Our boat was filling fast with icy water, and soon our precious cargo would float away and break up in the surf.

John now abandoned the engine and concentrated on baling but there was so much stuff in our boat it was hard to get the water out. He flung out a string of fish which we had caught the day before, and some smaller cooking items.

'I can't keep going for much longer,' I shouted to John. My arms were screaming with pain from the effort. He picked up the other paddle and between us we managed to push ourselves back into calmer waters. Still determined to get along the coast that night, John tried another plug, but all to no avail. To add to our problems Richard and Krister's engine also stopped and would not start again. We had to abandon the attempt that night. On our gloomy return to the beach where we had stopped for tea earlier we were observed by a haughty osprey, sitting high on a windblasted branch. Gimlet-eyed he judged us in a glance. Were he and the black killers of the narrows messengers from the gods, sent to watch us?

Exhausted, we hauled our boats up as high as we could, and looking through the contents of the boxes we found much of our rations were ruined. I felt almost too dazed to care, and my arms were aching and tender from the paddling. Surely it would all seem better in the morning.

After the previous day's efforts we did not wake until seven. We hurried to sort out and pack up our kit. We had to leave all the damp food – twenty packets of porridge and five of semolina, also two of the sledging boxes in which we stored the food. At least it made our loads for the boats lighter. We set off at 10.30. There was a slight breeze getting up but still the weather was fine. We crept along, fearful of waking the dozing giant, dreading the moment we would round the point. Again there was a big swell, but at least the overfalls were not as severe as the previous evening. Nevertheless much water slurped over the side. I baled with a ferocious monotony: anything was better than looking up and seeing the next big wave coming to swamp us; this way I could hide like an ostrich.

The engines miraculously kept going in spite of the odd splutter, but all the time the wind was freshening, and we knew a williwaw could send us hurtling out into the middle of the stormy Magellan Straits – and then what? But as the day wore on we became more confident, and could not help but marvel at the abundance of bird-life new to us. Giant albatrosses wheeled inquisitively towards us, their fourteen-foot wing tips lifting with the breeze. We disturbed flocks of black and white Magellan penguins diving at the very last minute as we approached. We saw one of the rare white kelp geese, and families of the flightless grey steamer ducks, their orange beaks showing bright as they shepherded their large families of fluffy young.

John had agreed the night before with Richard that we would try and reach Portaluppi, a long narrow fiord sheltered from the Pacific swell and shaped like a curled tail, and from there try and portage our kit over the pass shown by the contours of our much studied map. This route should take us down to a point where it looked as if we could make our ascent on to the ice-cap, avoiding more perilous ocean hops along the exposed coast.

The day wore on and the giant was waking. As we left the lee of Anderson Island the wind and the sea increased, but with more weight in the bow we found the engines less prone to swamping, and now we were able to push on in wild conditions so long as one of the two-man team was constantly baling out the water which came in green over the side. As the rising wind streaked the waves with ribbons of spindrift, on we battled passing islands that formed a lagoon, but not much shelter, off the headland where we must turn and head up the seven-mile Portaluppi fiord. Now sea was breaking all around us, the wind blowing violently from two opposite directions. Our boats bounced on, spray and rain making it difficult to see, and then when we felt we could take no more of this battering the wind started to drop and the sky cleared, just briefly to reveal the dazzling ice-cap way ahead above the green forest which fell steeply to the shore of this fiord. Suddenly there was a bump and then another: all around us was a school of dolphins escorting us to the beach where we had decided to stop.

Next day we found a route to carry our kit to the saddle. Up and up we went taking loads of food, fuel, the packed up boats, everything – all the time feeling we had sneaked past the sleeping giant in the sea. The weather deteriorated and again the wind shrieked, hurling rain and sleet, tearing at our tents and clothing, but at least the wet ground was firm.

Then the awful truth hit us. After many journeys and much effort we discovered our route to the ice-cap was blocked by a cliff, and it was not going to be possible to lower ourselves and our kit down. Cursing ourselves for not doing a proper recce, we set about carrying everything back down to our campsite on Portaluppi.

Nine days after arriving with our dolphin escort we set off again. It had been an interesting exercise, and we had learnt never to attempt anything without some kind of recce. We had learnt too that the map which we had believed in so implicitly could be wrong.

We were also now becoming an interdependent team. Over the weeks we had shared moments of such risk, danger, elation and despair that a strong bond of friendship was forming between the four of us, which would help us through the difficult times. As a woman there were times when I cursed my physical weakness – I could not carry the weights the other three were able to – but I tried hard to make up for it in other ways. I gathered and cooked our food; I tried to be cheerful and fair; I kept my fears and doubts to myself. We laughed and sang and throughout all the discomfort the spirit triumphed.

We packed up in the rain as usual. The wind still blew from the north-west, but we thought that if we could make some progress down the seven-mile fiord we would be in a better position to make the dash along the exposed ocean coast when it did drop calm.

Another day of heart stopping boating, I wrote in my diary. *Caught in the rip-tide our boats pitch and lurch, the engines splutter and stop when splashed. We can see waves breaking heavily on the islands that guard the mouth of the fiord. We must pass these to get round the point. Surely we will get some calm weather.*

We decide to stop. It is too stormy and we find a sheltered beach to camp, hoping for calm. We know now there isn't any other way except by sea.

We rise early. The wind has dropped; the sea is an oily green calm; our small boats lift and fall like feathers. The mighty giant slumbers, his chest the heaving swell, as we creep on, hardly daring to talk. Past Punta Janequeo, the point of no return, we lift and fall on the swell, hundreds of feet from the crest of one wall of water to the top of the next.

We motored together, rafting up every hour to refuel. The slow rain continued to flatten the ocean, and we passed albatrosses temporarily grounded because of the heaving calm. Another three hours and then we should be clear of the ocean, if only the weather would hold.

As the day wore on it began to brighten. The cloud lifted and by noon we had rounded Punta Cummings and were now making our way into the more sheltered waters of Fiordo Northbrook. The sky was blue; our spirits were high; euphoria took the place of anxiety. The rain had left the atmosphere sparkling clear along the coast and we gazed at the sharp mountains reaching up into the sky.

Then suddenly our good weather was replaced by a williwaw swooping off the mountains, whipping the water into spiky waves which once again slurped into our boats. Still, on we went through Canal Almirante Martinez into Bahia Beaufort. There was not much daylight left; we had been fourteen hours in the boats; we were getting tired – the classic situation for a mistake. I was bailing the icy water trying to keep ahead of it as it rushed in over the bows. Just a bit further and we were there, pulling our brave boats up the sandy beach of Xanadu and lashing them high above the tide. The gods had seen fit to let us through.

But now we must get on with what we had really come to Chile to do: to climb and cross the unexplored Gran Campo Nevado ice-cap. It lay brilliantly white beneath the sky: a bowl of ice and snow encircled by a necklace of jagged black peaks, its ring of glaciers squeezing through gaps in blue and white tumbles of ice, moving remorselessly towards the sea, five thousand feet below. We would have liked to have rested and restored ourselves after our harrowing sea journey, but that part was only incidental; now was the real challenge. Richard did a recce, and decided our best chance was to scale the three thousand-foot cliff near our camp and from there approach the ice-cap over a ridge.

'I reckon we should steer clear of the glacier,' he said. 'It looks very broken for a long way up from the foot: ice plates thrown against one another, with their ends forced into the air, and masses of crevasses. Nor are we an experienced team in glacier work.'

I had to agree. I had never done any snow and ice climbing. This would be my baptism of fire. I wrote in my diary: *Sat 2 December. Rise at 6.00. Plenty of mosquitoes biting us. Damp and rain starting. Pack kit and try fitting my crampons – much too small; John hammers the front wider. They'll do but far from perfect. Everyone edgy, and the odd sharp exchange between R and J. Finally leave at 10.30. Heavy pack. First we walk up through tangled trees, then start climbing. Near vertical cliff in most places. Ice axe very handy when dug in as hand hold, otherwise hold on to any branches, roots or clumps of grass and haul myself up. Encouragement from John, one above me which helps a lot. Daren't look down at the drop but keep scrambling up and up. How will I ever get down? Stop for breaks and lunch. Once John falls as his foothold gives way. Terrible feeling seeing him slip past, I am unable to help. I break down, pathetic but it is so shocking.*

Richard was in the lead, taking us up the route he had reconnoitred. He had left markers for us to follow, two stones placed on top of each other, sticks stuck into the turf. He had side stepped to check the next direction, when the soggy ledge that John was resting on suddenly gave way. John was powerless to stop himself. Falling, feet first with his face close to the cliff, he slid past me at high speed. Miraculously his fall was halted by his feet hitting a ledge which stuck out just before a sheer drop of hundreds of feet. Gingerly, he clambered up. We were all shaken.

Don't feel the weight of my load as I am so nervous, the steepest three-thousand-foot climb is over, we are now up in the snow, the climb has taken seven hours. We put up our tents and crawled inside. *Warmth and comfort returns, feel secure in my orange cocoon for the first time today. Cooked supper in tent; soup, mince and potatoes all together, with cocoa to follow. Boys squeezed in and we all had supper together. Went to sleep with wet clothes on in sleeping bag, but was warm enough.*

Sun 3 December. Up at 5.30. Make breakfast which J takes to boys. Pack up and set off. Poor visibility and windy. Weather gets steadily worse, after forty-five minutes there is a blizzard. Hard to see at all. Can just make out rocks so J sets off with compass counting paces in straight line. He waves and we follow. Very Bad hardly able to walk, and snow painful when blown on face. Difficult to breathe. Make way to small outcrop of rocks which will afford us some shelter and start tramping down flat spaces for tents and digging snow. Must keep moving, very cold. Worried about Krister; I can't make him talk, but find he is all right, only unable to talk because of his hat which is pulled up over his mouth. Finally get tents up takes TWO HOURS. Relief to be in – out of snow and wind – feet and hands freezing but soon thaw out. Lunch of four biscuits and two slices Kraft cheese in tent. Wind abates and mist clears to reveal that we are on the edge of a very steep snow hill dropping to a frozen lake hundreds of feet

below. Krister's bright pink polybag with kit nearly slides over edge.
Before bed I go out in wet boots and bare feet and fix fly sheet with snow and
bring in snow to melt for tomorrow's b'fast.

Mon 4 December. 5.00 make porridge and tea which John takes to
boys. While Richard takes down his tent his ridge pole slides down slope
and over edge at high speed with him after it. 'STOP,' J shouts and he
does just in time. R calls it 'a death blow'. Clear sky and bright sun. J and
R go off on a recce at 7.00, K and I make our way down round side of
steep hill and search for pole, much snow and steep slopes, K and I watch
out for avalanches, below where our tents are perched on the steep slope
there is the grimly smiling blue crack of a fissure. K finds pole on rock
after searching for an hour. Very lucky. We make our way back and meet
up with R. He and J have disagreed about the recce and R asks me to
persuade J not to go on.

I did not know what had been going on while Krister and I were
in the valley below searching for the tent pole, but judging by
John's and Richard's faces they were obviously not in agreement.
We were to hear they had set off along the ridge and after climbing
up and down through thick snow reached a point where they
could clearly see our proposed route to reach the ice-cap.

After a pause Richard had said: 'Scrub it. I wouldn't follow
anyone across that, let alone lead it.' I respected Richard's judgement – after all, of the four of us he was the one who knew most
about climbing – but also I knew how much this all meant to John:
the planning, expense, time. Surely we could manage it somehow. We all returned to our tent where the discussion raged on
and on. Eventually it was decided that Richard would go back to
our camp on the shore, making his own way down the three-
thousand-foot cliff. I am sure by taking this brave stand he felt he
would in the end win us over. But John was determined to go on
and I heard him mutter to no one in particular, 'We'd never have
rowed the Atlantic if we had listened to caution.'

We had a poor night. The wind changed direction and battered
our tents. Ours fell down twice in the night. I wasn't sleeping
much anyway, and John was all hyped up. So we started cooking
breakfast at 5.00. We packed up and tried to say goodbye to
Richard as the wind shrieked at us. The plan was that he would
wait four weeks and then set off for home if we did not return.

'If you don't show up on 4 January, Kris, I'll see you at the RV
in the great banana field up there!' he said, referring back to the

time they spent together on the kibbutz. I wanted desperately to ask him to keep an eye on Bec, but I could not speak.

We set off shortly after him but in the direction of the ice-cap. My pack was too heavy for me – it weighed more than seventy pounds – and I stumbled as I followed John, the deep snow slowing my steps. The wind blew fiercely and as one gust caught me off balance I slipped. Terrified I would never stop, I hurtled down the steep slope. We had our ice axes ready but somehow I could not get mine stuck into the snow to stop my fall, and our orange PVC suits were desperately slippery. I clawed my way back up, and John gruffly took six of my ration packs and fudge bars, lightening my load. Battling on we reached the high point where yesterday Richard decided against going on.

In the grey light it looked like a walk to the scaffold. The slope was crisscrossed with blue fissures and fell steeply down to a narrow snow bridge wide enough perhaps for one person to cross. It then dropped hundreds of feet down and out of sight, and we could see the nearly vertical climb on the far side was fraught with avalanche possibilities.

We stood and looked. I broke the silence: 'I'd rather put a pistol to my head – I'm sorry, Johnny.'

'Bloody hell!' John muttered through clenched teeth and stormed off hoping to find another route, and promptly fell up to his waist in a snowdrift.

I felt terrible: I had let him down. But I also thought, now that I had seen the route, that maybe Richard and I had saved him and Krister. We would never know. We set off immediately to return to our camp in the forest beneath the cliff. The trip down was as bad as I feared, looking down at the sheer drop of three thousand feet and knowing that at any point any of us could slip and fall. Richard was startled to see us – he had heard voices and thought he must be going mad.

That night we all slept fitfully. I woke screaming that I was falling over the edge. John held on to me tight. We were safe here, he said. But then we heard digging and scratching. In the morning Richard explained why. He had woken lathered in sweat, and all around his tent the ground was scarred with his shovel marks.

'We could still try and get up on to the ice-cap by the glacier,' I suggested. 'Shipton always goes up the glaciers.' I felt somewhat of an armchair expert, having read his book two and a half times.

'Well, it's that or nothing now,' John agreed.

In view of the shortage of rations it was decided that just Krister and John would make the attempt. Richard and I would hole up in the forest between the cliff and the water's edge with a minimum of food and wait for three weeks. If they were not back we were then to set off towards Skyring.

I waved goodbye till they disappeared out of sight round some rocks in the trusty rubber dinghy on their way to the foot of the glacier. And so started our strange time of waiting. Richard and I were both far too consumed with our own thoughts to feel much like conviviality. We met occasionally and shared meals from time to time but mostly we were caught up in our own dreams and hopes and fears. Our two single tents were pitched about forty yards apart, the trees and undergrowth almost obscuring their bright orange.

Some of the time I wandered about, listening to the sounds that were friendly by day: the birds, fish rising, the wind stirring the tops of the trees, waterfalls not very far away which I never went to find. But there was one sound which stalked and preyed on my imagination: the roar and crack and rumble of shifting ice from the glacier which sometimes shook the very ground we stood on. Other sinister sounds were at night. My tent was the centre of my universe and all around, outside in the darkness, were the scuffling, snuffling sounds of wild creatures. I would read until I felt my eyes heavy and then blow out the flame on my stub of a candle. My orange world was now black as I wrestled and reasoned against a rising panic.

Most of my courage had been used up, and it would take a while for the reservoir to refill. I felt an overwhelming desire to feel safe, to have my husband back by my side, to be home secure within the four strong walls of our croft house on the hill above the sea at Ardmore and to hold my trusting daughter close. Yet, I could not contemplate leaving here without John and Krister. Richard and I could survive far longer then the three weeks we were to wait. There were plenty of fish, an abundance of mussels, and now the bitter scarlet red calafate berry was beginning to sweeten with the early southern summer sun. I had even found a feathery bright green herb tasting like coriander. We had the .22 rifle and plenty of ammunition which we could use for shooting meat.

As I lay daydreaming in my tent on the eighth day since they left, there was a sudden *crack* which split the air, then a screaming yelping crashing sound. I leapt up, smelt gunpowder. Was somebody shooting at me? I was defenceless, trapped in my orange cocoon.

'It's all right, Marie Christine, it's all right.' It was Richard's voice calling from the other side of the trees.

'There was a wolf at your tent. I shot it.' We followed the drops of crimson blood and came across the wounded animal, its long fangs bared in a grimace of pain, its eyes half-glazed. Another shot rang out and all the birds of the forest flew up screaming into the sky. That night, as I lay tossing and hoping for sleep, I wondered if the she-wolf was waiting for her mate as I for John.

As each day dawned I thought that this would be the day they would return. I heard the sound of the outboard all the time, a cruel trick of the wind carrying to us the sound of a distant waterfall. I read and re-read everything we had with us, including the *RAMC 1952 Training Pamphlet for 1st Aid and Nursing For Other Ranks, November 1959 Country Life*, Henry Cooper's autobiography, *Doctor on Everest*. My precious anthology of poetry was lost. How I would have loved it now. But I had dreams in my head, and when the anxiety did not consume me, they were my solace.

Sitting very still on a rock warmed by the sun, and watching small black birds about the size of a wren flying in and out of the rocks below the trees and down to the icemelt milky water's edge, I tried to ignore the insistant 'outboard engine' background noise. This was day ten, and I had heard it every day up to now. Early on I would run expectantly out of the trees searching for the red and grey rubber boat. Not now. The disappointment was too hard to accept. Today it was even louder, perhaps the hum of the bees waking up to take nectar from early summer flowers was adding to the trick sound effect – I had found a vine clambering over the lower branches of the trees which had particularly sweet-scented pale yellow flowers just coming into bloom. Then, suddenly, I knew it was no trick. There was the boat, two figures waving wildly as I jumped up and down on the shore. I raced off to find Richard to give him the good news. We were all smiles, but the victors looked thin and gaunt, owl-eyed from wearing their goggles in the ice. We celebrated with a fine big supper of curried goose, shot by Richard a day or two before and plucked by me, and out of my rucksack I produced the bottle of Aguadiente I had been saving for a celebration. We drank it with the cherry red juice of the calafate berries. Legend has it that, once tasted, the calafate's magic juice will always lure that person back to Chile. But it was home that we all longed for now.

John had much to tell me as we lay together that night on the forest floor. I did not hear the wind in the tree tops now, nor the rumbling of the glacier, nor the owls and the animals. I listened only to his story of how they had cramponed their way up the crevassed glacier, and camped at the base of the ice fall. This was constantly avalanching, but they had to get up this to reach the ice-cap itself, scrambling through giant jumbled ice blocks the size of houses surrounded by yawning blue bottomless crevasses. A blizzard trapped them in their tent for twenty-nine hours, and they listened to avalanches rumbling and roaring close by, counting up to three in one minute. After five days they reached the top of the Gran Campo Nevado ice-cap and raced across the four miles, in perfect weather, the first humans ever to have set foot here. And now they were back.

With great care and deliberation John's ice-roughened fingers undid the many delicate mother of pearl buttons fastening the silk chemise that I wore beneath the rough army green shirt. Gently he pushed it off my shoulders, his blue eyes gazed intently at my nakedness. 'Oh, Marie Christine,' he whispered softly, holding me tight against his hard urgent body, 'I don't ever want to leave you again.'

Chapter Five

SAILING

Sometimes the wind would blow gently – rippling the surface of Loch a' Chad-Fi, our loch of the spindrift, between the houses and the mountains – mild summer winds whispering life into water, hill, sky. In summer we would welcome it. Chasing away the stinging midges, soft feathers of breeze blew cool on hot skin, causing the long grass to dance, and in the sky below the soaring clouds seagulls would display their skills as they banked and swooped full tilt, quivering at this invisible power, their sharp excited cries crowding the air.

Sometimes the wind would blow harder – cats' paws tumbling down from the hills pouncing across the water; heather and rushes nodding and bending with each gust, clinging with their anchoring roots to rocks and scanty soil; dead pale grass lifted and flung horizontal through the rushing air. The few trees spared by the sheep are victims to the wind's tearing fingers. Tender spring leaves have been burnt black in a single gale, branches ripped from thin trees, old thick trees tumbled over – their roots still clinging to moss and earth and now upended and levelled with the topmost branch, they lie conquered in battle by their invisible enemy.

The shipping forecast and gale warnings are listened to most carefully, particularly in spring and autumn: *Encyclopaedia Britannica* lists, 'Equinoctial storm, severe storm that, in Britain and North America, is popularly believed to accompany the vernal and autumnal equinoxes. The equinoxes do not actually cause any storms, but sometimes unusually violent weather does occur at those times of the year, caused by air masses' seasonal northward and southward shifts.'

'Rockall, Malin, Hebrides,' the impersonal voice from London reads out our fate over the air. We try to tie down as much as possible. Ropes are flung over roofs and lashed to the ground by pegs, or slung round boulders, the same for boats brought ashore. Nothing that can be lifted must be left unsecured. Boats staying in the water must take their chance, and moorings are checked each year by John who dives down to make sure the anchors are still in place, that every link of the chain is good – the adage of the weak link is of real relevance here.

When the glass drops and the wind starts to blow, and we hope all is secure, we can only sit and watch in fearful fascination as the tempest screams and hurls its power at everything that audaciously stands before it. Roofs have been prised up and sucked away; boats on land, even tied down to telegraph poles, have lifted and been thrown upside-down; whole huts have shifted, one landing like a crashed zeppelin on the beach a quarter of a mile away. Anything loose is sent cartwheeling in the path of the wind's fury. We watch from our house, one hundred feet up from the shore, through salt sprayed windowpanes at the smoking water of the loch, trying to tear away our boats as they valiantly cling and swing on their moorings.

To be out in it is exhilarating and terrifying. Trying to get along the path to the road, the really windy spot is coming down from Gentle's Brae over the wooden footbridge a few more yards and then to safety behind the rocks that give shelter from the south-west. The best plan is to sit down if the wind suddenly gusts, if you are caught unawares it can pick you up and throw you where it will into the heather or, worse, on to rocks. It has happened to us all – it is the hand of God or the Devil cuffing us. It always costs, however careful we think we have been. And when the wind is spent, talk in the neighbourhood is all of what was lost and who lost what.

We are at least protected from the savage wrath of the sea. The ocean swell does not penetrate our sheltered sea loch. Climbing up and over Cnoc na Suil on to the high ground of the Ardmore Peninsula, looking out towards the west across the Minch to the distant smudge of land that is Lewis, northernmost island of the Outer Hebrides, on windy days we can feel, hear, see the waves crashing on to the steep jagged rock that is Ardmore Point. I have stood with the wind buffeting me, watching in awe the power of the sea and, at different times in my life at Ardmore, fearful: for John somewhere out at sea, imagining him battling alone to pull a sail down on deck, knowing how easy it would be to make a false move and to slip forever into the rushing black water, singing into the wind the hymn we sang as children at the school for the daughters of naval officers:

'Eternal Father strong to save,
Whose arm doth bind the restless wave,
Who bidst the mighty ocean deep,
His own appointed limits keep.
Oh hear us when we cry to thee
For those in Peril on the sea!'

'Something to do with a sailor and a nurse,' was John's answer when people asked where he came from.

He'd been very lucky. Adopted as a baby, he had been given a good home and a first-class education. It was apparent the sea was in his blood; so he was sent to Pangbourne Nautical College for his education, and had been in uniform from the age of twelve. Then followed the Merchant Navy, Sandhurst and the Parachute Regiment, and that was when I met him.

In the early days of our courtship we would sometimes race down to the south coast and wander round boat yards, gazing at yachts. I knew nothing about yachting, but I had done some dinghy sailing whilst on holiday at Aldeburgh, where my sister and I used to crew for two large gangly boys called Marsden. It was fun, but the River Alde was full of shifting mud banks, and Suzie and I got fed up with always being the ones who had to get out and push the dinghy off the mud, getting very wet and dirty whilst the two boys issued orders from the boat.

When John was particularly bored or brassed off with the endless training and seeming futility of his army career, he would buy a yachting magazine and talk of sailing off around the world. This filled me with dread, it terrified me to think he was making plans that might not include me. To me he was a stern, awe-inspiring man. 'His heart was pure and terrible, and I think no other like it exists,' Emily Dickinson had said of her father. I could, had I the wit, have said it of John.

Once one of his fellow officers was admitted to hospital with asthma, and on one of our dates we went to visit him.

'Hi, Ridge. Hi, MC,' the chalky-faced young subaltern wheezed out from his bed. The talk was all of how they would both leave the army and pool what little savings they had to buy a yacht. As the afternoon wore on they were getting more and more enthusiastic and detailed with their plans.

Once outside on that cold wintry afternoon my pent-up jealousy spurted out: 'Well, if you and Carty go off to sail around the world, don't expect me to be waiting for you on your return.' I tossed my creamy lynx fur collar round my neck (it had originally bedecked a tennis coat belonging to my mother) and stormed off down the grey street, the tight skirt of my soft tweed suit, the colours of a moorland grouse (borrowed from one of my sisters) impeding a faster getaway. Once said, it could not be taken back, but I realised how stupid I had been to say this if I wanted us to stay pals.

John caught me up in two or three strides. 'Don't be daft,' he said. 'We can all go together.'

'Why, yes, Johnny,' I muttered weakly, as visions of mountainous seas, hurricane winds, crashing waves on unknown reefs filled my head.

Our life was beginning to fit into the pattern we had planned: an expedition every other winter – John rowing and sailing single-handed in 1966 and 1968, Amazon 1970, Chile 1972. Now, for winter 1974, we planned a sailing trip aboard our Nicholson 32' sloop, *English Rose V*, to the Spanish Sahara and on down to the Cape Verde Islands, then perhaps visiting the Azores before returning to Ardmore at the end of December. One of the aims was to take Bec, aged seven. She was due to start at the Kinlochbervie primary school later on in the school year, and this would open her eyes to a world beyond our mountains and Brighton where she had stayed with my mother. John was to write a book about our trip. It started off being called *Journey to the Sun* and ended up as *Storm Passage*.

To beef up our crew we invited along three of our instructors: dear Krister (24), the blond Swede who had been such a star on the Chile trip; Jamie Young (22), a shy gruff endearing giant of a young man – giant in the sense that there was nothing he could not face in terms of physical endurance and patience and diligence; and finally Stafford Morse (21), an Australian whose outstanding enthusiasm and zest for life had made us feel we would like to have him along with us on this trip. Jamie was a keen sailor and was to sail our 30' sloop *English Rose IV* in the single-handed transatlantic race out to Newport, Rhode Island, the following year, and, after a few days there, sail it straight back to Ardmore all on his own. The other two were not so experienced.

Because of a northerly airstream which would push us south we set off earlier than planned, on 28 September. The boat was loaded with food and sweet water which we had carried down from Granny Ross's well on the hill in five-gallon jerry cans. Six souls in such a small space – it would take some adjusting to.

Waving goodbye to Lance and Ada, we were soon heading out to sea into the rolling swell. It was a wretched first night and it was not long before the betting started on who would be sick first. Our small boat rolled around on the heaving sea, and, because of our rushed departure, heavy objects were not stowed correctly. Head down in the small cabin, wrestling with an active gas bottle which had a mind of its own, I knew I was in danger of coming first. Jamie steered on through the night, while Krister and Staff lay, a black bucket placed between them, in two small pipe cots forward of the tiny wash area which was curtained off from the saloon where Bec, John and I would sleep, and where in the day we would all eat, read, argue, play, laugh. There was not much privacy here.

Bec's bunk was on top of a large locker on the starboard side. She grew to hate the smell when the doors were opened to get out stores: it was sickly sweet, not unlike the smell of a greengrocer's shop full of overripe apples. But the first few nights she was squeezed in with John and me in our narrow double bunk, on the port side.

Bec complained of a sore tummy. 'Rub it, Mummy, rub it.' I rubbed her blue woollen jumper to the point where it all balled up into a tangle. Then she was finally violently sick, luckily into a plastic bowl we had handy. Poor Bec, what had we let her in for? I had severe doubts about the entire voyage, it was one thing us embarking on a fairly hazardous and uncomfortable journey in a small boat, with no engine, in the North Atlantic in winter, but were we right to take our small child? 'Aagghh!' said John impatiently as I murmured my doubts.

A gale warning had just been issued on Radio 2: 'Severe gale, force 9, imminent from the north for sea area Hebrides.' Us. The northerly gales blew us on as we started to settle in to our new life. Passing through the comparative calm of the Minch, and then out into the huge troughs and crests of the North Atlantic, all the while we were becoming accustomed to the discomfort. Staff was the most sick, and whenever the wind rose he would be retching over the lee rail, but he was immensely plucky and never used it as an excuse to get off his watch. Five years later Staff was to lose his life on a joint Australian and New Zealand climbing expedition in the Himalayas, swept away by an avalanche. Tragic though it was, I always felt that with his great verve, Staff had fitted into his short span probably more than most do in three score years and ten.

Once we were past Ireland and managing to clock up a good hundred miles or so a day – for there was not a second when we were not moving forward – each day the weather got warmer. This was what it was all meant to be about. The misery of the first few days was passing and our days and nights were fitting into a pattern. Now a routine was set up, we all seemed happier. The seasickness had faded more or less, though Bec, Staff and I still felt pretty queasy in the rather foetid atmosphere of the crowded cabin. But up on deck it was grand. Our fine boat felt sturdy and strong, and she seemed to cream along in all sea conditions, gliding when the wind blew gently, bouncing eagerly forward when the wind increased and the sea was rough. So we would muffle up and spend as much time as possible in that other world on deck.

I was cook, most of the time, but when I felt desperately sick Jamie often stood in for me. I remember thinking at the time, as I lay feeling weak in my bunk, talking him through each step of making bread in the pressure cooker, how I would make it up to him when I was well again. I don't suppose I ever did, but my gratitude towards him at the time was immense.

When meals and tidying below were over, we would venture out on deck. Bec and I had oceans of schoolwork to do, and seasickness was no excuse not to get on with it. Until we got further south and into warmer seas we would put on all our warmest gear. Bec had a heavy brown coat, a miniature version of a Royal Navy North Atlantic issue duffle, too hot for walking in but perfect for sitting in the cockpit and reading Peter and Jane books, of which there were thirty-six; she had got up to number twenty-five, so we still had a way to go. There was now lots of time to spend with each other at work and play, on stories and cuddles – such a contrast from the summer where it was perpetual motion just trying to keep abreast of the jobs. The three boys were endlessly patient and like three big brothers, Jamie and Staff reading her stories and Krister teaching her simple tricks and how to tie special knots.

John loved this time with his daughter. The plan to take Bec on this voyage had been his, and he was determined to make up for all time lost in the past because of his busy life. Together they would take their regulation spin around the deck. Bec in her blue safety harness would clip the karabiner on the end of her safety line to one of the lines that ran uninterrupted from the bow down either side of the deck to the cockpit. Then leading the way, with her bottom sticking firmly out behind her, she would creep carefully up towards the bow of the prancing boat followed closely by her dad. For hours they would hold on to the frame of the pulpit, riding the waves and watching the sea pass below, counting cuttlefish or whatever might be passing. As the weeks wore on she became more sure, and scampered like a monkey about the deck, but always linked by the safety harness.

We sped on, becoming more and more pleased with the boat. I was surprised to find how much I felt part of it and it of me: it was an extension of myself. This was my first sea voyage and I thought it wonderful. I am sure much of what John had said about sailing had rubbed off on me, for I liked the simplicity of our lifestyle: our world was this boat, and the sea around us; we were totally self-reliant and, providing we were careful and skilful, we would reach the places we had planned to visit. Layers of clothing were shed as with each day's progress it seemed a little warmer, and soon we were padding about the deck in our bathers.

It was grand to think what it must be like back at Ardmore now, but always at the back of my mind was the thought of heading home through the North Atlantic in December. It had been bad in October. It would be worse two months on. I tried to rationalise my fears, but I knew they were partly instinctive: I worried far more with Bec beside me than I would have on my own. I thought back to the time when she was less than one year old, and on a lovely hot sunny day John suggested we go down to Handa Island. We set off with some friends in a rubber dinghy. As we motored out into Loch Laxford before turning south to head down the coast, the unexpectedly hot sun swelled the air within the neoprene sections of our boat till they were tight.

'Please can we turn round, John,' I implored – in vain. 'Well, if we're not turning round, please put me and Bec off on an island.' I was getting into a mild panic, which was uncharacteristic of me, but I just felt terribly unsafe and feared the sections would burst and my baby would drown. I might have felt differently if it had been after our trip to Chile, which showed me how sturdy these craft are.

The party put us off and we spent our day stuck on a rocky islet enjoying the peace and isolation, but I felt rather foolish when several hours later they returned to pick us up. I could not help my anxiety, and nobody there would have understood. None of them were mothers.

Bec was thrilled with the flying fish which accompanied us as we sped along through blue bright translucent water eleven thousand feet above the sea bed. Their gossamer wings were a magic of genetic selection. Flying off the cresting waves, chased by an invisible menace below, unlucky ones sometimes hit our deck. We tried eating them but they were too bony.

We stopped at Madeira and the Canaries and then headed for the Spanish Sahara, for Vila Cisneros, a quiet Spanish colonial outpost of a port. Here, along the coast of Africa, the sand off the desert lent the sky a yellowish haze; we could hear the crashing surf as we sailed along the coastline; we could also see occasional wrecks of fishing boats and tankers along the empty beaches which stretched forever. This was no Blackpool. These sights sent a chill down my spine; I felt I should have crossed myself had I been a Roman Catholic.

We were rather apprehensive about this landfall. We could see on the chart it lay seven miles up the sheltered side of a peninsula, sheltered, that is, from the prevailing trade winds which were now blowing strongly, whipping up an ugly sea in the shallow coastal waters. Jamie drew up a plan of lights and buoys which he gleaned from our constantly read Admiralty Pilot. The daylight would soon be gone but the various lights would guide us safely to the pier.

Darkness comes fast in the tropics. I busied myself below cooking the supper. Bec was up and looking out on deck with the others, who were straining to read the lights and our route as they tacked up the channel. And then, two hundred yards from the safety of the pier, we hit an underground obstacle, and our precious boat began to bump up and down on the African continent. What were we going to lose in this god-forsaken place – our boat, our lives? Bec rushed down into my arms.

'Look after her,' John sternly ordered, as he and the three chaps pulled down the sails and put out anchors to prevent us being washed further on to this sandbank. They did not want my help.

In an attempt to calm Bec, I tried to drown the sound of the bumping and creaking of our battered boat by turning her favourite Rupert Bear tape on full volume. At the same time I read to her in a loud voice *The Owl who was afraid of the Dark*, while trying to listen out for what was going on on deck. We were listing badly; so I was also madly thinking what to take if we had to abandon ship. Eventually though, the tide started rising, we kedged ourselves off the sandbank, and anchored a short safe distance away for the night.

The following day we found out why we had gone aground. There sitting on the end of the pier were the lights we had been following. They should have given us a safe passage into harbour. Instead they had been taken ashore for maintenance and had lured us nearly to our doom. We did not learn much from the experience, except to be even more cautious.

It was here, the next day, that Bec nearly lost her life a second time, not even twenty-four hours after the first scrape. On going ashore she ran out on to a quiet dusty track, and suddenly a truck shot round a corner, missing her by millimetres. It was an entirely unexpected hazard, as there was hardly any traffic in this outpost, and Bec coming from traffic-free Ardmore was quite unaware of the possible danger.

We stayed a few days learning much about the Spanish Sahara from people we met, I was surprised how friendly everyone was towards us. Perhaps arriving by small yacht makes the difference, turning the visitors into modern-day pilgrims. One evening John and I were invited into the home of a young left-wing Saharoise. It had the air of an active guerilla headquarters, and we half expected to be raided by Spanish soldiers, as the Spanish were protecting their interests in this small state from Morocco, who were keen to take them over because of recently discovered rich deposits of phosphate. Two ideological friends joined us and talk was centred around their radical political views. They clearly wanted independence and to be free of Spanish interference.

During the conversation, a shy Arab cousin dressed in the traditional flowing blue *bousbous* set about making tea over a charcoal burner. Our host explained, as the first of the small cups were passed around: 'The first cup is without sugar; it is bitter like Life. The second cup has a little sugar; it is bittersweet like Love. And the third and last cup has much sugar, and is sweet like Death.' The maker of the tea sat with a faraway look in his eyes in the corner of this lushly furnished room between the giant television and the huge quadrophonic music centre. Our friend told us that his relation had come from a distant desert village to help in his father's chain of shops, and added wistfully: 'He will only sleep outside, where he can see the stars.'

I was surprised to find in all of the remote places we visited, how easy it was to make friends with the women. The men would often look suspiciously at us, but once the women saw I had a small child they would immediately come over and we would try and talk. Not sharing the same language, we would struggle through smatterings of French and Portuguese, but the talk did not matter – they would marvel at Bec's yellow hair and bring over their own dark children, and we would all be smiling at each other and touching hands, while the four men from our boat would look on as outsiders. We were united by a common bond, motherhood.

Sadly we could not stay long at any of the places we stopped at. From the Spanish Sahara we set sail for the Cape Verde Islands, 550 miles to the south-west, and 280 miles off the coast of Africa. We visited three of the islands.

The first, Sal, is the most north-easterly of the windward group, a rather desolate spot. When we arrived, we learned they had had no rain for seven years.

From Sal, which exported salt and fish, we moved on to Boa Vista. This island had been the capital of the archipelago, discovered by ships serving Prince Henry the Navigator of Portugal in the middle of the fifteenth century, but Praia on Sao Tiago replaced it in 1700. Before the drought, ships came here to collect salt, cattle, and castor oil seeds. Nowadays there was not much more than salt and poverty, only the remnants of tall elegant stone buildings shaded by spreading acacia trees reminding us of its long forgotten glorious past. Here we swam in the warm sea, snorkelling and gathering shells to take back to Ardmore, and we made friends with the lonely harbourmaster, Alfonso, a grey-haired old man, who spoke perfect measured English which he had taught himself. He was suffering from malaria and had run out of medicine, as the monthly visit from the doctor had been missed. We gave him what we could for relief and assured him that we would let the authorities at Praia know of his plight.

Praia was a modern city. John wanted to leave as soon as we arrived, but we stayed long enough for the boys to pick up their mail from poste restante and for us to send out over a thousand postcards which we had handwritten along the way. These were going to all those people who had attended courses in previous years, and, of course, to friends. It was quite a task, and much time was spent at the swelteringly hot post office, for the stamps had no glue on their backs and each one had to be carefully stuck on with rather smelly glue from a very sticky jar.

We left Sao Tiago late in the afternoon of 22 November, heading north for home via the Azores. All night we butted into the northeast trade winds, and the seasickness returned with a vengeance. Fifteen days and nights later we arrived at Ponta Delgada on the green and magnificent island of Sao Miguel in the Azores. The sufferers from seasickness had by then lost much weight. It had proved to be a very hard sail and we knew worse was to come.

Light-headed and light-footed we explored the town and countryside. We ate the best food in the world, grown close by on the island where they produced a wide variety of crops from tea to pineapples to every imaginable vegetable, as well as the best of beef. It seemed like paradise after the parched Cape Verde Islands. I wanted to come and live here. Once again we were lucky to make friends, and were taken out deep into the countryside. I was entranced to see fields encompassed by hedges of brilliant blue hydrangeas, which when in flower were cut and fed to the cattle. But our stay had to be short. We had the final leg of the journey to complete – Azores to Ardmore, nearly 1500 miles.

We waved goodbye to our new friends and their beautiful island and headed out to sea and the inevitable seasickness. For three days the wind blew hard and we bounced along falling off the heavy seas with a sickening thud. The boys moved into the centre cabin with us; they were being thrown out of their pipe cots up in the bows. In the small space meant for one, there were now six, if we were all below decks. The crush added to the squalor. The three boys were grand but all had bushy beards, and wherever I looked there were strands of wiry hair stuck to every damp surface. I longed now to be home, to be able to take my clothes off and bathe and lie between clean sheets, to pee without the whole boat knowing. Discovering my period had started was another nightmare of concealment. Yet all of this was minor – the main thing was to stay alive and get home safely.

We had all been worrying about this leg of the voyage, but now we were actually involved we found it exciting and, apart from the seasickness, spirits were high. Now we were constantly monitoring the barometer and listening out for weather forecasts. After the initial rough weather it dropped calm, and Staff was at last able to eat again: he had not been able to keep anything down for three days. This calm lasted an unbelievable five days, and on 14 December we logged only 5.2 miles. Would we ever get home? Then the barometer started to fall and the wind increased. Soon we were bowling along before a southerly gale under the storm jib, eating up the distance between us and the west coast of Ireland. The stormy weather increased daily and Christmas was getting nearer. Bec was busy making paper chains which we soon had festooned around the cabin – we were going to enjoy Christmas whatever.

On 23 December we were far out in the Atlantic but level with the southern shores of Donegal Bay. Krister was up on deck steering the boat, which was rollercoasting along in heavy grey seas, while below John and Staff were trying to sleep. Jamie was reading, Bec was playing beside her dad and I had gingerly nursed a bowl of hot water into the loo compartment for a wash – just another ordinary day in the North Atlantic. Then suddenly our world was shattered, a giant gush of icy water came rushing at us. Horror! The sea had penetrated our safe world below decks.

In the first instant I could not believe what I felt. I was almost in the bow of the boat, standing up washing at the basin, when the spurt of seawater soaked me from my hair down, like a bucketful of water being thrown with great force. Had we a hole? Where was this water coming from? My mind panicked and raced desperate for the answer.

'Block it – Jamie – block it,' yelled John.

An enormous freak wave had raced up from behind, lifting Krister off his feet, and John had watched mesmerised as it forced its icy way through the gap in the hatch which we should have had shut down. Jamie, clad only in his now sodden underwear, was already up reaching for the teak drop boards, shoving them into place before another wave came and filled our boat. Simultaneously Staff leapt up from his drenched sleeping bag as the boat righted itself and the rush of water subsided to a trickle from the well in the filled cockpit. At all costs, we must pump out the water before more was forced into our waterlogged boat; a second wave would undoubtedly sink us.

Bec was distraught. She screamed: 'We're sinking, Mummy, we're sinking.'

I picked her out of the icy water that was swilling around our legs and held her close. 'Don't worry, we'll be all right.' I tried to sound calm, but I thought: 'One false move and we are all drowned.'

Krister would have been washed overboard were it not for his life harness. Now, lashing the tiller, he made a quick tour of the deck once he had baled out the water from the cockpit. Just as he was reporting the damage he shouted out, 'Look out,' and another enormous wave hit, and swamped our small craft. This time it did not penetrate our bubble of a cabin, but we were knocked over once again by its mighty strength.

'Lash the tiller firmly, Krister, and come below. We'll let the boat lie a-hull for a bit,' John shouted from below.

As the boat rose and fell on mountainous seas, the six of us took three hours to sort out the chaos below. Just about everything was wet. Luckily I had put some extra clothing into a waterproof bag which had remained dry, so I was able to dish this out and put Bec into my fibre-pile jacket which came to below her knees. She wore John's mitts for shoes, and a Damart hood to keep her wet head warm. She sat on top of her food-locker bed and through chattering teeth kept asking: 'Whatever is the world coming to?' in between wails of despair.

I made hot sweet tea, the great panacea, and we continued with our wringing and mopping. The shipping forecast warned of 'South-south-east gale force 8 to storm 10, veering west 9,' and we heard on the news that the weather was so severe that the Swansea to Cork ferry was cancelled. I fervently hoped nobody who knew us thought we were in this area. We had made our boat secure and we should be all right, but we did fear the cross seas that would build up with the wind veering. This time, though, we were lucky: the storm abated and our fears were unfounded. That wild night, four of us tried to sleep together for warmth in our tiny double bunk wearing our wet clothing. It was the only way we would get it dry.

By Christmas Day we were almost back to normal, except that Bec's decorations hung in tatters, the bright colours streaked from their wetting. We celebrated it as best we could. I hung out stockings filled with chocolate, tangerines and miniature bottles of liqueur for the three boys, and special ones for Bec and John. Breakfast was French toast made with real eggs. Lunch was frankfurter sausages and Jamie's bread – he was now expert. A

slightly salty soggy Christmas cake followed, and for supper we
had tuna fish pie, spinach and mashed real potatoes, all cooked in
the one and only remaining pot – the rest had been washed over the
side. We finished off with a bottle of wine bought from a soldier on
the Cape Verde Islands, and the last of the pineapples we had
brought with us from the Azores.

'It's the rottenest Christmas ever!' Bec pronounced shortly after
losing at a game of cards, but later on she said, 'I quite like it really.
I'd rather be with you,' looking seriously at John and me.

On Boxing Day we put into Castlebay, on the island of Barra.
Wearily we made our way ashore in search of a bath and a night in a
dry bed. Everything except the bars was shut, but I had stuffed
some dryish clothing under my coat and suddenly realised why one
landlady took pity on us and opened up: she was gazing at my bump
sympathetically. It had not been done on purpose, and I felt a bit
embarrassed once we got inside and I took off my coat.

The next day we set off at 4.30 in the afternoon in failing light on
the last leg – 120 miles up the Minch to Loch Laxford. Once again
the wind rose, the forecast was 'South-west 7 to severe gale force 9,'
but at least it was from the right direction.

For me, this part of the trip was more frightening than anything
else, ever. During the hours of darkness we prepared to abandon
ship twice, for we were heading through narrow channels in fierce
squalls which until the last minute obscured the navigation lights –
we all remembered Vila Cisneros. Throughout the journey we
were dressed in full oilskins and life jackets, even the sleeping Bec,
who was propped up on our bunk with the Callbuoy emergency
radio strapped to her – she had been instructed on how to use it if by
some miracle she was saved. My knees truly shook with fear. I felt
worn down by the chances we had taken – surely we had used up
our share of luck. Yet, with the tide and the fierce wind behind us,
we miraculously navigated past Skye between the Neist Point and
Vaternish Point lighthouses and across the mouth of Loch Snizort
on towards the Trodday light which in sectors marks the position
of the unlit rocks of Ant-Iasgair. If we were unable to see these
lights we would likely be shipwrecked. As the squalls came
through on that pitch-black December night the visibility was
terrible, but miraculously they cleared briefly to allow us safely
past. After a dark eternity we began to feel safer as dawn broke, and
by noon we found ourselves looking at a familiar coastline, past

Stoer Head, then Handa. The last few miles to Laxford seemed to take forever and finally we were sailing into the narrow waters of home.

How small it all looked after the ocean – how safe! Heckie Ross, with his dog Mona standing as usual in the bow of his painted green boat, came round the point, as Lance Bell appeared from the direction of the school. It was 4.30 in the afternoon; he had finished work. It was wonderful to see our two friends.

I felt a traitor leaving our trusty yacht at last at her anchor beneath the wood. She had been part of me for three whole months and had safely carried my family and three friends on a magic journey of six thousand miles.

We walked up the hill and into our house. The Rayburn was lit, and Ada was expecting us for supper and beer. Our adventure was already just a fading memory.

Chapter Six

OVERDRIVE

'A change is as good as a rest.'

It was certainly a change coming home and enjoying the small luxuries that are soon taken for granted. Water flowing from the tap was the best – hot when the Rayburn is well-stoked, or the gas bottle is full enough to power the Valiant gas water heater. Every evening for the first few days I luxuriated in the bath, the peaty steaming water almost slurping over its brim. I would lie back, reflecting with pleasure on my new slender shape – the only advantage of seasickness – and wondering how long it would be before my body got rounder.

The small chill bathroom would be full of steam, and my candle would splutter and burn low through lack of oxygen. A touch more hot, then lying back again I would look at the foxy face of the Valiant logo staring down at me from the white enamelled heater. 'Yes, I'm back. I'm still alive,' I would say to it.

'Did you say something, Marie Christine?' John would call from the other room.

'No nothing,' I would holler back, winking at my friend to whom I confided my secrets.

I would have liked a body that was straight, hard and, above all, strong. I was built with soft curves, but at least my legs were strong from skiing and climbing up our hill. I could lift quite heavy weights, which surprised visitors, who thought me delicate.

We seemed always to have a constant flow of people staying in our small house, and now we were back from the sea the flow increased. John had so many schemes afoot: the school had been going seven years; we had survived a difficult year or two after the postal strike and recession; now we must surge forward. The bookings for our forthcoming season were very encouraging: we had only two places left out of two hundred and fifty. Still, we went into a sort of frenzied overdrive.

I am sure I would have missed the interest if people had not come, but being cook and provisioner I would groan when John told me who was coming and whom they were bringing with them. For me, it was like living in the front line, a battle to be fought and won against jobs and time and energy. Whether I warmed to the visitors or not depended not so much on how entertaining they were, more on how helpful they were. Many was the time that I would struggle up the hill with a sack of peat or a gas bottle to be met at the top by a beefy chap offering to help, when he knew he was safe and that the weighty article was now up. Perhaps I should not generalise, but it was often the officer/executive type that seemed least keen to lift a finger to help with the menial tasks. I could not help but feel scorn for them. Ardmore is no place for posturing or assuming rank and position. Motor cars and fine suits were left at the road end. People's qualities shone through or not, and out here a different set of values counted.

We had been married eleven years on 21 March 1975, years of fighting to establish the school and to keep John's name to the fore. (I had to agree the two were closely linked, although at times it was hard for me to swallow how everything centred on him.) Bec was now weekly boarding at Kinlochbervie. She put up with it bravely but I know she would have preferred to be at home.

That spring we met Arun Bose, a shy, soft-spoken young man born of an Indian father but now living with his English mother at Durness, fifteen miles to the north. It was to be one of those rare lucky encounters. He was a boat builder of extraordinary skill and resourcefulness. He had been awarded a prestigious medal on passing his final national exams, and here he was on our doorstep. After long discussions, we decided to buy a bigger boat, a bare hull that Arun would fit out. We would have to sell our Nicholson 32' sloop and pool all our savings, but it seemed the courageous thing to do, and John was hell bent on the idea. I could think of a thousand other things I wanted to make our life more efficient and – dare I say it? – easier, but once again I was carried along by John's great plans.

I looked back on the Cape Verde trip with mixed feelings. It had been wonderful at times, but I had hated the squalor and crush of so many people in so small a space. Unlike the chaps, I did not get much of a buzz from the danger, which had so excited them. I realised I was made differently. My overriding instincts were for the preservation of myself and my child. And now with plans for a new boat there would be more sailing. 'No, not for me,' I thought. But then if I opted out, I would be left in the back seat. I wrestled with my doubts; John made it all sound so exciting that inevitably I would just get swept along with his tide of enthusiasm.

A plan was developing: if Arun could fit out the Bowman 57′ ketch in time, we would celebrate our tenth year of running the school by entering her in the 1977/78 Whitbread Round the World Yacht Race. That made up my mind: I could not possibly miss out on the chance of sailing round the world.

It was a big project for us, and we would have to do it on a shoestring. Later that winter, I decided to have my appendix removed – just in case. John followed suit a few weeks later. Work continued in a frenzy. 'Whatever else, Marie Christine,' John would say. 'It isn't boring.'

Another season passed in between bouts of exhaustion, and on 3 October 1976 we set off in the new boat on a three-month trial voyage to the Azores. We had such wonderful memories of these islands that we thought it would be good to visit them again and test ourselves, our crew and the new boat.

Bec and I, however, set off with heavy hearts, as we both knew well what it would be like to start with – the last trip was still clear in our memories. Still, we did not want to miss the action, and the education authorities had reluctantly agreed to my teaching her once again for this three-month period.

There were to be thirteen of us on board, and as the boat was barely fitted out below we were all prepared for it to be tough. In a rush, on the day following the end of the season, we loaded enough provisions for the crew for three months – and a lot of black buckets – and set off once again out into the Minch in October.

The weather was appalling. Mountainous seas knocked us down off Ireland, causing enough damage to make us realise we were not ready for this pounding. Six days later, having made no contact with anybody, we were sailing back into Laxford.

We unloaded the mountains of food into the store. At least we would not go hungry this winter. Then, as the crew went back to their homes, I set about making chutney from the boxes of tomatoes and cucumbers.

'Sorry, John, I'm not coming on the big trip,' I said. I knew he would be disappointed, but Bec and I had been so sick during the six stormy days that I felt I could not face the ordeal. We had spent most of the time in the bare stern cabin with water dripping through the aft hatch, sharing our hard triangular bed with a box of rattling tools and the huge bolt croppers, which were there in case the mast came down and we needed to cut the wire stays to prevent it from holing the hull. Bec and I agreed we would have preferred a teddy bear.

But ten months later, despite my resolution to stay at home, I was back on the boat, waving farewell to Bec and my mother and all our friends as we sailed out of Loch Laxford. We were heading for Portsmouth, for final preparations and then the start of the Whitbread Round the World Yacht Race. John had prevailed upon me to go. It was a unique opportunity, I would never forgive myself if I did not take it. After all, what was seasickness and a bit of discomfort and missing my child compared to the great experience of circumnavigating the globe? Almost more important – John wanted me to be by his side.

Before we left, I stole out in a quiet moment. I climbed the hill behind our house and wandered out to the end of the rocky peninsula, past the dark loch where we swam, disturbing the pair of red-throated divers with their now almost fully grown chick gliding low in the water, past the lazy-beds and the worked-out peat cuttings, past Loch Eileanach where we sometimes fished for small brown trout, each one speckled with pink spots – not one of them alike – out to the high cliff where Ardmore finishes and the great ocean begins. I looked out to the horizon and tried to imagine the scale of our journey. When I next stood on this point, I would be very different, I felt: I would have sailed round the entire globe. But what was to happen between now and that future moment? Would I be staunch, and have sufficient fortitude? Would I survive?

It was not going to be easy – thirteen of us on board the 57' ketch, with me the only female, and the skipper's wife at that. It was not a plum role. I had always been treated as the headmaster's wife by most of the instructors, and I expected it would be a similar experience, but this time our world was reduced to a living space of ten feet by nine feet, the saloon a microcosm of emotions which would intensify as the weeks passed by.

How right I proved to be. Throughout that voyage we were locked together. We were theoretically united by a common aim to sail round the world, but what in fact emerged were quite varying attitudes to this goal. John wanted to take our beautiful and precious boat safely from start to finish, and give us and the crew an experience of a lifetime. Others wanted to race, and felt frustrated and disappointed when he would not push harder and risk expensive damage to sails and equipment. The TV crew on board wanted to get dramatic material, not so much of sailing but of the tensions that build up amongst people living at such close quarters. John and I also had the job of writing a book. We needed sponsorship just to get to the start, not to mention covering the entire nine months of feeding the crew and replacing damaged gear. Without the book and the TV film we would not have got the support. We had all of this, and we still had the struggle with the winds and the seas.

As I look back now on that nine months, I see it quite differently from how I felt at the time. In spite of everything, it was grand and glorious. We did achieve what we set out to do; we did sail our boat round the world; we did not come last in a race which was as much about seamanship and endurance as racing skills and unlimited funds. Certainly we had personality problems throughout, which other crews also experienced, but ours were being recorded on film and written about, which spotlighted and exacerbated them. On our second stop, in Auckland, we even had a mutiny. Just about the whole crew wanted to jump ship, and it looked as though John and I would be sailing the boat back to Britain on our own. With alacrity, the television producer flew out from Britain. He did a fine job as mediator, helping to air grievances and bring us all together again. As a result, we set off from Auckland on Boxing Day 1977, less only two of the original team.

During the second half of the trip we were all more cautious about what we said. Nothing was discussed that could be controversial, yet everything that was talked about seemed to be potentially controversial – from pet expressions, to personal habits, to normally innocuous comments. I had read a book about cruising before the start, which had warned the reader about repeatedly using the same expressions. The example given was, 'That's the way the grapefruit squirts.' It was not long before I appreciated exactly the message the author was getting over. Out here there was time to dissect every nuance. When, for instance, I confessed to never having eaten a chip butty, scorn was poured on me from all quarters. Probably what enraged some of my fellow travellers was that I had never been in a situation where chip butties were being dished out.

I tried to steer a middle course. Sometimes it was a help being female: I tried to be more of a sister/mother figure. I wasn't competing with the chaps, but I felt they were wary of me. I could not decide whether this was because I was the skipper's wife. Certainly, I often had to stick up for him, which I could not help but do in a most vehement fashion, although I tried hard to be fair in all things. Perhaps though it was because I was female and they did not feel easy with me. We were all cooped up for four periods each of up to six weeks, eleven men and me. Padding around in the intense heat, lightly clad, did my presence disturb them? I could not know how they felt, and, anyway, what else could I do?

As John and I had worked very hard to get to the starting line, he had rather thoughtfully said to me, 'You've done enough cooking over the years at Ardmore, MC. We'll get somebody to come and cook on this journey. I want you just to enjoy it.' So, although I helped sail the boat, mend sails, even cook once I got over my seasickness, and was not in either of the watches, I didn't have a definite role. I realise now that this was a mistake. I had too much time to worry about the atmosphere, my position, how people reacted to me. Another factor that did not help was John's attitude towards me: never demonstratively affectionate, he was distinctly impartial. I would not have wanted preferential treatment, but I felt isolated and lonely.

The problems increased when, on the second leg, we took on an older navigator. He did not freeze me out like some of the younger crew, and we immediately became good friends. It was fun to have someone to talk to and laugh with, but this came to a head when we got stuck in the pack-ice off Antarctica, losing an advantage which we had hoped to gain by taking the more southerly shorter route. A new course had to be set to take us further north and out of the ice. John was annoyed and then depressed at this lost chance, and I stupidly did not realise that he was also annoyed and depressed by my friendship with the navigator, and at a time when he needed my support most. All of this was a struggle, every bit as much as sailing our boat and staying alive.

In spite of all the difficulties, however, there were truly memorable experiences: watching a whale jump high out of the water to get a better look at us, his baleful eye, the size of a dinner plate, staring straight into mine; albatross, white-tailed tropic birds, silver-grey petrels, killer-whales, dolphins, porpoises, and icebergs; square three-hundred-foot tabular bergs brilliant white against the storm-grey sky with dark indigo fissures tracing from their tops to where the booming surf broke below, their blue strata lines denoting their ancient glacial lineage.

On the third leg we also saw bergs quite different from the square-topped tabulars – bergs fantastically shaped like fairy castles with spires and minarets floating on their fateful journey north. One of the crew and I were put off into the rubber dinghy to take photos of the yacht passing one of these bergs.

It was an uncanny sight to see the yacht disappearing behind the swell as she sailed away from us, I wrote in my diary. *The sky was overcast now, dark patches of snow cloud hung heavily on the horizon, the air was full of silver-grey petrels circling around us inquisitively. Close to the berg a whale surfaced and blew. We could smell its fishy breath in the chill air, it would be feeding on the krill to be found there, which sometimes colours the whole sea purple. 'What if they don't come back for us Tony?' I speculated. The boat was now out of sight. 'Well, we would just have to prepare for death,' he replied solemnly.* Then the yacht appeared like a swan, on the crest of the swell to pick us up, her sails yellow and worn against the sharp blue-white castellated peaks of the ice mountain, and we got our photos.

I felt cross with John for not worrying about me taking such a risk – we could have been spilled out of our dinghy by the passing whale. On the other hand perhaps it was a compliment. Maybe he thought he had trained me to the point where I was well able to cope with such risky endeavours.

From the Roaring Forties, to the Shrieking Fifties, to the Screaming Sixties, we shot along in the Southern Ocean, managing to average two hundred miles a day. We would have been delighted with a distance of one hundred miles a day in the Nicholson 32' – a greater hull length meant a greater speed. Each day we spoke to the other boats on the evening radio chat show, reporting positions, any ice spotted, general chit-chat. The French skipper of one of the faster boats, who was quite a friend of mine, would politely enquire of John, 'And 'ow eez Marie Christine?' John's reply, quick as a flash, would crackle back, 'Better than nothing.' So inevitably I was nicknamed 'Better-than-nothing' by the other crews who listened in.

It was terribly cold. Sometimes we had ice forming below inside our cabin, where the condensation froze, and everything was damp. My chilblains were playing up, probably due to the fact that I did not want to abandon my hot-water bottle. I would heat the same water up day after day and put it back into the bottle. It was a source of great comfort.

Two days after my thirty-fourth birthday we rounded Cape Horn. The night was dark, the little light shed from a slip of a moon hidden by frequent squalls. We had watched as land came into sight on several occasions but we were waiting to see the actual light on Cape Horn which should flash every ten seconds. The squalls cleared just enough and squinting through spray and wind we could make out the flash of light. It was to many of us the dream of a lifetime, most especially to John and to me. I had spent the last two days and nights with one of the crew sewing the mainsail together – it had been split right across from luff to leech. It was the heaviest of sails and I nursed my tender fingers in the chill damp air, as wearily but triumphant we looked towards the Cape.

We all wanted now to get on to Rio for the carnival. It was our last stop before turning the corner and heading up the Atlantic for home. Excitement mounted. After weeks aboard the boat, it was hard to imagine anything more different than Rio. The boys were getting wildly excited. I think they imagined it would be one long orgy.

Suddenly the sailing took on a different dimension. On deck there was not a moment when the boat was not being finely tuned to get the maximum speed. We sailed past the Falkland Islands, passing so close to one of the islands, Grand Jason, that we disturbed the penguins standing on rocks above the shore; in a wave they all jumped back in the water. The wind was blowing strongly, and John was concerned that the crew were piling on too much sail and straining the boat. He was in an unenviable position. It was not easy to be always cautioning the younger, keen ones, but at the same time we could not just sit back and see our boat wrecked.

On what John called 'The day of the punch on the nose', when the wind was gusting well over sixty knots, we had two bad broaches where the boat was flung on to its side. Then a cry went up: 'Rudder's gone, rudder's gone.' I could see John was furious. Just for the hell of it the crew had far too much sail up, and now the strain had broken the rudder. It was a dangerous and expensive lesson for us all caused by 'the young Turks', as John had started to call our crew. The boat was vibrating wildly with the flapping sails rising and falling heavily on giant seas.

We were now riding the breaking waves broadside, and water was cascading over the deck as the boys battled at getting the sails down and secured. As the wind shrieked through the rigging, we set to repairing the damage. We found that the rudder was still intact, but the quadrant, between the wheel and the rudder, had been subjected to such enormous strain that two of the four stainless steel bolts holding a vital plate had sheared off. I felt for John who was depressed at what he saw as vandalism. Once again, things were getting tense. It would be good for everybody to have a break from each other and the boat.

Then, at last, we were there. Rio was ours for three whole weeks. I loved it. Just getting off the boat and away from each other was a treat. Here it was carnival time, and the Race organisers had done a good job trying to make sure we were looked after at this stop – as indeed they had at the other two. John and I were taken in by a kind British couple who lived in a magnificent apartment overlooking the Copacabana. They gave us a bed, food and a shower and the freedom to come and go as we pleased. We were immensely grateful to have this time to ourselves – up to now the trip had been quite a strain on our relationship. Each day I would come back from doing jobs on the yacht with bags of dirty washing, which I offered to do for the boys. It was such a luxury to have clean dry clothes again.

Rio was the world of the body-beautiful, for the lucky ones. I felt distinctly overdressed on our first night, wearing a light cotton skirt and a sleeveless cotton blouse, as a voluptuous girl swung her naked hips inches past our table while we were having our first meal ashore. She was stunning – her smooth dark skin sprinkled lightly with gold dust. Wearing the briefest of lamé bras and only a tiny G-string, exposing rounded buttocks, polished and smooth, she ambled out into the velvet night vibrating with the rhythm of the samba, casually clicking her fingers in time to its insistent beat. How would our chaps cope? I thought ruefully. This was going to be wilder than any fantasy they had in the Southern Ocean. The whole of Brazil seemed to have reached a fever pitch, the excitement was infectious, and contests raged between districts as to who was putting on the best show. After looking at the sea for six weeks this was truly a shocking feast for our starved senses.

We also had the run of the exclusive Rio Yacht Club, where our boats were moored alongside. Here we rested and repaired ourselves and our boat in between enjoying the spectacle of the carnival. During the last week John asked me to collect some money from the bank. Before going I tried to telephone from the Club – I remembered similar fruitless visits in other South American spots.

'Allow me to help you.' I looked round to see a well-dressed Brazilian gentleman. He had noticed I was not getting through to the right person.

'Oh, thank you,' I gratefully replied, and explained my predicament. I did not want to fail John – he had enough on his plate without me not getting the money.

'In fact, I am going that way myself. I can give you a lift.'

I gratefully got into his sleek Mercedes, the ultimate status symbol in Rio, and we purred away. Not knowing the city, I was not very sure, but I did not think we were taking the quickest route, and I did not have much time before the bank would be shut. My companion clearly thought the same.

'Oh, my God, we will not get to your bank in time – they close at three,' he said.

'Oh dear,' I thought – more bad news for John. 'I'll just have to try again tomorrow.' My chauffeur interrupted my anxious thoughts, and suggested I might like a drink. I was feeling thirsty and said a glass of orange would be lovely, perhaps near the Copacabana where I could get out, and buy a few things I needed and then make my way back to the flat.

My companion put his foot down on the accelerator, and off we shot, in and out of the traffic at high speed. Where were we going? My suspicions began to be aroused, and, glancing at the suave Brazilian, I wondered what else was beginning to be aroused. No, surely not, what an unworthy thought. He was just trying to be helpful.

'We're well past Copacabana, aren't we?'

'Oh, just a bit, but I wish to take you to a quiet place for a drink. The cafés here are noisy and dirty.'

'Well, please not too far. I have a lot to do and I can't spend all afternoon out.' I could just imagine what John would say if I arrived back late with no money collected, with none of the things that we needed on the shopping list bought, and an explanation of how I had spent the afternoon drinking orange with a charming Brazilian gent. He would be furious. I was not very happy – particularly when the charming Brazilian gent screeched to a halt just past a motel, reversed and drove up to the office to pick up keys.

I had walked naively into a trap. Now what? Sitting frozen with horror in the passenger seat, I tried to decide what to do. Surely I could appeal to him and make him understand that it would not look good if I was to complain about his behaviour to the yacht club secretary. But then for all I knew he probably owned the yacht club.

On getting back into the car he leant over towards me. I could smell a mixture of cologne, sweat and peppermint, as his soft hands started to paw at my body. Enraged, I shouted at him. The boy from the office sauntered out on to the sweltering forecourt for a better look, and grinned as he watched me push the Brazilian away. I then summoned up all my dignity and warned him I would report him to all the authorities if he continued to pester me. I had not sailed round three Capes, been stuck in the pack-ice, gone through hell, to be intimidated by this man. My tirade seemed to do the trick. He was furious, his ridiculous pride injured. Muttering dark and dire threats, he drove me back to the outskirts of Rio. I was furious too – at my own stupidity – and I was shaken. I did not tell John for two days.

The three weeks drew to a close with a finale party held at the yacht club. It was quite a grand affair, and we had dressed up for the occasion. Waiters swirled around the many tables offering glasses of coconut milk and rum, or passion fruit laced with some mysterious liquor. I went to the Ladies before the prize-giving and was amazed to see four semi-naked women, screaming at the top of their voices, sticking sequins on to various parts of each other's anatomy. Feeling somewhat overdressed in my bare-back low-cut evening dress I smiled politely at them and returned to our table to tell the boys to expect some entertainment later. Prizes were handed out, and the victors of Leg Three had a long walk up under the spotlights to receive their awards. Finally, all the women taking part were called up in turn to receive giant bunches of roses. The drinks had taken effect and there was rowdy cheering and stamping from the other crews as each of us went forward to accept the flowers. It all seemed a far cry from the often frightening and squalid times we had endured at sea.

The evening progressed, the band struck up, and the sequinned dancing girls came on. Some of the bolder chaps joined in, and before long nearly everyone was being thrown into the swimming pool. John and I just escaped, but as we ran from the scene we were nearly bowled over by the riot police who had been called by the maître d'hôtel. Waving truncheons and letting off tear gas, they soon established order. There were lots of red eyes wandering around the next day – the day before the start of the final leg, home to Portsmouth and back to our families and loved ones.

On Wednesday 22 February 1978, an overcast but still sweltering hot day, we loaded the boat with last-minute fresh food and sorted out the final stowage. We would soon be bucking up and down on the ocean again. With plenty of time in hand we cast off and headed into the bay to practise starts. There was a festive air as we tucked into a delicious lunch of cold chicken and salad. I was at the wheel when one of the crew came up and, smiling shyly, said, 'Well, if I don't speak to you again, have a good trip.' I laughed, but I knew what he meant, and I so hoped that we had become wiser and would manage the last seven thousand miles in harmony.

I felt we were drawn as if by a magnet now. It was not Cape Town, Auckland or Rio we were dreaming of – it was home. We passed the Equator, going north this time, and toasted the occasion with warm beer. The heat drilled into us, but it seemed a bit more bearable in the knowledge that we would soon be 'Butting up the Channel in the mad March days,' and it would be a while before we would want to swim again. Then the wind came and blew us on. We clocked up our best day's run of our trip: 233 miles. But we were always chasing the weather and trying to avoid the Azores High. I had always considered it beneficial, but now it was the work of the Devil, as far as I was concerned, for with it came calm and no progress.

Our crew number was now down to ten. It seemed to make quite a difference from the thirteen of the last three legs. We did not get under each others' feet so much. There always seemed to be somewhere one could go and sit and be alone, and for me it meant more to do. I wished I had pushed myself forward a bit more earlier because I really came to enjoy the sailing. It was like driving a chariot, standing with my legs braced on the lockers either side of the cockpit, feeling this mighty boat creaming along the waves, responding to the slightest turn on the wheel held by my thin brown hands.

We arrived back at Portsmouth on 29 March in the middle of the night after a journey of thirty thousand miles which had taken nearly nine months. Unexpectedly, there was a terrific welcome party waiting for us, particularly our friends and families. In the darkness I searched the crowd for two special figures. Suddenly there they were, and I was picking up Bec who hugged me as though she never wanted to let me go again, and my dear mother, without whose help I could never have gone. Bec, who was very close to her granny, had gone to a new boarding school in Brighton, near where my mother lived. She had started the previous autumn when we were on our way to Cape Town. My mother had stepped in and done all the things I should have been doing: organising the school uniform and extra maths coaching, getting to know the headmistress and matron, attending the carol service and going to watch freezingly cold lacrosse matches. She did so much, I will never be able to thank her enough.

Then there was the final leg from Portsmouth to Ardmore, and we were home. A day or two later, while it was all still fresh in my mind, I walked out to Ardmore Point, once again to look out at the ocean that had spared me. The months of struggle had passed, and I was still me, yet irrevocably changed. 'I am moved from where I used to be: and can never go back.'

Was I at last beginning to know myself, to face my weaknesses to stand alone. The struggle would continue, the struggle to keep the school alive, to keep living our unusual life at Ardmore. But once again, John had given me the chance to accompany him on his quest for adventure and excitement. I would surely have never done it on my own, and through these testing times I think I had grown stronger and more sure. Was this not the point where the real struggle should begin – where I should strike out and be more my own person? Or were our lives so linked by the school, that any ideas I had of doing things I particularly wanted to were just not yet possible?

Chapter Seven

RUNNING

Two weeks to the day of our return from the Whitbread Race we started running our summer season; it was quite a rush. We had had plenty of time on the boat to think about how things were going and what we wanted to improve.

We agreed that I had done enough cooking over the last ten years; so we set about employing the girlfriend of one of those on the trip, as cook. We continued this system on and off for a few years, until I found that really it was best if I did it. We carried out other plans too. We put in a 12-KVA generator to power a new dishwasher. It was buying a sledgehammer to crack a nut, but after years over the sink with not very willing helpers, we felt it was a necessary step in taking some of the drudgery out of my life. We had also decided to invest in a 30′ fishing boat with a tough 6-hp engine.

During the summer we also decided to build a second timber house on the shore to improve the accommodation for the courses. Times had changed – people did not want to sleep in tents or huts anymore.

With every surge forward, however, there always seemed to be something to pull us back. We had arrived at Ardmore full of plans and very pleased to be home and delighting in the song of the birds in the wood, but our summer season was mostly a struggle with personalities. Many of the instructors were those who had sailed around the world with us – as John put it, 'They'd had the carrot first with the sailing trip' – and we had all got tired of each other. Then, on the last day of the season, our Land Rover was written off. Unknown to us, one of the chaps had taken his girlfriend to a local dance. Luckily they were both unharmed, but it was an expensive blow as we had only third-party insurance. Then we started to lose many of our salmon to shags and cormorants.

We had started a small salmon farm in the loch below our croft in

1976, growing silvery smolts into fine salmon weighing sometimes up to twenty-five pounds. These were early days in the fish farming industry and not much was known about predator nets. Losses were expensive and heartbreaking.

More serious by far, and most worrying, was that John kept on getting bad bouts of backache which had him confined to bed, when he felt all around needed his attention. Lance would sagely comment, 'The only man that was indispensable was Adam,' but John would fret, and not rest and let things improve as he should. In black moments he would mutter: 'My back is broken. How will I live at Ardmore as a cripple?' My heart went out to him. It was so ironic that after all the struggle and consolidation of the business, when things should have been looking brighter, there was this bitter and unexpected blow. By Christmas it was decided he should have an operation, and in January I took him down to the King Edward VII hospital for 'very old officers' in London, and they performed a laminectomy.

The film of the trip came out at the same time, and it unfairly cast John in a poor light. I had returned north, and the night after its showing nationwide the phone was jammed with calls from friends and acquaintances. 'How could you let them show it?' was the question everyone put to me. And there was my poor Johnny raving from his hospital bed, high on painkillers and sedatives. All that glorious effort seemed to have crumbled away.

Still, we had to keep struggling on. There did not seem to be much of an alternative. John could not contemplate living any-where other than Ardmore, while I thought that maybe if his back did not improve we could move down to one of the two wooden houses on the shore, where he could sit at a window with a fishing line dangling out into the loch. A wheelchair would have been impossible without any flat paths. I dreaded and feared his not getting better. Some people cope with disability better than others and I worried that depression would swamp him. We got him back to Ardmore, and, with the spring, he began to mend, but it had been a terrible blow and his confidence was shaken.

The day to day business of keeping the salmon farm going now fell to me. We had had one or two strange young men up to help but they had not worked out. It was easier to look after the fish myself. We got in help when it came to harvesting. I had hoped for some little bit of time to myself after getting a cook and dishwasher, but it was not to be.

But John's fighting spirit, which was an inspiration to so many of us, had not deserted him and, once the unusually long spell of snow in February melted, he was out training his body, shuffling along the track, calling back the strength that he so needed to keep the dream of living at Ardmore alive. He had decided that running was the way to rebuild that strength, and all he needed was a challenge. He chose the biggest challenge he could find – the marathon. It was a challenge we could both take on, for by then I was a runner too.

When we first started the school, early each morning before the businessmen came up for breakfast at our croft house, John would take them out to the lobster creels in the old double ender eighteen-foot black boat called the *Ada Bell*, the ancient Kelvin petro-paraffin engine chugging under Lance's expert care. It was fun on pearly mornings when the haul produced the blue-black beauties, but when it was wet and there were none it was not a very thrilling start to the day. So we abandoned the lobster fishing, and the following year decided to start the day with a jog or walk around the loch. The reasoning behind this early-morning activity was that to make the most of the short day, people should be fully awake at breakfast, and the run certainly woke people up.

At the same time we abandoned tents and put bunk beds in the wooden house which we had taken over when the Liddons left. There was also the double garage which we had erected on the shore, and turned into a museum for the rowing boat. One half was curtained off and used as sleeping quarters. People thought it quite a joke to be put into the museum to sleep. Old timers would rush for the beds there, and it was usually the wilder ones who appreciated this spot, with plenty of space to stow the bottles they had carted in. Great parties would go on most of the night, and when John arrived at ten to six with his flask of hot tea to wake them he did not always get a brilliant reception. But most days everyone would clamber out, put on damp gear, and make their way to the waiting boats, engines primed by sleepy instructors, and then across the loch to the southern shore where the run would commence.

In the early 1970s I never considered joining them. I was too busy getting breakfast ready, and getting Bec up to go to school. There was always plenty to do. But then my eyes were opened. One year on the women's course there was a slim attractive woman called

Leonora; she was German and typically self-disciplined. She lived in Dulwich and managed to run regularly. She loved our hilly track, and she loved the fresh clean air, the views to the mountains and beyond, and no sign of another human being.

'Marie Christine, you must make time to do it,' she urged.

'I doubt you could,' John challenged.

With that I started. I had a pair of Green Flash white Dunlop gymshoes, a pair of white towelling shorts and a yellow T-shirt. Rather self-consciously, when everyone was out, I set off from the house through the wood and eventually along the track. I was surprised to find how much easier it was than walking. Being dressed lightly and carrying nothing made it almost a pleasure – except when it came to going up the hills. Then I would stop, my lungs bursting, my legs aching, and think: 'This is terrible. I am never going to do this again.' But John's words ringing through my head spurred me to do it again and again. I am sure now he said it knowing it was the best form of encouragement he could give me.

It was not long before I could manage to run quite a way without stopping, nor long before I started to enjoy it and feel the benefits – and the benefits were various. It was good to see how my body firmed and strengthened. I lost weight, particularly round my tummy and thighs. Initially, when I was just running a daily three miles, I probably lost about half a stone, but with all the work and worry I was not overweight anyway. My legs became even stronger than they already were – living at the top of a hundred-foot steep hill involved a lot of exercising, just from going up and down to get provisions from the store. My complexion brightened, and my circulation was stepped up, so that in winter the chilblains on my toes in our cold damp house which had once so tormented me, hardly bothered me now. Generally my physical condition improved; my body felt tuned.

I did not lose my temper now to the degree I had before. Poor John was often at the receiving end of missiles, such as rocks and frying pans although he did sometimes ask for it. On one famous occasion when I was distraught over some slight, I flung a cup of coffee at him. In my rage the direction went awry, the cup hit the ceiling, broke and the contents drenched me. 'What on earth are you doing, Marie Christine?' he calmly asked. He put my fiery tempers down to me being half Irish. John may often have been at the receiving end of my rages, but there have been occasions when I

have stuck up for him in an equally ferocious fashion catching
people unawares, as normally I am politely quiet in a group.
Injustice brings my blood to the boil very fast.

My energy also increased. It seems a paradox that by using up
energy you increase your reserves, but that is exactly what I found
happens. Coming back to my tasks after running for an hour during
the day, I had the energy to get on with them, feeling brighter, and I
could keep going longer without feeling tired. Strangely too, if I
felt tired in the day it was often more beneficial to go out and run,
rather than sit in a chair to relax. To be able to get out and run for
oneself is a wonderfully selfish occupation, and my hour out was a
time to ponder matters without interruption. Surprisingly, often
the answers to problems that had been troubling me came then, just
out of the blue.

People who already run regularly will know all of this, but I was
just amazed to find it out for myself and to find how it helped me
cope with my life. My confidence increased.

'OK, I'll come on the morning run,' I told John. I could get most
of the breakfast organised the night before, and it would not take
long to finish it off when I got back.

In the early days, my appearance on the scene was greeted with
disbelief and dismay.

'What about the porridge?'

'Don't worry, I'll get back in time,' I would answer as I bent to
stretch and tie my laces in the double knot – never let your shoes
come undone. Meeting at the boat in the early dawn, muffled for
the cool trip across the loch, mercifully hardly light, I would shrink
into the collar of my down jacket. Sitting uneasily on the wet
thwart, sandwiched between sleepy businessmen, I hoped the
Adonis instructor would start his Seagull engine on the first pull.
Otherwise John, his patience short-fused at this time of the
morning, would push his way to the stern of the boat, the
emasculated instructor moving to let John bring the engine to life;
under his hands it would not dare not choke into a roar. Across we
would go to the other side of the loch, with mumbled comments
about running shoes and training programmes from the keen
contenders. Hoping to keep the feet dry, we would hop ashore, lean
against the rocks to remove outer garments, strip down to the
minimum, shorts and singlet. Stretch and then off. Pounding along
the track, we would jockey for position so as not to get boxed in for

the uphill path which leads the pack to the road, over a couple of stiles and up and up past the fuel tanks and the BMWs and Jaguars, their panting owners glancing at them anxiously. Then up to the mail box, and, turning left on to the main single track road, Foinaven stretching into the distant bowl of early morning sky. Groups would now be forming. A fit young instructor would be running with the fastest course members – it would never do for our team not to be able to keep up with someone on the course; great emphasis is put on this and instructors are honed to be tireless, fast and uninjured. To become injured is almost a crime. Somewhere in the middle I would be busting my guts to run as fast as I could.

There are always plenty in the field who hate to be overtaken by a female, and view it as the ultimate humiliation. If I passed a dismayed gent on the route I would save just enough breath to shout, 'Sorry got to hurry; got to get the breakfast.'

Now I did not care about being stuck indoors so much. I had lungfuls of wonderful fresh air; my body felt relaxed and strong; and I was now accepted in a different light by those on the course. My self-respect mattered a lot to me.

Then came the marathon running. A friend who had been on a previous course returned unrecognisable. His appearance and manner had completely changed. Before he had been slightly overweight and rather soggy-looking. Now he was bright, much more energetic, and stones lighter. He told us his week at Ardmore two years before made him realise how he had let himself go. Determined to do something about it, he had become fitter and now was into marathon running.

'You've got to do it, John,' he said to my husband. I bristled.

'I might try too,' I butted in, almost regretting the impetuous words the moment I had uttered them.

'Twenty-six miles is a very long way, Marie Christine,' John cautioned, a phrase he was to repeat again and again in the months ahead. But once again it was the spur I needed.

We enlisted to run in the 1980 New York Marathon. The interest in long distance running had not really started in Britain, but Central Television thought it a good idea to make a film of us taking part. This would also make it into more of an event for us, and was a great idea for publicity for the school. But it meant we had to do it. I used to wake in the night in terror wondering what I had let myself in for. Failing is bad enough, but failing in public, on the television screen for all to see . . .

Chris Brasher, Olympic gold medallist and well-known writer, came to advise us on our training. It was clear there were no short cuts – we had to get the miles in. John took it all most seriously. He has always kept fastidious daily records of his running: distance, time, comments about his condition. It now assumed the import-ance of the Peninsular Campaign. Though I was a bit less organised – perhaps to offset John's intense approach – and it was a while before I got a stop watch, I covered the distance that John did. I did not run with him – it just became all too competitive – but my aim was the same: to complete the distance, to run a marathon. I had doubts that I could, particularly when early on in the year I would come in exhausted after ten miles and then think that in October I would have to double that distance and more.

The summer wore on, and we gradually increased our distances. We would leave the house at five-thirty each morning to run round to the petrol tanks and back, a distance of ten miles, and then once a week we would try and do a fifteen-mile run to Laxford Bridge. I tucked squares of strawberry jelly tied up in clingfilm into the small pocket on my shorts to eat if I started to feel weak. Stronger and stronger we got, until finally I managed to run to the Tarbet junction on the Scourie road and back, a distance of twenty-two miles. I crawled back up beside the waterfall, my feet and armpits chafed raw but feeling triumphant. I knew I could run the twenty-six miles.

I was all right – my temperament helped me to go at it fairly steadily, and with my light frame I had not developed any injuries. John, though, was beginning to show signs of stress. Much of the plan to do this marathon was to restore his confidence in his physical ability, but we should perhaps have contented ourselves with a lesser challenge that did not require such mileage training, for the sciatic nerve in his left leg now became very painful. We kept hoping the pain would go away, but it just became worse.

Our understanding local doctor referred John to Squadron Leader Iain MacAulay, a physiotherapist and osteopath down at Drumbeg, south of Kylesku ferry, at least an hour and a half away. The journey time depended on how long it took for the ferry man to come out of the pub on the other shore. Iain greeted us with a broad smile. His unruly white hair was topped by a fine Highland bonnet and he sported a kilt around his burly girth. He was a legendary figure. During the war he had been captured by the Japanese and had seen two thousand of his companions die from malnutrition and disease. His own weight decreased from twelve to five stone, and fearing blindness he trained to become a physiotherapist. He was just the person John needed to see, for his enthusiasm was infectious. A bit of manipulation and then some heat treatment, and we were on our way back up the winding coastal road across the ferry and home. It all helped, but there was no getting away from the truth – John should really abandon the whole plan.

By this stage we had got well involved with the film-making. The director had become a good friend and he was counting on this film to help his career which at that point was in the doldrums. I had become very friendly too with his French girlfriend, Eva. She was such fun, and made us laugh. We felt we could not let them down. We were caught in a terrible dilemma. When the film crew arrived in September to take some more training shots, John was hardly able to move and spent much of the time resting his sore leg in bed. He was in despair, yet he was determined to do the marathon in spite of my entreaties to leave it for another year.

Meanwhile the crew took endless shots of me having imaginary telephone calls with my mother in Brighton. With all the tension in the house, I found it hard not to collapse into hysterical giggles.

Brasher came up for a filmed interview. It was decided we would do the scene in our matchboard-lined kitchen, sitting round the supper table with a wine bottle or two. Brasher insisted on smoking a cigar, as he was keen to promote the view that you did not have to give up everything in order to run marathons. I do not think John shared his view, but now was not the time for a philosophical discussion on lifestyles. I was feeling hot, having had to cook supper for the quite large film crew party, and my pale blue Rayburn, next to the kitchen table, was pulsing out the heat, the oven needle up to 450. Adding to the heat were special filming lights to illuminate the scene. The generator powering these was outside, and in spite of shutting all the windows and doors we could still hear its hum. The soundman looked troubled; tape was found, and soon we had taped the windows and door and put up extra cardboard baffles. We were now sealed into an airless, overheated box. John and Brasher may have been feeling hot, but at least they were not running with sweat like I was. What could I do? I could not be filmed with my hair sticking to my face and drops of sweat making dark patches on my smart blue silk blouse. In the end I got two buckets of icy water, took off my shoes, and plunged my feet and legs into them, all safely out of sight under the table, out of camera.

The wet and stormy autumn days raced on, with John's back and leg giving more and more trouble. I could not think of anything to say that would console him. Even 'It's not as bad as facing the death sentence,' seemed hollow. I think we both looked on 26 October as the day we would climb the scaffold and face public shame. Iain MacAulay came regularly to Skerricha to give John further treatment but, for it to work, he said John should rest for weeks to allow the damaged tissue to heal. We were still in the throes of the autumn courses and John felt he just could not ease up.

We decided to go south as soon as our season was over at the end of September. There must be someone there who had the magic cure. We trailed round the different treatments: short-wave diothermy, microwave, epidural injections. Twenty-four hours before flying to New York John was even under general anaesthetic receiving osteopathic manipulation. My poor darling Johnny, it was tough. The TV director knew John was having problems but not how severe they were. He kindly laid on limousines to take us to Heathrow and to meet us at JFK in New York. John could not even sit down on the flight, as the smallest vibration caused him terrible pain.

The day of the marathon dawned with a sickening inevitability. The film crew now had expanded to a major production unit; in fact there were to be nine separate film crews filming us as we passed the various mile posts. We had been installed in a luxurious suite on the forty-second floor of the Sheraton Center looking out over the vast teeming city of New York. John had been restless all night, and neither of us felt very bright. Carefully we put on the silky running singlets and shorts we had been given. We needed braver colours than the lilac and pale yellow chosen for us. I bent down, first to tie John's running shoes and then mine. Imaginary twinges were breaking out all over me now too.

'I think my back and leg feel easier,' John said cautiously, as we waited for the elevator to take us down. By chance John had met a masseur who had worked for many years on the QEII, and he had offered to try and ease John's pain. His magic hands had pushed, pulled and coaxed John's muscles and tendons. They were both tired by the end of the three-hour session, but John felt a warm relaxed glow spread over his back and legs for the first time in a long while.

'Maybe the massage has done the trick,' I answered hopefully, unsure if it was the elevator which was causing the sinking feeling in my stomach, as I noticed John fingering the pain killers he had tucked into his shorts pocket. Our film director was now fully aware of John's condition. Trying to salvage something from our attempted run, he suggested that if John did not manage the twenty-six miles, he could always come in with a dramatic statement from his wheelchair. 'Tell 'em this, John,' he'd grin. '"I'll never walk again".'

A great roar went up as we set off together with sixteen thousand other competitors, across the giant Verrazano Narrows Bridge. Every runner knew what everyone else had put in to get to this point. There were no barriers here: black, white, male, female, old, young, rich, poor, fat, thin. We were all united by this common effort. John's old 'big match temperament' came to the fore. We ran together for the entire twenty-six miles. He took one of the strong pain killers at mile thirteen, and glucose at mile twenty-one. I was all right – I could only think of John. Finally we were in Central Park, and it looked like we would make it. Then jubilation, as we passed the finishing line in under four hours. Whatever the pain to follow, he had – we had – succeeded.

After this, John took it a bit easier for a while, and the sciatic nerve trouble subsided. Our film was shown on the night before the first-ever London Marathon, in 1981. And in the autumn of that year we ran two more marathons. We thought we would try the New York one again, without the hassle of the film, and it was again a great experience. This time, John and I ran separately – only first-time men were started with the women competitors – and I got to know some of the others running. They were so friendly that I hardly noticed the miles passing. Also we both managed a slightly better time.

My final marathon was in Boise, Idaho: John had an awful scheme that we should hire a car and run marathons all across America. New York was first, then two weeks later came Boise. The other competitors were from Boise athletics clubs and they took it all pretty seriously. At the start-line I heard over the public address system, 'and we have, representing Scotland . . . John and Marie Ridgway.'

'Oh dear,' I thought. We were both still quite tired from New York, and I had the distinction of coming in last, and with a Boise Police escort for the final three miles. Los Angeles was to be next. We did not show.

Back at home now in the early morning, when I am all alone out on the single track road, I sometimes remember the New York crowds cheering everyone on: 'You can do it, you can do it.' Maybe that was what I learnt most from the whole business: that really anyone *can* do anything.

PART TWO

Elizabeth

Chapter Eight

ELVIN

Sometimes the rain would fall, gently and insidiously, its drops tip-tapping into the old iron guttering from rivulets trickling off our patched roof, and running down the rowans on to stones worn smooth and clean over many years. With diligence it would inevitably seek out cracked and slipped slates and invade our house with insistent drips, filling buckets, basins – pity the man with a leaking roof and a cross wife.

Sometimes the rain would batter our roof, accompanied by a shrieking south-westerly wind. Curtains of near horizontal rain would lash the hill, the house; the peaty ground would become entirely saturated; the burns would rush with a fury of frothing yellow spate water; waterfalls would cascade over lips of steep rocks – everything wet spilling and racing down towards the accommodating welcome of the sea loch.

In June though, it hardly rained at all. It was our driest month, our only real month of summer. Sometimes May was good too, but we all banked on June being pearly, with the complete stillness of early morning, the heavens a canopy of bluest silk embroidered with lingering silvery stars and one pale-faced moon, her moment of glory past as the big orange sun outshining her started its mighty ascent rising between Bein Spionnaidh and the ridge of Foinaven, ancient landmarks, old as the world itself.

One day in June we left the house, and walked down through the dew-wet meadow grass to the shore. The bird song was loud: a blackbird had nested close by in a deserted byre, a crevice between grey stones below the thickly tarred black roof. She vied with the mavis, most speckled thrush, for sweetest song, piercing the cool morning air. The smooth loch that is more sky than water shattered as we ploughed along, leaving in our wake an ever-widening chevron of ripples journeying to each shore. Oyster catchers screeched in rage at us as we passed their private island nests, firing themselves into the air, triangles of jagged black and white, their furious bold orange beaks and legs skimming the silky sky water. And still the sun kept rising up higher and higher in the summer sky, leaving the grey mountains far below.

And on that day far away over many other mountains and seas, in a different land by the rushing streams fed from the high snow peaks racing to join the 'great speaker', jungle shadows hid jaguar, monkey, snuffling armadillo, snakes and spiders; jungle trees were host to clouds of brilliant parakeets, toucans, vampire bats, butterflies of every hue; dense forest was choked with hanging moss, rope-like lianas, bromeliads, strangely beautiful orchids. Here, deep in a valley beside a curve in the river, nestled a cluster of thatched huts. From one there came a strangled cry which echoed across the valley to be swallowed by the surrounding dense green jungle. Two women helped another bring into the world: a small girl child.

The baby's whimper and then lusty yell were never heard by her mother, for she was profoundly deaf. After the umbilical cord was cut with the customary potsherd and tied to the mother's big toe, to prevent it returning to the womb, *ama kutiykurqonanpaq*, the placenta was examined in an attempt to read the child's future. Then after piercing with thorns it was burnt, the ashes being carefully kept as a cure for penetration by the spirits.

The mother, Leocadia, held her baby close, for she knew it would soon be taken by its granny and aunt and ritually bathed in the icy water of the rushing river. Past the silent huts they crept, too early yet even for the crowing cockerels, and down to the edge of waters which had only last year altered their course, for Lucmahuayco means in Quechua 'Place of the Lukma fruit trees where the flash floods occur.'

Before the girl child was washed clean the spirits must be honoured, so no evil should enter her soul. Coca leaves – three for each person present – some fat, a waxy-leafed plant and ash from the placenta were all burnt and blown to the winds – '*fa, fa, fa*' – to the spirits who must always be honoured. Here there were spirits everywhere, the mighty river, the mountains, the trees, the fertile valley's earth. As dawn brightened the sky, the baby was wrapped tightly in swaddling bands, but only after the two women, Josephina and her elder daughter Marcelina, had examined her closely. She was perfectly formed, she looked strong enough to survive. But she was not like other babies of this village: this infant had pale skin not dark, and the down covering her head was gingery. They knew then that Elvin Berg would accept this child as his daughter.

This was the eighth day of June 1979. On the other side of the world as my day proceeded I was ignorant of the birth of this child that would one day call me Mama and run to me for comfort and love, that in parallel we would struggle on with our lives, and meet six years later by the remotest thread of chance.

In the summer of 1985, Bec left school. She was just eighteen, and John thought it would be good if we were all to go on an expedition together that winter to Peru, on 'a family holiday': we had drifted and needed something to bring us close again.

Since the Whitbread Round the World Race, seven years of titanic struggle had passed: John's back had collapsed and mended; we had run our marathons; John and Andy Briggs had sailed non-stop around the world, setting a new world record of 202 days; we had pushed on at Ardmore and had built two more houses; the mains electricity had come, and the Valiant Heater – my Foxy friend – lay rusting on the midden, cast out and forgotten. In between we had suffered from another recession and poor bookings, and our fish farm had nearly gone under, losing many salmon to seals.

For years John had talked about Osambre and Elvin. I was disappointed not to have been with him on the earlier part of the Amazon expedition in 1970, and to have missed meeting the Bergs who sounded so intriguing. I had often heard the story of how they had carved out a farm from virgin forest in the 'eyebrow of the jungle', and of a life self-sufficient, even to the point of washing with nuts which fell to the ground from a soap-nut tree planted in the area between their huts and where a stream had been diverted to run. Although the time John and Abel Berg's eldest son Elvin spent together was short, they had both recognised in each other a matching spirit of adventure, and Elvin had steered John and his expedition to safety down the rushing Apurimac – without this young man's knowledge and skill they would likely have perished.

'I must go back to Osambre. I want you to meet Elvin, Marie Christine,' John would sometimes say in the fifteen intervening years. Something else always cropped up, but now at last we had made our plan.

There were five of us: John, myself, Bec, Edward Ley-Wilson, our chief instructor, and Justin Matterson, who had come to help at the school and on the yacht on and off for the past five years. They were sterling chaps, much in the mould of those gone before. I thought back to thirteen years earlier to Krister and Richard in Chile – Richard now long married with two growing boys – to the late Staff Morse of the Cape Verde sailing trip eleven years before, of all the good fellows on the round-the-world trip. And how would this trip work out? I was feeling worn down by the struggle at Ardmore. Maybe this was what I needed, to go away and see a different world and a different, simpler way of life.

Bec was very excited about the proposed trip and it would be lovely for me, for once, to have another woman for company. That summer of 1985, whenever we had a moment from running the courses, we spent it preparing for our trip. There were weekly visits to the local doctor at Scourie for the necessary injections. We had to be prepared for anything, and John talked a lot about vampire bats, which were known to carry rabies. Our doctor inoculated us with a costly vaccine, which, in the event of our being bitten, would give us protection for twenty-four hours. We packed in our medical kits the next huge dose, in case we could not get medical help within that period. The ghost of a worry haunted me once again: it was fine for me to take risks with my life, but what about Bec?

She had finished her last two years of schooling at Gordonstoun. John and I were so proud of her. She had grown into a sweet, considerate, amusing young woman, athletic and conscientious; and she still loved Ardmore. I regretted the time I had not spent with her as she grew up, the long spells when we had gone off on our expeditions, the shorter times when my work had kept me busy, and (because of our location at Ardmore) the two thirds of every year since she was eleven that she had spent away at boarding school, first in Brighton, then in Morayshire on the east coast of Scotland – a bit nearer but still a six-hour round drive.

In 1984 Bec had asked me to go to see her in a school production of *Carmen*. After a busy day I had set off in the late afternoon. I arrived a little early, parked my car close to a near by wood, and fell asleep in a mossy clearing. I awoke with a start and looked at my watch – only ten minutes before the curtain went up.

Pink and flustered, I was ushered to my seat and sat gingerly feeling for bits of dried leaves in the back of my hair. It was a spirited performance, and I was pleased Bec had taken part in it. She would always remember this occasion when she heard *Carmen* playing in the future. I left Gordonstoun at ten that evening, arriving at Lairg just after midnight. The next forty-seven miles took all night. I just could not keep awake. As I drove along the deserted single-track road, I bit my lip till it bled, shouted songs at the top of my voice, but nothing would keep me awake. Finally, just after the watershed where all the rain that falls runs west, joining streams spilling into lochs and rivers, and runs eventually out into the Minch, I succumbed and fell into a deep sleep. Suddenly there was a great roar and I awoke, shocked to see in the darkness the dim but close outline of a magnificent stag, acknowledging my presence. I set off again, and at five that morning, with only an hour before the daily work would begin, I crept in beside the sleeping form of my husband.

Just before we left Britain, by the merest thread of a chance, Elvin's relations in Norway heard of our proposed journey to Peru. A brief mention in a daily paper led to a Norwegian journalist contacting us and asking who was this friend Elvin Berg we were planning to visit. Out came the story of how Elvin had saved John's life all those years before and how in the autumn John was taking me and Bec to visit him in his jungle stronghold. Then we received a telephone call from Norway. John who is slightly deaf, thanks to the self-loading rifle of his army days, strained to hear the halting English.

'Alexander Berg speaking. We would be very pleased to hear news of Elvin Berg. We have not heard from him now for quite a while, and we are worried . . . he was always a good letter writer, after his parents Abel and Rosa died.'

Our suspicions that not all was well in Peru were confirmed on our arrival – the British Embassy expressly warning us against going into the area of Osambre.

'You go at your own risk, against our advice,' they said. 'Do not expect us to come and look for you if you go missing.' The message was clear.

We now learnt of the terrorist group *Sendero Luminoso*, Shining Path. Set up by a University professor in Ayacucho, it is similar to the Khmer Rouge in Kampuchea. These extremists stop at nothing to spread chaos and fear. They start history again, at Year One. Their strategy is to capture the support of the countryside first. Then the towns will fall when supplies are cut. There follows the complete destruction of established authority.

The people who were suffering most were the *campesinos*, the very people who surely the terrorists were trying to help. If a raid was made on an outlying village, those that did not vow allegiance to the *Senderos* would be brutally murdered. People were hung up naked by their feet and burnt to death, and one twelve-year-old boy had confessed to dismembering nine adults. It was a dirty, terrifying war. The peasants died if they did not become terrorists; they died if they did, for if those in the village were allowed to live the soldiers assumed they had harboured the terrorists and they were then killed by the military. Numbers of dead and missing were mounting daily.

We were faced with a dilemma. It would be foolhardy to go straight into the *Zona Roca* – the war zone that we had expressly been warned against – yet this was where Osambre was. We could not afford to hang around Lima and Cuzco: there were five of us to feed and house, and the two boys could eat like horses. John felt that if we were to face difficult challenges in a dangerous situation we should train up and become tougher, quicker and generally more efficient. So after a day in Lima we flew to Cuzco, the ancient Inca capital and 'Navel of the World', and from there we took a train down to Sicuani. Even here at eight thousand feet we were beginning to feel the effect of the altitude: headaches and lassitude. But our plan was to take us higher. We wanted to get to the old silver mine at Cailloma at fourteen thousand feet, where, fifteen years before, John and his team had gone to find the furthest source of the Amazon. A period of walking at this altitude, where there were apparently no terrorists, should prepare us well for the next phase which would be more dangerous. This was to try to get to Osambre, which was situated near the same river on which we now stood, but many many miles downstream, where it had tumbled eight thousand feet on its journey to meet up with the Amazon.

We carried basic food: rice, tea, sugar, milk and tinned fish, which we supplemented with anything we could buy along the way, although there was not much, just potatoes and an egg or two if we were lucky. Day after day we walked, gradually accustoming our bodies to a simpler but more demanding way of life. We were self-sufficient and carried all we needed. High up on the roof of the world this Altiplano stretched forever in rolling hills of bleached ichu-grass with patches of poor soil turned and cultivated by a people who expected little from life. In spite of what seemed to us a hard and unrewarding life, their spirit shone through. The Quechua women wore the brightest of clothes: woven voluminous skirts in shades of vermilion, poppy scarlet, trimmed with saffron yellow and orange braid, of shocking cobalt blue and black and emerald, proclaiming their presence in this empty land under a huge and empty sky.

We plodded on, cheered by the greetings we got, but many people were suspicious of us and some were hostile. Why were *gringos* carrying their own kit? Surely we would have horses and guides. We were a puzzle to them, and perhaps a threat. Rumour and fear abounded in these troubled times. Much of the time we wore khaki clothing and 'belt order' – a webbing belt with pouches hanging from it. The idea was that if we were attacked we would throw off our rucksacks and be able to get away faster with just the belt order, as the pouches contained emergency supplies to last us for a while: malaria pills, basic first-aid kit, fishing hooks and line, knife, emergency rations.

John had briefed us on how to confuse the enemy. We usually walked in single file along the narrow tracks, but on attack we were to scatter, the first person to the left, the second to the right and so on. Bec and I listened intently. Judging from the talk in Lima and Cuzco we could become a target. People told us the terrorists were not in the Altiplano but to watch out for robbers – our clothing, boots, and rucksacks would be attractive to them, and we would surely have money.

We continued very much in the footsteps of John's previous expedition. Some people would greet John, remembering '*quinze anos ante*', but at other places there were changes. The much needed Agrarian Reforms of 1973, where land had been parcelled out to the people where previously it had been owned in large chunks by rich landowners, had completely altered the order of things. It was now outstandingly fairer, but a system which had once reigned was now gone and with its departure much of the land, buildings, paths had all fallen into disrepair. People were content to produce enough just for themselves, but this meant not enough for the community. We passed villages where there was poverty, and we also passed a few communes which worked well, but these tended to be run by one strong leader.

Throughout this whole area an immense effort had been made to build and run schools. However remote the settlement – and there were no roads here – there would be a school, and children would come from great distances each day to attend. We managed to stay at the schools and we met many of the teachers, mostly idealistic but disappointed young people doing their very best far from home, but frequently isolated by the community who saw them as instruments of a government they did not trust. Further down in terrorist country it was the teachers who were often assassinated first – they and other officials were called *yana uma* black heads – and who could blame those who returned to their homes in the cities, disillusioned? So the fine schools would be locked up, shutting out a whole generation of children who would never know the meaning of *oportunidad*.

As we walked over the rolling Peruvian plains, we were getting stronger, our bodies leaner and tougher, but the altitude was hard to adjust to. At times, we all suffered from headaches and shortness of breath. My nose bled frequently, while Bec developed a cold which gradually got worse. She suffered with it stoically, but John and I worried about her. As we continued walking one morning after a customary stop, I noticed her in tears.

'It's my ear, Mum.' I knew it must be bad for her to cry.

John insisted we stop, and find somewhere for her to rest, keep warm and recover. We both understood how much more serious illnesses like these are at altitude. Bec looked so defenceless.

We limped into Ccotana the nearest village, to find the teacher was away, and *el presidente*, who lived in a low mud hovel, was drunk. The village was poor, the children thin and the adults distressed. No key could be found for the school, so we were shown to a small adjacent hut, poorly thatched and not much bigger than a dog kennel – eight foot by seven. The rough earth floor was littered with broken glass and animal droppings. We cleaned it as best we could, then covering it we laid Bec down in her sleeping bag. She was in much pain, her face screwed up with each spasm, tears trickling from the corners of her tightly shut eyes.

Outside the villagers stood trying to catch sight of us. What was going on? Who were these foreign people? Had the young *gringa* a disease? Would it spread to their children? Understandably, they were far from friendly, but with our poor Spanish we could not explain to them anything, and in this situation would it have helped?

It was decided Justin and Ed would walk to Tunga Suca to try to get medical help – people talked of a missionary nurse. I set off up the rutted path to get water. The village supply was just a drain running along the main street, the haunt of pigs and dogs. A bleached human skull rested on a wall close by.

As the night wore on, John and I took it in turns to hold our daughter in our arms. At 2.30 a.m. her ear began to discharge a pale liquid tinged with blood. We feverishly searched through the *Traveller's Guide to Health*. The symptoms fitted otitis media, a severe infection spreading up from the Eustachian tube resulting in pus bursting the ear drum.

During that long night I would have bartered my soul to the Devil for Bec's pain to be lessened. John and I were consumed with remorse. Why had we brought her? Why were we putting her life at such risk? Only two days before we had watched a funeral procession, the mourners throwing themselves to the ground overcome by grief. We were no different from these people. They knew about death, about losing a precious, loved child. If we did not give Bec the right treatment, she too might die in this god-forsaken place.

Justin and Ed returned the next morning having met a *médico* who confirmed our diagnosis. We had – correctly, they confirmed – started Bec on antibiotics in the night, and hourly she improved. We got the key to the school and moved in. A black twenty-four hours of nightmare was over, but it was a warning that, out here, we could not always expect things to work out how we hoped. But curiously Bec's illness was to play a small part in the story that unfolded later on.

We had been walking along the roof of the world now for twenty-two days, and John felt it was time to tackle the next phase and head into the jungle. On our way back to Cuzco, we met a sad-faced girl at an empty railway station. She came over to help Bec get off a truck, as Bec had her head wrapped in an army head-warmer which was covering a bulging pad over her sore ear. Whilst waiting for the train, we discovered her name was Elizabeth Paullo, and that she was a teacher going to Cuzco for four days' holiday. It transpired John had met her family fifteen years before: they had lived a great distance from where we were now sitting, but close to Osambre. She knew Elvin. She told us the property belonging to the Bergs and the Paullos had all been destroyed, and that her father had been murdered. Elvin, she said, was alive and living in Lucmahuayaco.

The story about Señor Paullo was terrible but the news of Elvin was just what John wanted to hear, a signpost, pointing us in the direction of the 'Red Zone'. We planned a day or two of lying low in Cuzco, as we did not want the authorities to discover our whereabouts. John had been interviewed by the secret police when we were first in Cuzco, and the military had issued us with a pass to go into the Zone, but we heard things had changed in the four weeks we had been away. All personnel had been stopped entering the Zone, and it would be unlikely they would grant us permission now.

Once John is set on an idea it is hard to dissuade him. I knew that if it was humanly possible we would find Elvin. It had become a quest, and 'Let no cause or persuasion deter you from your task' was the message John carried in his heart. Bec was better, still a little deaf, but her old chirpy self; the boys were raring to go; as for myself, I just felt carried along.

We set off on phase two of our journey. We were now lean, mean, and, if not quite fighting machines, we felt we could cope with most situations. With John's knowledge of the area we would approach our destination by a back door, crossing the Apurimac River at a point where fifteen years ago they had found a raft. We had heard that there was now an aerial wire on which we could hoist ourselves over, in case the raft crossing was out, as the river would be coming into flood. It was hot now. Biting flies, thirst, poisonous tarantulas replaced altitude problems, but still there was the ever-threatening menace of an ambush.

At the bottom of a treacherous cliff, where Bec and I nearly fell to our deaths, was the Apurimac River. This was where we planned to put into action John's plan to enter the war zone through a back door. But it was fifteen years on, and there was no sign of a raft, nor a wire, just a big river full of coffee-coloured water rushing down through gorges with rapids at frequent intervals. Justin had been a good swimmer at school, and he now implored John to allow him to swim the river. John was reluctant. He knew the terrible risk, how easy it would be to drown, but also he knew how important it was to a young blood like Justin. This was a great challenge, just as rowing the Atlantic had been to John.

They studied the river closely and devised a plan. Justin would allow the eddy on our bank to carry him upstream swimming with a measured breaststroke. Then, on hitting the edge of the rapids in the middle, he was to allow the river to carry him downstream thirty yards, where he must put in a twenty-five-yard sprint to the far bank where he could scramble out and make his way into the forest and up to a clearing where we felt there must be a house and help.

Wearing a white T-shirt and jungle trousers, with running shoes tied around his waist, and in his pocket a sealed plastic bag containing some money and Bec's phrase book, he waded into the water. At once the water seized him. We watched, mesmerised, as the river took hold of him. He was not in control. The rushing water was master now. Too fast he was hurled out of the eddy and into the main stream. We watched him as he tried in vain to return to our bank, his arms flailing uselessly in the torrent, then he was gone. Sickened we watched and waited.

'Look, there he is,' Bec screamed from far off down the river. With Ed she had dashed downstream, hopping over the rounded boulders, desperately anxious for her friend. Yes. There he was. We could just make out the shape of his dark head in the brown water. He had been washed through the second set of rapids. Was he alive? Conscious? He was now far beyond our help. Then we saw his arms moving in an exhausted crawl. He was making a last enormous effort to reach the far bank and escape the grip of this monster river.

Miraculously he was washed ashore on to the only place he could have got out – beyond were the sheer cliffs at the bend of the river. For a long time he lay like a corpse on the short sandy beach, then we watched him clamber wearily up into the dense undergrowth to try to find help, while the four of us huddled together shaking with the horror of what we had nearly witnessed.

Justin managed to find some people who came rushing down to rebuild the raft, and by the following day we were all safely across the river. We were now in the war zone. Our presence was reported by a runner to the military headquarters two days' walk away. A message came back for us to be escorted to *el commandante* at Amaybamba.

The people on this side of the river were in a high state of excitement. They had been thrilled at Justin's extraordinary swim across the river – probably nobody had ever done this before and survived – and because of this they helped the rest of us to cross the river. Yet we felt terrible when we realised the position we had put them in, for now we were on their territory we were told that the penalty for harbouring strangers was to be shot.

The young *Gobernador* allowed us to spend one night in the school, where only twenty out of the normal one hundred pupils remained. Many families had left for the slums of the cities, terrified for their lives, and in going had forfeited their land and homes. On the second day just as it was getting dark we set off, with an escort of ten of the toughest men. One was almost in tears when pressed into service. What were we heading into? We kept asking about Elvin. The answers were conflicting, but most people believed Osambre was one of the first farms to be attacked by the *Senderos* and that Elvin had been murdered, although his brother Olaf might have escaped, they thought.

We fervently hoped these stories were incorrect and that Elvin was alive. His presence drew us on. I felt all would be fine once we got to Osambre. We were allowed to stop for a few hours' sleep at a village where the people were distinctly hostile. We could not blame them. The next day under heavy guard we set off on a gruelling march. We had an immense five-hour climb to a tiny *pueblo*. I was suffering from severe period pains but there was no question of slowing down or stopping. By mid–afternoon the horse carrying our rucksacks collapsed and we had to manage for ourselves, Justin, Ed and John taking nearly everything. Up and up we climbed. Finally we could go no further and reluctantly our guards allowed us to stop at an impoverished village just over a ridge at over eleven thousand feet. Again these poor people were alarmed to see us and we spent a miserable cold night frightened and hungry, sleeping under a rough porch.

Late that afternoon we arrived at Amaybamba, not knowing what to expect. As we approached, a military troop-carrying helicopter swooped in and out, and we heard ragged rifle and machine-gun fire. Were we all to be shot?

We were led through a throng of four hundred people who had gathered to discuss with the military the defence of their villages. Would we be lynched, made an example of? We had heard stories of foreigners who had been caught helping terrorists. With our poor Spanish, we would not be able to put up much of a case for our defence. It was late afternoon, and we were led to the front of the only large mud-block building. The most senior man present, who looked like an elderly Baden-Powell, came forward. John produced all his papers. He then thought it might help if we were to show we were carrying no weapons or ammunition by publicly emptying the entire contents of each of our rucksacks. It is bad enough being searched by the customs, but here we were with four hundred onlookers all peering for a peep, as every single item was taken out and turned over and closely examined. If it was to save our lives, any feelings of delicacy or shyness I might have harboured were of little consequence. We were cleared. We obviously had nothing that these people need worry about. They must have thought we were just rather foolish eccentric travellers.

We felt pretty low. We could not move on. We had only rumours that Osambre was burnt and Elvin killed. Then two days later a small army patrol of black-balaclava-helmeted soldiers returned from a sortie. The lieutenant had been kicked by a mule. We wasted no time in introducing ourselves by offering him a good slug of our Johnny Walker whisky and arnica for his bruise. He could have taken us out and had us shot, but I think he was rather relieved to see us, and we talked of inconsequential matters such as the fine restaurant at the yacht club at Callao, Lima's old port, and of how his colonel favoured our particular brand of whisky. He then looked grim.

'This whole area is full of terrorists,' he warned us, waving his arm at the jungle all around. 'Osambre is burned to the ground. We were there yesterday. Your friend is dead. You must leave. You are at great risk.'

We set off with heavy hearts in the opposite direction from Osambre. There was nothing else we could do. We had been given a letter dictated and signed by 'Baden-Powell' which would help when we stopped at any villages on our way out of the area. With our heavy packs and on foot, this journey would easily take us three days. It was an old Inca trail, which included two high *abras*, mountain passes, one at sixteen thousand feet. Until the trouble had started, this path had been the main route for transporting the coffee crop, the best coffee in the world, grown high. Now we passed plantations which had been abandoned, the sweet scent from the white flowers intoxicatingly fragrant.

The heat bored into us, as we wearily walked up and up, cooling ourselves with Ed's trick of plunging our heads into the rushing icy waters of mountain streams. One of the team would always keep a lookout, as we feared the terrorists were in the trees all around watching the path, and felt they could attack whenever they wanted. We tried to look strong and fierce, which was difficult in the intense heat with our heavy loads. Our talk seemed to revolve around the report from a young man who had escaped from the *Senderos*, after his village, close to Lucmahuayco and Osambre, had been attacked. He had overheard the *Senderos* claim that they would control the whole of this valley by 1 December. We had just under a week to get out.

Studying our map we decided we would try and get to Accobamba, a small village at eight thousand feet, for the night. Here we hoped it would be cooler and we would be free of the biting black fly which had plagued us for so long. All day we walked up and up, and finally at four in the afternoon, just as the sun was disappearing behind the snow-capped mountains, we straggled into Accobamba.

Our first impression was one of tranquillity: smoke curled up from some of the thatched roofs; on a gentle slope surrounded by steep jungle there were green meadows where cows and donkeys were tethered; we breathed in the cool air scented with aromatic eucalyptus and sweet spicy wood smoke. On closer inspection many of the simple houses were padlocked and empty. It was the usual story – their owners would have fled for their lives. What a paradox! I had hardly seen a more beautiful place and yet the lurking air of menace and fear made it seem like hell. We met a kindly young schoolteacher who allowed us once again to sleep in the school. Again the numbers of children had diminished to a third, and those that attended were too frightened and hungry to concentrate. We felt guilty that we were passing through and leaving these innocent people to their fate.

Unaccustomed to the chill air, that night John sneezed and sneezed, and by morning he was looking wretched, wrapped up in his sleeping bag, wearing his hat and scarf. A black depression had settled heavily on him – I knew he was grieving for his friend Elvin. We all agreed he had better stay put – Bec's ear problem was still fresh in our memories. The same could happen to John on a high pass. Anyway it was a lovely place to stop. There were Inca ruins on the hill behind the village; there were tiny trout in the Mapito River that rushed down from the glaciers of Choquesapra, 'The Beard of Gold' which joined the Apurimac, days away down the valley near Lucmahuayco.

Leaving John sleeping, we went out to have a look around. Bec and I wandered amongst the few houses and found an old couple who were baking rolls in a beehive-shaped oven. We could not believe our luck. We had not seen bread in a long time, and this was just freshly baked with a crisp crust and soft doughy centre. We bought some and could not resist nibbling at it.

On our way back to the school with our treasure, we stopped at a small tumbledown shack on the side of the path and bought two glasses of *chicha*, a type of maize beer, from a couple of friendly women. The younger of the two was so crippled she could only pull herself around on the floor. Bec is no boozer, and we had been so careful about what we ate and drank. To stop here was a rash move, but I just felt drawn to this small hut. We talked and rested; we all smiled at each other – these rather beautiful strong-faced women were friendly. Lightheaded, we made our way back to the school and John, expecting some sort of a reprimand. John was sitting up looking brighter and writing up his diary.

'Come on, Dad, come and have a walk,' the words spilled out of Bec. 'It's a lovely place, and we've found somewhere you can buy *chicha* and coffee.' We were soon sitting inside the small traveller's stop, the smoke curling from the open fire up through the low rafters and out through the thatch. Only the crippled young woman was in, but she seemed pleased to see Bec and me again and welcomed us and John warmly. In the course of the conversation we mentioned Elvin, and our reason for being in this area. Yes, she had known Elvin – he would stop on his way through, taking the coffee crop out to sell at Quillabamba. Then as an afterthought she said, 'You know Elvin's daughter is living here.'

We could not believe what we were hearing – a piercing ray of light after all the wretched misery. At least he was survived by his own blood. We asked if it would be possible to visit the family.

'Yes, but they have suffered much. The girl, who is now six, is living with her grandparents, as her mother is unable to look after her.'

In the midst of our conversation the other friend from earlier arrived with her sister, and they all joined in with more details

which we desperately tried to understand. It seemed that the family
had lived in Lucmahuayco, where the grandfather was *gobernador*.
The terrorists had attacked, and the grandfather had to flee into the
jungle. In reprisal his mother was murdered, and his only son
brutally dismembered. The child, as Elvin's daughter, could have
quite likely been singled out and killed, but had survived. Now they
were living here as refugees with nothing except their fear and their
memories of terror in a hut near where we had bought the bread. The
child's mother was simple, like a child – perhaps the horrors had been
more than she could cope with. She was also stone deaf. She could
not care for her child and was being looked after by relatives in a
village far away.

Later that afternoon the women took us to visit these people. We
passed a small graveyard with freshly dug graves. We were all
nervous. We scrambled over a broken wall through a meadow and
round the side of a simple hut. In a central section, open to the air, sat a
family: two women and three children. A fire smoked in the corner.

Straight away it was clear which was Elvin's daughter. Her skin
was paler than her cousins, the hair under her grubby crocheted hat
was wavy and browner, not the blue-black straight hair of the others.
I did not want to stare but I was mesmerised by this small child who
looked up at us inquisitively, her head tilted to one side, her almond
eyes peeping and then looking away. Sitting on a sheepskin and
drinking watery soup from a chipped enamel bowl, she looked
hungry and thin.

The older lady stopped weaving. Apart from a couple of black
pots this loom seemed to be their only possession. She was the grandmother, Josephina. We were introduced to her and to her daughter,
Marcelina. The grandmother looked particularly anxious. She was
breathing fast and unevenly and kept touching her throat, her
handsome but careworn face creased with anxiety. What did we
want? Our two friends explained that we had come to Peru to visit
Elvin Berg, who had saved the life of this man, pointing to John
'*quinze anos ante*', and how we had heard of his death and how sad we
were. She smiled, she stood up and took our hands, and told us this
child was Elvin's, that her name was Elizabeth: Elizabeth Berg.

Without thinking I slipped off my silver ring, which had belonged
to my Irish grandmother, also called Elizabeth, and we hung it
around the child's neck on Bec's silver confirmation chain. If it was
not stolen or sold, perhaps this would mark her out from others. We

turned to leave, and Josephina began talking rapidly in Quechua to
our two friends. 'She wants you to take the child,' they explained.
'She says they are too old to care for her and the child's mother is not
well.'

As we stepped down from their simple shelter of a home a small
forlorn voice called out to John: 'Ciao, Pappi!'

We all turned round to see the pitifully thin child looking
wistfully at us as we walked away. Bec and I stumbled up the path,
too overcome to speak. When I caught up with her, I could see her
thin shoulders shaking and her cheeks wet from rain and tears. John
was close behind, trying to understand what our two lady friends
were saying. Did we really understand right? Did they want us to
take the child?

Without thinking for a moment, I knew instantly this was what I
wanted, more than anything. But what about John? I knew it
would not work unless the three of us felt the same.

'I would like to see my friend Elvin right,' he said. 'Had it been
the other way round, I am sure he would have taken Bec; so, if it is
what you and Bec want, we will say yes.' There was nothing more
to be said between us.

We returned later that evening and sat in the alcove looking out
on a papaya tree and the green jungle stretching to the rushing river
below, thunder and bright flashes of lightning brightening the
darkening dusk sky. Elizabeth's hair was slicked down now and her
dirty pink dress had been covered by a cleaner green one. My heart
went out to her. I hoped they realised it did not matter at all to us
how she looked. I wanted to pick her up, to talk to her, to hold her,
but I hardly dared look at this child who might one day call me
Mama. Aware of everyone's fragile emotions in a situation fraught
with possible misunderstanding, we were tongue-tied and had to
rely on our interpreter's sensitivity and discretion.

Now present was Juan Huaman Chavez, Elizabeth's grandfather, wearing a fine brown poncho and brightly coloured *chulio*.
He shook our hands warmly and with dignity, but he buried his
face in his hands with anxiety from time to time as he tried to talk to
us. He spoke a little Spanish, which we desperately tried to
understand. It was the same story as before. They were too old and
too poor now to look after this child, and they feared for her safety.
He smiled softly at us from a face that had suffered more than I
could imagine, and then murmured in Quechua, 'The stars are

burning at midday for me.' Tragedy had overtaken these two proud people. Of course we would help.

I wrote in my diary: *We are handed tin mugs of sweet coffee in the semi-darkness, the only light is from the glow of the fire. Looking at this small child who might become so much of my life – such a strange change of direction – I feel if events move towards her coming to us, then it is fate and unquestionable. We are borne along on a tide, there are too many coincidences for us to ignore.*

Was this small girl to be my second daughter, foretold so many years before? The tide of destiny had carried me safely to this point.

Chapter Nine

ARRIVAL

It was 5 October 1986, and there was frenzied activity at Ardmore. Nick Asheshov and his son, Igor, were due to land that morning in London, having flown from Peru via Florida on a special mission – they were bringing Elizabeth to Britain, to us. We were worried that something – anything – might go wrong, above all that Home Office Clearance might not be granted and that Elizabeth would be placed in custody until arrangements could be made for her return to Peru. She was fragile, utterly our responsibility, for her grandparents had handed her over to Nick to bring her to us.

It seemed unbelievable that we had actually got to the point where she was so nearly here. I remembered the first of several visits from our social worker, Kay Allinson. It was on St Valentine's day, eight months before. Kay was a delicate and pretty woman, with dark curly hair, blue eyes and a luminous skin. Her looks belied a steely resolve, which she needed to deal with the problems she had to tackle in her daily rounds. Kay had walked out along the winding hilly track, and sitting at the kitchen table eating a lunch of home-made soup and scones – winter meals are rustled up from what's left in the store cupboard – we talked around and around the subject of Elizabeth. At that point it all seemed so hypothetical to me. I wondered if this child would ever come to Ardmore – if she was even still living, for that matter. However, John was far more practical and was the instigator of this meeting. With the attention to detail which is his hallmark it was he who got in touch with the necessary authorities, in good time.

We, and our home, were under close scrutiny. It was reassuring to know that in Britain any child who is adopted is going to a home and family that have been so carefully checked out. We were to learn that, above all, it is the child's needs which come first and must be suited, rather than those of the potential parents.

We had not been having so much luck with the Home Office regarding Entry Clearance for Elizabeth. Nick Asheshov, we hoped, would be able to arrange for her exit from Peru, but immigration into Britain was our task. Resulting from our initial enquiry, we received a lengthy letter headed 'Draft Home Office Stock Letter: For Adoption Cases.' Early on, it states: 'There is no provision in the Immigration Rules for a child to come to the United Kingdom for adoption. However, the Home Secretary may exceptionally exercise his discretion to allow a child to come here for this purpose, if he is satisfied that this is appropriate in all the circumstances of the case.' We had to satisfy him.

Many forms had to be completed: detailed medical reports on both John and myself, statements from the local minister on our spiritual health, from our accountant on our financial well-being, and from the police, including trying to get an Interpol certificate detailing the existence or otherwise of criminal records. Detailed health reports on Elizabeth and her family were also required. One on her we had, but reports on her family were an impossibility, so long as they were still in terrorist-infested jungle.

The bureaucratic delays could have halted the vital Entry Clearance being issued. As it was, it took from our initial telephone call on 7 January until 29 August before it was provisionally granted. John's father kindly spent many hours queueing at Lunar House – 'Loonie House' he re-christened it. There are so many applications that sending one through the post can result in weeks before it even goes on to the file. On 14 July, Reg, an old campaigner, took his place in the queue of over six hundred immigrants waiting patiently for their turn to plead their case in one of the forty booths. He returned again on the 21 and 22 July and finally got us placed on record with a reference number. Only the very determined succeed.

Eventually, after much help from many people, we received a letter saying that Entry Clearance might be authorised for Elizabeth to come to the United Kingdom for adoption. We were not home and dry yet, but it was looking hopeful, especially as we had heard from Nick that Elizabeth had been issued with a precious, thin green Peruvian passport, giving Lucmahuayco as her place of birth. We hoped nothing would go wrong at our end with the Entry Clearance.

At ten-thirty the phone rang. 'Everything's fine, John,' Nick's excited voice shouted down the phone. 'We're at Heathrow – no problem with immigration. She's been given an Entry Clearance visa. No, she's not exhausted at all. She loved the flight. The air hostesses made a great fuss of her, and she's crackers about Igor. We'll phone when we land at Inverness.'

That was it. She would in all probability be here that afternoon. After all the planning and uncertainty, the hopes and fears, it was actually going to happen – Elizabeth, the small child we had last seen in Accobamba eight thousand feet up in the Andes, was following her extraordinary destiny and being brought to Ardmore to be part of our family.

If they kept to Nick's schedule, and the weather remained kind, it seemed they would arrive here at Ardmore in the afternoon. October is always a windy month in north-west Scotland and we just hoped the clear weather would hold for the rest of the day.

The frenzy within the thick croft house walls hid the nervousness that all three of us were feeling – there was no going back now. It was no longer notional. Elizabeth herself would soon be here. Bec put the finishing touches to Elizabeth's room, which adjoined her own: a chest of drawers with new clothes (we had to guess the size); a small bed with a brilliantly coloured crocheted blanket (wouldn't she find everything here rather grey?); a rug on the floor with ancient Inca patterns woven into it (wouldn't she feel far from home?). We were all tormented by doubt, but Bec knew that at least the dolls on her bed would thrill any small child.

The telephone went a second time. It was a slightly wearier Nick, checking in from Inverness Airport. They were still on schedule.

John took out the hoover, and did the entire house, the droning noise adding to the general air of anxiety. In times of stress, this is John's panacea. He has admitted that Heaven for him would be to spend the rest of eternity hoovering. How has he managed all these years to live with Bec and myself, magpies who collect and bring back to our nest anything bright and glittery to clutter up our life? Then his ingrained sense of order led him on to change any faulty lightbulbs. My entreaties from the kitchen went unheeded.

In moments the worst had happened: the light circuit had fused. The telephone rang a third time. This was Nick's final call from Achfary, the Grosvenor Estate village belonging to the Duchess of Westminster, where the mountains Arkle and Ben Stack stand sentinel over Loch More and the road drops to the west coast twenty minutes from our road end.

In the half-light of late afternoon, I luckily found the fuse wire and hastily repaired the fuse, and just remembered to turn off the stove, having cooked a mountain of food. This was to be a feast of celebration. Then grabbing all the waterproofs we had hanging in the hall, we rushed down the hill to the shore. Pulling in the wooden yawlie we hurried across to our bright red thirty-foot fishing boat.

John started up the big 60-hp engine and motored across the loch. The sun was dipping in the autumn sky, its colour drenching the bracken and rocks red. I was grateful it would not seem grey to our new child. I so wanted everything to be perfect.

At Portlevorchy, John waited offshore in the boat, while Bec and I rowed into the beach. The yawlie crunched on the pebbles. Our hearts bumping, we hastily secured the painter and I ran up on to the grass, where, quite composed, a small figure was heading purposefully towards us, followed by Nick and Igor.

Doubts and fears gone, I ran to greet her. In that moment I recognised our need of each other. I kissed her cold cheek and took her hand. How different she was from the raggedy thin child we remembered. Now she was looking almost sturdy, and beneath a warm blue jacket I could see she was wearing a red corduroy skirt, a white frilled blouse, and a tightly laced black waistcoat, with a frilled white pinny over the skirt. Conchy, Nick Asheshov's wife, had cared for her well over the two months she had had her staying in their home in Lima, and had grown so fond of Elizabeth that she would have willingly kept her as one of her own large family of five daughters and two boys.

Bec kissed her and said hello, and I could see her turning away to wipe her tears. Then Elizabeth, holding on tightly to my hand, carefully walked over the green croft to the yawlie. We all climbed in and Bec rowed us out to where John was waiting in the dusk for his new daughter.

As John lifted Elizabeth up on to the fishing boat and held her close, I thought of how, all those years ago, Elvin had kept him alive on another stretch of water – not the gin-clear water of Loch a' Chad-Fi where we were about to commence the final phase of a journey for Elizabeth to her new life at Ardmore – but the muddy brown torrent of the Apurimac. The threads of this tapestry were strongly coloured, and the weaving begun even before this seven-year-old child had been born.

Once into the house Elizabeth amazed us. We had expected a

frightened withdrawn child, terrified by so many new experiences. Not at all. She wanted to see everything. Off came the trainers, and out of her pink travelling bag she produced a pair of soft kid white party shoes. With these on, she led a procession round the house inspecting her new home, thrilled with her bedroom and the lights. It was lucky we had managed to mend the fuse in the lighting circuit. On and off, on and off she switched them in total fascination.

Into the kitchen we went for supper, where she sat to the left of John whom she gazed at in obvious admiration. There was much chat and laughter, though Elizabeth spoke only Quechua, with a little Spanish which she had learnt in Lima, and one or two English words that the Asheshovs had taught her before starting off on her great journey to Scotland. She decided there and then to call John 'Danny'. Her erstwhile 'sister', Tabby Asheshov, had a tall and good-looking boyfriend called Danny, whom she con-fused with John. So Danny was at the head of the table, Elizabeth next to him, and then me. Coming over in the boat in the dark she had sat on my knee, kept her small hand tightly held in mine, and called me Mama. All women in the Altiplano are called Mama so it was nothing special, but I was delighted. Opposite sat her big sister, slender and blonde, who would be 'Rebeeka' as soon as Elizabeth could manage the strange three-syllable name.

It was a grand night. The home team had been knotted up for days with a mixture of great excitement and fear, but now with Igor and Nick there, and with Elizabeth safely handed over, it all seemed so right.

On reaching Lima some weeks before, Elizabeth had been taken to a doctor, who found that she had the usual worms, had lice in her hair, was three foot six inches tall and weighed a meagre thirty-nine pounds. Now a great deal bigger, but with the memory of her lifetime of six years of chronic malnutrition, she set about eating her leg of chicken with a fearsome concentration. She had not yet learnt the intricacies of using a knife and fork, but with small neat fingers she pulled the juicy meat from the bone, popping morsels into her mouth. Then when all was gone, she picked up the drumstick and with relish chewed away all the gristle at the top of the joint. We did not want her to feel self-conscious, so purposefully talked louder over the crunching sounds that came from her contented face.

I thought of how delighted Elizabeth's Great Aunt Victoria would be at this scene. When we had come out of the jungle the year before, we had been keen to make contact with any Berg relation, to tell them about Elvin and Elizabeth. We had felt there might be Bergs in Lima, so we looked up the name in the thick telephone directory. There were two. A very helpful Spanish-speaking lady from the British Embassy made the initial call, as our Spanish would not have been good enough to explain our extraordinary story, and we did not want to worry the person we were calling. The first and only number we called was answered by Victoria Berg, who invited us around.

We arrived in a chauffeur-driven limousine kindly lent by the British Embassy, and stopped in front of a detached modern house in a smart residential area. As soon as we entered the house, John knew we had come to see the right person. Victoria strongly resembled her brother Abel, Elvin's father, and Elizabeth's grandfather. She had spent thirty years nursing in California but had kept strong links with her family here in Peru. She owned this smart house which she was now hoping to sell, for she had retired and wanted to spend the rest of her days in America. Luckily for us she spoke excellent English. She had feared that Elvin, her favourite nephew, was dead, and her voice faltered when she spoke of him. He had visited her sometimes here in Lima, and she had watched him grow up from a bright and spirited boy into a strong and fearless man. We told her of Elizabeth, and I think she felt, as we had, that a light suddenly shone again in the dark.

We met as many times as we could before we had to leave for Britain, and on the morning of our departure she telephoned to say she must come and see us once more. She was quite arthritic and it was not an easy journey. She produced from her bag three small parcels: silver bracelets for Bec and me, and a silver spoon for John. The bracelets seemed like further links in the silver chain that we had hung around Elizabeth's neck. She held my hands and looked deep into my eyes. She knew we had her trust, and we would do our best for Elizabeth. The bright silver spoon marked with the ancient Peruvian Inti now sat in the sugar bowl on the laden table before us.

If I had just flown from Peru via Miami and London, and driven three hours from Inverness, and finally reached my new home by boat, and been re-acquainted with three people who were to be my new family, I would have been whacked. Not so Elizabeth.

Nick laughingly said: 'She's tough. Hers is a super breed. She could walk to Inverness without batting an eyelid.'

Above: Round the World with Ridgway – John and me on the pulpit of our 57′ ketch in the 1977/8 Whitbread race

Right: Bec aged eight and me on a rare trip to London

Above: Refugee Elizabeth aged six in Accobamba, Peru

Left: Elizabeth and her mother, Leocadia, at Accobamba

Below: Crossing the Andes at 15,000 feet – Elizabeth takes a last look back

'It's a good thing she is,' Bec laughed ruefully, remembering her upbringing at Ardmore – three miles from the road along a rocky track skirting the loch, boat trips in all weathers, no electricity, no television. Like a northern silver birch Bec had grown straight and true, her roots struck deep here. Although she had been away to school and spent a period in London doing a secretarial course, she had come back to her beloved Ardmore whenever she could, and now she was here to get to know her new sister.

I took the happy and replete child upstairs to her tiny room. Would now be the moment when she would suddenly realise it was not just a game but for real? I felt so intensely protective towards this small girl. We did not speak the same language, but I talked to her as I had talked to Bec when she was small, and Elizabeth chatted to me in Quechua, which I did not understand at all. It did not matter. She seemed happy. We laughed and smiled – that was universal.

I helped her take off the pretty red, white and black dress, which had been specially made at her request. She had seen a picture of Snow White in a story book in Lima and had wanted to come to us dressed for a fairy-tale. As the blouse came off, I saw the silver chain and ring that Bec and I had given her when we said goodbye in the jungle. I called to Bec who came up, and Elizabeth shyly showed us what she had kept hidden all this time. We had been told she would not let anybody touch or even look at what she wore around her neck. Bec and I looked at each other, remembering the moment in that other world when, to mark her apart from other children, we had placed the chain and ring around her neck. A new life was starting for us all as we tucked this trusting child into her cosy bed, switched off the light and kissed her goodnight. She lay looking at the bright stars through the skylight knowing that she was safe, warm and not hungry.

Late that evening, lying in our bed next to Elizabeth's room, I strained to hear any sound of sorrow, but there was nothing – only John's steady breathing. At Ardmore during the day there are always sounds, chaffinches and tits quarrelling over food on the old ruined mound outside the kitchen, gulls calling into the empty sky, the only surviving duck resident on our doorstep alert to any chance of food, and in the winter early morning the curlew's loneliest of calls. On calm nights, however, the silence almost overwhelms me. There is nothing to disturb or distract my thoughts. So now inside my head the noise was loud with impressions of this day. I now knew what our new daughter looked like. I was immensely grateful that she was being positive – what a long journey it would be if she had decided she did not like us! There was going to be so much we would learn about each other over the months to come, but her trust was all we needed to proceed with, and I knew that was there the moment I saw her.

I was intensely curious about every detail of Elizabeth before she arrived at Ardmore. This total stranger was to be our daughter, and all of a sudden I was jealous of all the time in her seven years that was lost to me. Nick had told us more at supper about the journey out of Accobamba. He and Igor had ridden into the village, but had not dared remain there long as word would not take long to reach the terrorists. Elizabeth's family quickly signed the adoption papers before a District Justice of the Peace. Elizabeth was hastily handed over to Nick, placed on his saddle and they rode off along that path we had so wearily climbed on foot six months previously.

She had cried like any child in such shocking circumstances would have done.

The path took them over two high mountain passes, but eventually she stopped crying and whimpered only occasionally and then went silent. When they stopped at a cluster of huts for the night, Elizabeth was handed over to a Quechua woman. Elizabeth said nothing and at dawn when handing her back to the two *gringos*, the lady voiced her fears that Elizabeth was a deaf-mute. She had retreated far into herself. Hunger and fear had been constantly at her side all her short life. Only ailing grandparents who had suffered much themselves had cared for her, with her girl-mother occasionally there, but in greater need of being looked after herself than able to care for her child.

They finally reached Quillabamba where the child brightened. Thrilled at the sight of electricity, she sat on the kerb gazing in wonder at the dazzling lights of this her first town. More was to come. She was taken out for supper and ate one plate of chicken and then another. She squatted in the street when she had to, watching in fascination as wheeled vehicles sped past her. When on the train to Cuzco, she ducked to avoid the branches that hit the windows, for she had never even seen glass. In three days she had passed from the simplest style of life right into the twentieth century.

The next morning we crept in early to find that she had wrapped herself in the duvet and that she had moved from the bed to the floor. Her wonderful thick dark hair was all we could see of her head until she turned and, waking, smiled. In moments she was in our warm bed.

As I held her trusting small body close to mine, I thought back to Accobamba, to the lady who had first taken us to see Elizabeth and had said to us, '*Pobre Elizabeth, no tiene Mama, no tiene Papa, muy triste.*' I vowed then to give her all the love she needed to grow into a secure and happy person.

Holding her close, I could examine her minutely. She had pale olive skin. Her almost-black eyes were set wide apart and were almond-shaped and fringed with thick lashes. Her nose was short and not bony like ours; it wrinkled a lot with her changing expressions. Her mouth had a perfect cupid's bow, and was quite the same as Elvin's in the one or two photographs we had of her murdered father. Her arms were still thin, and her chest was deep, a feature of a race who have adapted to high altitude living where the air is thin. She smelt very different to my own now grown-up child. She had a fragrant spicy smell which would change over the weeks to come as she adjusted to different food. She snuggled in, like any young creature getting the warmth and reassurance she needed. The three of us lay there waiting for the dawn to brighten our room.

Nick and Igor were leaving that morning. I wondered how we could console Elizabeth once she found that she had been left with the three strangers: John, Bec and me. Explanations were impossible; our only comfort could be physical. We need not have worried. She was too delighted with the dolls she now owned and was absorbed with them, chattering to them and giving them the odd bash.

As we waved farewell to the two men who had played such a vital role in bringing Elizabeth out of the jungle and arranging for her exit from Peru, I thought back to Dr Jane Asheshov, Nick's English mother, and wondered what she would have thought of this twist of fate, had she still been living. Many years back she and my mother had become friends, both living close in Brighton. By chance one stormy winter's day on the way to the shops they had bumped into each other. My mother said, 'I'm rather worried about my son-in-law. He is leading an expedition in South America, and we have heard nothing from him now for quite a while.' To which Jane replied, 'How strange! My daughter Anna is somewhere out in Peru, and we are getting rather anxious about her as we have not heard any news from her for some time.'

The cold wind off the sea whipped some of the words away as they battled their way to the shops. Still the conversation continued and revealed the coincidence that both were on the same expedition – an expedition on which John's and Elvin's lives became so inextricably linked that Nick Asheshov had now brought Elvin's daughter here to John.

We started our first full day. Helping to dress Elizabeth was a bit of a mystery: she was determined to put on all her four skirts. They looked wonderful, as we had been given some outgrown kilts and the different tartans showed like a vivid petticoat as she rushed up and down the stairs. We later learned that Quechua women on the Altiplano do wear their entire wardrobe. Breakfast was easy. After the treat of chicken for supper, an egg for breakfast was the next best thing. Back home for Elizabeth, meat or eggs would have been a rare treat. We watched, without her noticing, as once again with her delicate fingers she carefully peeled off half of the shell and then pulled out morsels of the hard boiled egg until she had eaten it all.

Apart from playing with the dolls, her favourite game turned out to be 'Escapee'. This involved a complicated course usually round the kitchen table, with the odd chair being flung in the way by Elizabeth if we were catching her up. She liked best to be chased by John, and it soon became a game of great roaring by the chaser and screaming with excitement by Elizabeth. 'Escapee, Escapee, Danny?' Elizabeth would implore, and would nimbly and with great speed evade the chaser for ages, and then suddenly rush over to Bec or me and cling on for dear life screaming even louder for help. This was no normal child's game. It was enacting and getting out of her system the terror she had experienced in Peru. We heard later that on at least two occasions the terrorists had attacked the village where she had been. One time, only a couple of days after we had left Accobamba, Elizabeth and her granny, Josephina, had run and hid in the jungle for two days and nights. An earlier attack had resulted in the massacre of half the village of Lucmahuayco where she had been born. Death to Elizabeth was violent and terrifying.

After the hectic build up of Elizabeth's arrival, life settled into a more gentle rhythm. Each day there was progress. Living twenty minutes from us by boat, or an hour's walk and drive away, our great friends Sandee and Sinclair Mackintosh had been waiting with great anticipation for Elizabeth to arrive. They lived in nearly as remote a setting, at the mouth of the River Laxford. Sometimes we would sit together at the end of the day, gazing down the sea loch watching the sun dip below the horizon and talk. Sinclair had spent some of his childhood in Lima where his father was involved with the church. He knew Miraflores, the smart suburb where Elizabeth had stayed with the Asheshovs. Elizabeth became very attached to their daughter Mary B, who was wise for her ten years. 'Mariposa, Mariposa,' we would hear Elizabeth's throaty voice calling to her friend round the big house.

In early November we travelled down to London. It was time to introduce Elizabeth to her grandparents. John's father lived in Wimbledon and we went to stay with him first. Elizabeth looked shyly up at the big man with the twinkling blue eyes who smiled down at her and gave her another doll. It was clear that they would be firm friends. She could not quite manage the word grandpa; instead she called him Rambo. He liked that. Reg had in his time been a great sportsman and had led an active life as an extremely successful civil engineer.

We then went down to Brighton to introduce Elizabeth as ninth grandchild to her grandmother. I knew that the moment my mother saw her, any reservations she had would disappear. Reservations were certainly there, as my mother felt we were taking on too many responsibilities and I would be busier than ever. After lunch John fell asleep in the high ceilinged Regency drawing room, while Bec, Mum and I finished washing up. Elizabeth, sitting on the stairs scolding one of the dolls, called to her new grandmother as we walked past. Putting one finger to her lips, she cautioned: 'Sshh! Danny sneepy, Danny tard.' My mum was entranced at this small brave girl from the jungle – 'The Inca Princess,' as she aptly christened her – who was telling her new relations what to do.

Elizabeth, we discovered, was always delighted to be the centre of attention. In only a few weeks she had become very much part of our small family and now bossed us all. It worried us to think she might become spoiled with all the attention, but we tried to maintain the balance between giving her the love and attention she so desperately needed and yet not letting her have her own way all the time, which was not easy when we could not make any explanations. Sitting cross-legged on the sofa, which in any house she usually took over as her domain, she would imperiously order us about. Friends, knowing her history were naturally curious and indulgent. Poor child, she had been through so much suffering, now she had to learn about another way of life so very different to her past seven years, of which we knew so little.

It was to help in this that on our return to Scotland Bec attended a week-long course in Quechua at St Andrew's University. It was desperately frustrating for us all – and I am sure most of all for Elizabeth – not to be able to communicate beyond the simplest of phrases. We would be unable to find any form of dictionary until we found one in Cuzco three years later.

Bec set off in her small white Renault. The weather was cold, snow was in the air, and she had only passed her driving test that summer. She completed the 200-mile journey and set about her task of learning as much of her new sister's language as possible. The three other fellow students were missionaries about to take up posts in Peru. The class was conducted in Spanish so Bec had first to translate the Spanish to English with her dictionary before she was able to reach the meaning of the word or phrase.

Professor Douglas Gifford was the director of the Centre for Latin-American Linguistics at St Andrew's and Bec's teacher. He and his wife very kindly had Bec to supper a few times and were interested to hear her story. She returned home after her week on the bitter Fife coast full of words and phrases to use on Elizabeth, only to find that Elizabeth wanted none of it. It seemed as though she had put a barrier up between her old life in Peru and the one she now lived where she was no longer hungry, frightened or wanting. That ancient language of the Incas was just one other reminder that she wanted to forget. 'Saksasqa wiksayuqpaqa, sonqompas kusisqan' is 'Full stomach and a contented heart'. The filling of the stomach was easy; the contented heart we had to help her achieve.

We had some photographs of Elizabeth and her family taken the first day we met in Accobamba. Pointing to the small girl looking straight at the camera in the raggedy green dress, I would say, 'Who is that?' In a husky voice she would answer, 'Monikaja' – 'dolly'. It was as if she wanted to distance herself from her past.

Of more importance than the words that Bec had learnt on her course were the traditional beliefs the Giffords were able to tell her about. As with all Indian tribes, the Quechua people were

Animists: they believed that everything was possessed of a spirit; the future unfolded as a result of what had occurred in the past. If you fell ill, it was because you had done something bad in a previous life and the spirits were punishing you. This helped us to understand Elizabeth's extraordinarily stoical approach to getting hurt. One day she twisted her ankle. She did not cry but bravely hobbled back home and said nothing; even when I removed her small boot and examined the swelling ankle she kept quiet. She never cried. I worried that inside she had frozen, and when the tears did come, over something small and months after she had been with us, it was just one more step forward.

Chapter Ten

BEGINNING

Each day Elizabeth's story and our story intertwined, the threads of our lives weaving into this cloth of many colours.

It was coming to the end of November and Elizabeth had been with us at Ardmore for six weeks. Sometimes she would reach for the *manta* we had brought back from Accobamba. She would lay the closely woven dark cloth on the floor, carefully smoothing out the wrinkles so that she could see the bright strips of intricate weaving down each side. The significance of these coloured strips was centuries old, and interwoven was a pattern of ancient Inca spirits: birds, mountains, flowers, snakes, rabbits, fish. Intent on her task, she would fold the cloth, take a favourite doll, wrap it in it tightly, then toss it on to her back, tying the ends around her shoulders. *Monikaja* was safe and secure on her small back.

Returning to and observing a simpler way of life could teach us much. Here was Elizabeth, uprooted at the age of seven, half-starved and in fear of her life. Her grandparents had implored us to take her into our own family where she would be safe and would have the opportunity to grow and flourish. But emotionally would the change be so traumatic as to be harmful? We had agonised long over this and were still not certain. My own view was that Elizabeth had received such a head start in terms of physical comforting and love as a baby from her granny that she would have within her a great capacity to love and be loved. Not for her a sterile nursery where she would be placed in a cot surrounded with fluffy surrogate comforts and left to cry herself to sleep. No, she had been always just a few inches from the heartbeat and warmth of her granny. Swaddled in just such a *manta* she would be there out in the fields as her granny worked away at crops, in the semi-darkness of their primitive home preparing food, outside weaving or spinning, walking along the ancient Inca route in sun and rain, but with a constant physical comfort and reassurance.

Life now in Scotland was not so very different from Peru. 'Come on, Elizabeth, darling. Time to feed the fish.' The boots would go on, and the jacket and hat and gloves. Finally dolly would be swung on to the back again, and we would make our way gingerly down the now slippery green hill to the boat on which we would pull ourselves out to the salmon cages.

'*Hatun mayu*,' Elizabeth gasped the first time we went to the fish cages. Yes it was a big river, this sheltered sea loch which extended through narrows into Loch Laxford, the salmon fiord, so named by the Vikings who had come in their long boats centuries before to Sutherland, the South Land, round Cape Wrath, Norse for turning point. And here in this small, partly Norwegian girl coursed the same blood as these ancestors.

'One two, three four five, once I caught a fish alive.' We sang the counting song as we took buckets of fish food to the numbered cages. We had such a huge area to cover if Elizabeth was ever to catch up with her age-group, that we had to make the most of every chance to learn. 'Six seven, eight nine ten, then I let it go again.' Elizabeth would stand on the top bar and excitedly throw the pellets to the silver fish as they rose in a swirl to the surface. 'Why did you let it go? Because it bit my finger so.' Another fistful was flung at the salmon. 'Which finger did it bite? This little finger on the right.' Elizabeth would gleefully hold up one small gloved little finger.

I doubt if she understood the concept of numbers. To her it was one or many – we had a very long way to go. She had never seen such an abundance of fish before, just the few tiny trout that were caught on the tumbling river that rushed down from Choquesapra. Back in Accobamba they were highly prized, and everything was eaten even the head. It surprised us how neatly this child could eat a fish. She would leave a perfect backbone picked quite clean and even eat the skin. I thought of British children who complain of bones and can only eat fish filleted into fingers, but then they have never been hungry.

We spent a great deal of time on the fish cages that autumn. Elizabeth did not really mind where she was as long as she was with us and had the dolls along too, although she was getting pretty keen on the television. It was magic to her.

One evening the perfect opportunity for explaining where she came from presented itself – the Miss World contest. Always intrigued by pretty clothes, Elizabeth sat enthralled as the contestants paraded up and down the catwalk, and half way through I could tell she wanted to take part – because of limited conversation we tended to act out situations. We rushed up and found Elizabeth's prettiest dress. 'Mama too,' the husky voice insisted. We paraded up and down in front of the telly mimicking the contestants. When it came to the bathing costume section, not to be outdone, Elizabeth rushed upstairs again grabbing my hand, and donning our bathing costumes we continued to parade. 'Miss Peru – Peruana Elizabeth.' We cheered loudly. I was thankful that it was unlikely anyone would be walking past our sitting room windows that evening three miles from the road, and grateful that the installation of electricity five years previously made such events bearable. Elizabeth was delighted, and to this day has called her bathing costume a peruana.

However one thing bothered her greatly. 'Why Danny no horse?' We were not hungry; we had clean clothes to wear; the house did not leak here like it had in Accobamba – 'Me like house' – she often exclaimed. By her standards we were affluent, and any self-respecting person had a horse, or at least a mule. I tried to tell her that Danny's Land Rover was our equivalent but I could feel she was not impressed. We still had to walk the three miles out from Ardmore to the tarmac, where the vehicles were parked. A horse could easily manage that, and was it not altogether nobler to be seated high on a horse, than clamber aboard a noisy smelly metal box on wheels?

I was tempted to indulge Elizabeth and try and get her a pony, but John reminded me of Bec's Connemara pony, Boy Blue, who had caused us two years of havoc, eating washing off the clothes line, forcing his way into buildings and eating the stores, galloping through the wood and terrifying anybody walking through. He was a beautiful creature, but the gradients at Ardmore were too severe and any flattish ground was bog for most of the year, so riding was difficult. 'This has got to stop.' I remembered John's statement, all those years ago, as he returned from carrying a bale of hay all the way from the shore on Lower Ardmore up through the wood and along the windy path to Upper Ardmore where Boy Blue had decided to stay one winter. It had not quite worked out as

John had planned, in fact the reverse – we worked harder than the pony. We just were not good enough with horses to start all over again.

After much consultation with Kay Allinson, and the Highland Regional Council Education Authority, it was decided that Elizabeth should attend the local school at Kinlochbervie. Bec had been to the same school from the age of seven till ten. It was decided that initially Elizabeth would attend school on Tuesday and Thursday mornings and that Bec would take her, sit nearby for reassurance and bring her home again.

Early on the morning of 4 December the two sisters set off along the path, Elizabeth clutching her new red, blue and yellow satchel. Once at the fine new school situated at the bottom of the long brae on the shore of Loch Innes, Elizabeth and Bec were taken into one of the two classrooms by the headteacher Mrs Rookes. She explained that Miss Mackay would be Elizabeth's teacher, another teacher having been taken on to allow Miss Mackay extra time with Elizabeth. Memories of Bec's schooldays came rushing back, for it was Miss Mackay who had also first taught the shy fair-haired girl from Ardmore all those years ago.

Elizabeth sat at one of the small desks, totally bewildered by everything around her. It was a small school with only forty children who had all been told the story of the little Peruvian girl who had come to live nearby. Generously built, with her long hair twisted into a bun, Miss Mackay, or 'Miss Kay' as Elizabeth called her teacher, was ideally suited to this situation, as she had spent several years in Africa as a missionary teacher. Whilst those Africans did not have quite the same language problems as Elizabeth, there were other similarities of differing culture and background. In the classroom of her youth Bec sat once again at her small desk, helping the other children in the class, while Miss Mackay set about the mammoth task of initiating Elizabeth's education.

At first Elizabeth was frightened of everything, particularly the other children. They could not have been kinder or more helpful, but she clung to Rebeeka when they entered the school each day. Gradually her confidence grew and it was decided she would be able to concentrate better if she and Miss Mackay were in a separate room; so the tiny staffroom became their classroom. They listened to songs on the cassette player and clapped their hands and sang and acted out the stories. Some of Elizabeth's words we had to translate to her teacher. Elizabeth went on and on to Miss Mackay about an *arranya*, and we were able to link this to the mural on the wall in the recreation room in the middle of which was a huge spider. *Crocodillos* and *arranyas* were still very much on Elizabeth's mind. After two months it was decided she was able to go on her own each day to school. The time Bec had given was invaluable, but her big sister was no longer needed as escort.

One of us would set off each morning with Elizabeth to catch the white school bus. It was a hilly half-hour's walk to where the tarmac began and generally it rained, which frightened her. Elizabeth had a horror of rain. We felt it must go back to her previous life when to be caught out in the rain was devastating. She would have had no adequate waterproof clothing – just a torn polythene sheet if she were lucky – and not much hope of getting dry easily. She now had good wet weather gear and strong rubber boots, but nevertheless she could not shake off the anxiety.

We would hurry along '*Rapido, rapido*', 'Wickely, wickely', through the wood, past the Blue House where Lance's flock would wait. Most pampered in all of the north, his seven beauties received toast each morning, and crisped potato skin snacks to cheer them on glum days. If the weather was particularly horrid they would be allowed into the byre to sit on old carpet and munch the sweet hay gathered from last year's fragrant summer. His hens would be busy down towards Monshalls' standfast grey stone croft at the top of the waterfall. Barbara and Gordon Monshall, our good friends, had retired from teaching in Kent, but were busier here than ever before with their garden, their home and friends who came in a non-stop stream to stay. Tammy their black-and-white cat would watch us inscrutably from her perch on the dry stone wall into which they had set a ship's compass. Beyond our two hurrying figures Tammy could see the loch with the mountains beyond to the south and the east.

Carefully, we would clamber down the waterfall as the minutes ticked away, through the gate and on to the path, up and up the long brae, hearts pumping and lungs bursting, Elizabeth getting hotter and pinker. At the top, we would spin round and look out to the north-west into Loch Dughaill, watching the ocean waves breaking on to the rocky coast of Ceathramh Garbh, the empty quarter. 'Hurry, hurry,' we would gasp, 'We'll miss the bus.' Past the giant

frog rock we would speed, sentinel of the summit, then uncontroll-
ably run down the steep but beautifully constructed Gentle's Brae
watching for the white quartz arrow embedded in the granite rock.
Next the bridge. If we were not at this point by ten minutes past the
hour we were in trouble. Once we saw an otter making its way up
the burn, holding our breath as we watched its sleek body swim
away.

Not much further now: one or two hills, past the peat cuttings,
and then on down towards the road. Over the last hill we would
strain to see whether the white bus was already parked – relief if it
was not there. Elizabeth would then take off gloves, hat and scarf
and, standing on the toe of her boot, pull out one white-socked
square foot and carefully place it into one smart black patent leather
strap-shoe. Then she would repeat the operation with her other
foot. Looking casual and undoing the buttons of her coat, she
appeared to all the world as though she had just walked out of her
front door when the bus finally halted in front of us, her friends
grinning in the back.

That first winter I kept thinking of Kay Allinson's words: 'She'll
take up a lot of your time, Marie Christine.' I knew this, but we
would just have to make time. 'Priorities, it's just a question of
priorities,' I would mutter, trying to reassure myself, as if coming
up with a grand sounding formula would miraculously help.
Elizabeth had to play her part as well. After all, a child of seven back
in Peru would be expected to do her share of the chores in the
running of the home and fields, and we felt she would feel more part
of our team if we could find little jobs for her to do here. Elizabeth
had other plans. The Inca Princess muttered darkly when coerced
into helping sweep the floor, wash-up, tidy her room. She probably
thought she had left all that behind, along with the hunger and
poverty and fear. Adjustments were having to be made all round. It
was all so different for her, and we could not even explain it to her in
words.

It was an interesting time for self-examination, for us to decide
afresh what was important in the way we lived. For a start, how
could she understand that the floors should be completely free of
dust, when all she had ever known was hard earth floors littered
with husks of corn and scuttling guinea pigs? How could Elizabeth
understand why we should so spoil our three precious cats,
allowing them to curl up on chairs and feeding them meat from tins

that would have kept a family alive for a day where she had come from? Animals that did not justify their existence in some productive way just had not featured in Elizabeth's life up to now. So the poor cats were rather pushed around, and when there was a chance and we were not looking she would shoo them out of the door, saying something awful – no doubt – to them in Quechua. I wondered if in time she would ever grow to like them. Certainly John had some sympathy with her. He believed them to be the cause of his occasional wheeziness and would gloomily mutter: 'It's the cats or me – I suppose it'll be me.' Then he had an allergy test and the cats got a reprieve: household dust was found to be the culprit.

Washing-up Elizabeth came round to: it was a novelty, and easy for her to turn into a game. Back in Peru, the chipped enamel bowls were just rinsed, as there was not much left on them to wash off, for not a scrap of food was ever wasted. But here at Ardmore, with an apron tied around her middle, Elizabeth would stand on a stool and spend hours delighting in the bubbles and warm water, playing magical games with the cups and plates, her little fingers crinkling up like washerwomen's. Again, it was hard to explain that they had to be quite clean, and that the bubbles should be rinsed off with more hot water.

As for tidying her room, instilling this into her would have required the patience of a saint. If I felt short on this I would just do it for her, but then I would think: 'This isn't what is best for Elizabeth. If she is ever going to fit in, she must learn to do it for herself.' Here again she had to learn a whole new way of doing things. I remembered how, when we first of all saw her in Accobamba, her aunt went into the gloom of the sleeping area of their home and rummaged in a dark corner scattering the guinea pigs in a great squeaking flurry and brought out a slightly newer green dress for Elizabeth to wear for her photograph. Nothing there was hung up or folded; the rags and scraps were just pushed into a corner.

What a fusspot I must have seemed to Elizabeth, insisting that only her clean clothes were put back into drawers, that they should be folded, that knickers and vests and socks – which she had only been wearing for the last four months – went into the top drawer, that T-shirts and blouses were in the next one down, thick jumpers in the bottom drawer, and that her dresses were hung up so they would not crease. Nobody had ever worried about creases before; just having something to wear was what was important. Her books, too, must be put on the bookshelf in reasonable order, her shoes left neatly together. Poor baby, how odd it must all have seemed. I did not labour the point, but she had come to live in our world and she would eventually have to conform if she was ever to fit in.

There was so much I could not explain. I so wished for her to understand that we had not brought her to a place where the sun never shone and it was always windy, wet and cold. Where was the sun, she must have wondered. I did not know the words to tell her that soon we would turn the corner of the year and that our dreary short northern days would lengthen, that it would get light before we left the house in the morning at eight-thirty and it would not always darken by four in the afternoon, that with the spring she would feel the soft warm sun, that our own birch wood would be loud with the song of birds. Still, they had called her home Kingdom of the Clouds. Perhaps this was why she settled so well.

The eight weeks before Christmas involved me in my usual salmon-smoking panic. I was not a fragrant smelling mummy she came to for cuddles anymore; I smelt of oak chip smoke from the top of my head to my toes. I tried to keep my smoking clothing separate from everything else but it was not always possible.

I smoked salmon for a mail order Christmas market, at the bottom of the hill on the shore. We had modified the store under the wooden house. It was my pride and joy, tiled throughout and with the very best stainless steel equipment, which included a kiln, slicer and vacuum packer, much of which John's father had helped us buy. My day had to start early. When the house – in fact it seemed like the rest of the world – was fast asleep, I would make my way down the slippery hill with my torch, to get going on the process.

First I would light the smoker. I would sift the oak chips with my garden riddle, one bin of coarse, one of fine. To the fine I would add water to moisten, and these would be sprinkled on the layer of coarse dry chips which were then lit, burning slowly and making smoke. The smoking took the longest of all the different processes, so it had to be started first. It could take eight hours or more to cold smoke gently a side of brined drained salmon. With the smoker purring at one end of my brightly lit empire, I would then lift out the beautiful pink filleted sides that had been soaking overnight in the brine and place them to drain on wire trays – sufficient draining helps a beautiful golden salt glaze form on the sides whilst they are smoking. Later on in the afternoon, these would be moved into the kiln, taking the place of the sides which had been smoking during the day. I tried to keep the process going almost round the clock.

My yellow Sony water-resistant cassette player filled the tiled chamber with Mozart as I prepared the next batch of silver fish for brining. I would marvel at their beauty as I cut off their heads and slit open their pale bellies to ease out the slippery entrails. Gently, so as not to puncture the firm flesh, I would scoop away the dark blood clotted along the inside of the backbone. My hands would be half-numb with cold. I would warm them by pouring hot water into the tiny sink, but the kettle took forever to boil. I had to be careful not to cut myself – one nick with the sharp filleting knife would make my job difficult. The two knives I used were sharpened every time I filleted a fish. I would lay the fish, now gutted and headless, away from me, insert the knife and, feeling the pressure of the backbone pressing down on its cold razor-sharp edge, move the steel from head to tail. Holding my breath, I would lift the first fillet and examine the backbone – not bad – then turn the fish over and repeat the process. I hoped to leave as little flesh on the backbone as I could, and I hoped to find I had cut two perfect fillets for the brining tub.

Absorbed in my job, I found the time raced by. From upstairs I would hear a thump as 'Webbo', one of the fish farm workers, jumped down from his top bunk, to start another day. I would anxiously glance at my watch lying on the windowsill – seven, still dark outside. I had another half hour. I must get the last of the fish gutted and filleted before I started up the hill. I was not alone; I knew that Pussy Ridgway, the old grey tabby, would be sitting fluffed up in her winter fur outside on the step, half hoping for a morsel. The ducks too would not be far away, Mrs Duck, the greedy muscovy, at the front of the queue. At least if there was any flesh left on the backbone it would go to an appreciative crowd outside the door.

A faint grey light circling Ben Stack proclaimed dawn, and the instant I opened the door the flock of curlews grazing early on the cropped grass exploded into the still dark sky. I hurried up the hill to help Bec get Elizabeth up for breakfast. As I stood in the hall taking off my coat, I could hear Bec's voice, 'No, Isso darling, you can't wear all those skirts.' It was her day for taking her little sister off to the school bus. Without thinking we talked all the time to Elizabeth. She could not have understood all the words, but she very soon understood the meaning. After breakfast in the cosy chaotic kitchen, they were gone, and I would return to my task.

My salmon smoking business had been born out of adversity. First John had bought a large Afos stainless steel smoker, which we could run off our 12-KVA Lister generator, thinking that one day I might be interested in smoking a few fish. A winter or two later I had attended an interesting four-day course run by the Highlands and Islands Development Board at the Inverness Technical College. Staying at a Bed and Breakfast in the town, I was able to go to the cinema and theatre in the evenings. It was like a holiday and it was fun only having to think of myself. I returned to Ardmore with my diploma and notes, and soon got caught up with the next season.

A year or two later, on returning from six weeks' walking in Nepal, we found disaster had hit our small salmon farm. A sickly oily smell floated in the air above the salmon cages. We knew immediately it was the smell of death. We hauled up the nets to find the rotting carcasses of fish at varying stages of decomposition.

In spite of outside nets, which would normally deter predators, the nightly slaughter had been going on for some time. Probably two seals working as a pair would swim strongly at the outer net. One would hold it close to the inner net which held the fish while the other would snatch at the fish caught panicking at the bottom. Fish naturally dive if they are under attack, the wily seal used this to his advantage. The salmon would have their protein rich liver sucked out by the seal, through the netting which surprisingly he did not tear, and the mutilated salmon would then be left to die at the bottom of the net. John and I felt we should have never gone away. Would it have happened if we had stayed at Ardmore? Once more the spectre of financial doom was stalking us, closer than ever this time.

To salvage something from this disaster, I decided that I would just have to smoke the mutilated fish and try to sell them. We did not have enough freezer space to store them fresh. The slaughter continued for another two weeks, until we were able to fox the seals with curtains of nets. Each day I would stand outside the store with a big box of savaged fish which I would then prepare for smoking.

As I gutted them, I would glance nervously out at the loch and watch John lifting the nets of the six cages and dread seeing him pick up the big landing net, knowing that he was going to scoop out more freshly killed fish. I would shout across the water 'How many?' and John would hold up his hands. Snow flurries bowled across the grey loch and the battle seemed unending.

I sent out free samples to hotels north of Inverness and received back quite a number of orders. Meanwhile the smoked sides were taken out by boat and kept frozen in friends' freezers until we were able to sort something out at Ardmore.

It was just at the time we were being put on to the National Grid. The magic of electricity was coming to Ardmore. No more lugging and humping up the hill of gas bottles, jerrycans of paraffin, sacks of peat. The invisible power would just hum in along the wires. We had to agree to pay for a minimum amount each year, which had John worried.

'What if we are faced with ruin and can't meet the bills?' Bankruptcy was always his horror.

'Well we would just have to go out and get a proper job, like other people,' I would answer impatiently. I did not nurture John's anxieties. I blithely felt there would always be some solution.

But John had cause for worry, as there was now an extra house to guarantee a minimum payment for. As well as the wooden house and the bunk house, we had re-built an old ruin next door to our croft house. Building it had been a major operation and involved carting tens of tons of building material up the one-hundred-foot-steep hill from the shore. It was a fine house, secure and dry, and when our chief instructor Jamie Young, and his wife, who had lived there for a short while, left to start a new life in Ireland I decided we should move out of our own very leaky croft house into the 'ruin'. Bec and John, both Cancerians and resistant to change, were not keen. But we all realised the old house desperately needed a new roof, and, what was more, the new house was all wired up for electricity. After seventeen years without, for me electricity was magical. We moved over, and we stayed.

My first proper mains freezers were not, however, filled with the stores I had dreamed of: joints of beef, legs of pork, summer fruits, ice cream. They were packed solid with carefully wrapped smoked salmon. Later that year I sold nearly all of it to businessmen who came on our courses. It happened to taste delicious and I did not charge much. It was the start of my smoked salmon business.

I spread the word that I would be smoking fish for the following Christmas – this time fish that we had carefully selected and harvested ourselves without the help of the seals. I sent out our printed order form to the two thousand customers or so who had attended courses at Ardmore over the years and whose names and addresses were on our mailing list. Once again, each day the new young postman, George – several years on from pebble-spectacled Willie – was weighted down with envelopes containing orders for Ardmore Smoked Salmon.

In conjunction with an old friend, John McConnell, partner at the illustrious firm of designers, Pentagram (whose other clients included Japanese Railways, Faber & Faber, and a sprinkling of Saudi banks) we came up with a beautiful box to parcel it up in. It was all very carefully thought out. It had to look and feel right for the product it was to package, a product that had been 'hand-tooled' for a 'niche market'. We were thrilled when John told us we had been awarded the prestigious Design Council's Award for Excellence and were to feature in a book called *The Best of British Packaging*. Now and again lucky breaks do occur; though it did not seem to tie up with my recent memories of standing out in the snow, gutting boxes of savaged fish, in despair, and panicking over how I would get the sides smoked before a fresh lot were dumped in front of me.

Having turned the situation round in this rather unexpected way, I now found myself with masses of orders and a wintertime, which should have been a quieter phase for me, busier than ever. As I progressed with the smoking we decided to invest in plant. With help from Reg, we bought a vacuum packer, a brilliant slicing machine, a fine stainless steel filleting table, proper digital scales, and we made plans to erect a cold store that could take up to ten tons of frozen fish. Perhaps we rushed into it all rather hastily, but suddenly having mains electricity, after seventeen years without, made so much seem possible, added to which I had lots of encouraging letters and phone calls from people who wanted more, and all the year round as well. It seemed daft not to go for it. Surely I could employ a cook and spend my time between the office and the smoke room.

It is thrilling setting up a new business, particularly in such a remote area where it is so hard to make a living, but keeping it going, week in and week out with the same problems over lack of help and never having enough time to spend on what has to be done, was a big effort. I thought endlessly about training another person up to help, but there were two major problems. The first was accommodation: out at Ardmore we had only just enough room for ourselves, with a few huts dotted around for summer staff, but nowhere substantial for a permanent assistant to stay comfortably during the winter. Even if we had, it is so remote. Would they have remained happy out here, with very little laid on in the way of entertainment? One young man, who came to help on his own one winter, left saying he was suffering from 'social stress'. It could be lonely if you were not of a self-sufficient cast of mind.

The other problem was that I was a ridiculous perfectionist. I could not bear to see the job being done if it was not to my own, almost impossible to achieve, standard. It is almost impossible because, of course, each fish varied, so no hard and fast rules could be applied. Instinctively and by experience I knew if the brine had penetrated the fillets sufficiently, at what point it was time to start smoking them, and for how long and where in the kiln they should be placed. It mattered terribly to me that each side was as good as it could be. Apart from Bec who took to it all quite naturally I seemed unable to teach anyone unless I knew them really well. It nearly killed me seeing it done wrong, curbing my natural impatience and agonising over having to say: 'It does not matter, but try and do it this way,' while knowing the value of the fish which had just been wrecked.

Ada would come and help with the slicing and interleaving at which she excelled.

'I do hope this batch is all right,' I would mutter anxiously.

'Of course they will be,' she would reassure me. 'Stop worrying.'

During the hectic build-up to the last postal day before Christmas, Elizabeth would come down the hill at the end of the day after school, to see what was going on – sometimes on her own in the dark, without a torch. I felt this to be terribly brave for a small person, but I did not make a fuss. I did not want to influence her trusting attitude. I am rather superstitious over darkness. For me a benign place in daylight assumes a sinister cloak at night. Hiding in its dark velvet folds are goblins, ghosts, evil spirits, requiring all possible self-control to quell a rising panic.

'Mamalita!' She would bustle in, dipping her black boots in the bucket of disinfectant, and then rush over to me. I was woolly-hatted, my long white rubber apron covering layers of jumpers, plastic gauntlets protecting my cuffs, in knee-length white rubber boots, a size too large so that I could insert a sheepskin sole and an extra pair of socks. 'Me like pish,' she would archly comment, eyeing the big pile of trimmings which I would be about to weigh and then vacuum pack into pounds to sell for pâté. I would select some nice juicy bits and she guzzled them hungrily. How the wheel of fortune had spun for Elizabeth, I thought: this time last year half starved and in danger, now fit to burst on smoked salmon.

'Time to call it a day.' We would dismantle and wash the slicer, my least favourite fiddly job, when home and sitting down was all I could think of. Isso would pick up the hard bristled brush and vigorously sweep the floor in between sluicing it down with water from a hose which had a mind of its own, and if not held firmly would spray its icy jet in any direction. Then, at last, with everything tidied and the final fire-box made up for the night, we would climb up the hill, followed by a retinue of three cats and listening to the heron's awful cry as it screeched its utter loneliness into the night.

Eventually it was all over. The last boxes had gone to Lairg for franking and I could sit back and look forward to Christmas. Elizabeth seemed happy and so loving – it was she who had adopted me. Whenever she could, she would come and hug me tight, and sit on my knee. I think she really loved the idea of at last having her own mummy. But the dark side to this bright coin was her jealousy. Feeling utterly rejected she would sulk if I put my arm around Bec or John. It even extended to the cats. If any of them were petted she would say crossly: 'Why you do that?' I was sure it was something we could overcome in time, and luckily John and Bec were magnanimous enough not to let it bother them.

We did not know what Christmas meant to Elizabeth. It could not have been much of a joyous affair before. She gazed in amazement as we brought in the Christmas tree and garlanded it with twinkling coloured lights. She helped hang the silver balls and laughed in a rich deep chortle as the cats tried hard to knock them off.

On Christmas Eve 'Rebeeka' tried to explain that Father Christmas would come when all good children were fast asleep and fill the stockings left at the foot of each bed with presents. Later that night she crept into her big sister's bed shivering and scared, 'Me 'rightened – me no like Father Christmas.' Life had taught Elizabeth early that strangers at night were not friendly. The next day, though, all was well, the heavy lumpy stocking opened and the presents around the Christmas tree torn open and carried off to her bedroom for closer inspection. Owning so much was novel and thrilling.

For the three of us it was very special. The past year had been filled with doubt and uncertainties. There seemed still many more hurdles to overcome, the greatest and the one most out of our control being whether the authorities would allow Elizabeth to stay in Britain and whether legal adoption would be approved. The period of waiting was twelve months – a year of anxiety.

We had all grown to love this special child, tough yet vulnerable, wise beyond her years yet still a baby, vivid and bright yet sometimes shy and quite withdrawn: contradictions at every turn. By next Christmas we would know if she was to be legally ours. She seemed in every other sense to be part of our family. Indeed it was hard to imagine what life was like before she came to us so bravely and with such trust. Elizabeth coming into our lives had so changed our circumstances. Sitting around the table with a fourth place laid, Bec, John and I all felt our lives would be so empty without her. We could not bear to contemplate her being taken from us now.

After the excitement of Christmas I realised I did feel tired – from the salmon smoking stint coupled with my re-entry into motherhood. I just hoped that my energy and enthusiasm would return with the New Year. After our excesses of drink and food, Bec, John and I decided to try to decoke our systems by going on to a fruit diet. The first forty-eight hours we had to drink only water and just eat one type of fruit. For us it was dreary anaemic Golden Delicious apples, all we could get from the greengrocers. We felt weak and light-headed. Isso was still chomping normal food, and could not understand what we were up to. After this initial shock to our system we were allowed to go on to raw vegetables and different kinds of fruit. Again we could not get much in the north. It would probably be quite appealing in London sitting down to a plate of papaya, mango, out-of-season strawberries, pineapple, grapes. We were just stuck with more tasteless French apples, wizened oranges and grapefruit and lots of shredded cabbage and carrot.

I began to feel quite unwell. The diet *must* be doing me good, I thought, it was so horrid. My stomach seemed to blow up with painful wind. Well what could I expect, I reasoned, I was only eating indigestible chlorophyll? I did not have a cow's double stomach. Promises in the diet book of clearer skin, brighter eyes, amazing weight loss lured us all on to extend our deprivation. Two nights before my birthday on 18 January, the pain got worse and worse. I crept downstairs knowing my restlessness was stopping John from sleeping. I searched through the bathroom cupboard for pain killers: Aspirin, Paracetamol, Paramol, which we had not touched since the Whitbread Race nearly seven years before. Would they be out of date? It was so painful now I did not care. I swallowed three. I should feel some relief in twenty minutes, but the pain increased. I took a swig of whisky, then another, vowing to ring the doctor first thing. The pain was eating into the very core of my body. Just as rags tied to a string are pulled through the barrel of a gun to clean it, so the pain tugged at my entrails. At last the relief of morning. Hardly able to speak, I rang the doctor. He was brought over by boat. The weather was calm and the loch not frozen nor snow on the roads. He looked worried as he examined me, and said that I should be taken straight away to Raigmore Hospital, one hundred miles away in Inverness.

'But we've got the planning officer coming for lunch,' I said. He dismissed my weak entreaties, and I knew I needed help, urgently. Bec got a few things together and we left. I waved goodbye to little Isso, staring forlornly out of the window. The pain gripped me again and again as we slowly motored across the loch. With help I reached my car and the doctor gave me a large jab of morphine.

'Drive quickly,' he said to Bec. 'The hospital will be expecting her.'

Bec told me later that I talked a lot about dying on the long journey down to the hospital, how she was to have my precious brooch which Reg had just given me, that Isso was to have my grandmother Elizabeth's gold snake necklace with the emerald eyes and ruby head, how they must look after each other and not be sad.

On our arrival, the surgeon sat beside my bed and held my hand as he explained what they thought was wrong: a possible poisoning of my ovaries from using an IUD. 'We could take them both out while you are asleep, and save you any further bother,' he suggested.

'No – please don't remove anything you don't have to,' I sobbed, thinking of all my unborn babies.

They operated on me that evening, I came round later tied up to tubes, and so sore. My kind surgeon, whom I was already half in love with, said, 'You've been lucky. A chronic condition turned acute. Another twenty-four hours and you wouldn't have survived.' I was too drowsy to take it in. 'Probably due to your IUD, you have had a long-standing infection in one of your ovaries, which we have had to remove – it was gangrenous.'

How foolish I had been. Of course this was nothing to do with the fruit diet. I had stupidly ignored all those warning pains with my periods in recent years. I could have so easily died in Peru. My mind went back to that spell of great pain when we were route marched all day and night. No prizes for being stoical.

John, Bec and Isso briefly visited me. They all looked shocked. Isso stood close to Bec. Her eyes would not really meet mine. She would not come near me. Did she think I would leave her? Was this to be another of life's cruel tricks?

I did get better slowly, and all the time I lay in my bed healing, she would not come near me. The warmth and love we had shared was not there any more. She had frozen towards me. I could not pretend it did not hurt, but I tried to understand what she must be feeling. She was still Quechua, brought up with all the taboos relating to illness. I was an outsider now. I had brought on me the displeasure of the guardian spirit Uywaq, and *coca* should be burnt and blown away to the spirit Uywaqman, and the names of the hills should be invoked, saying *nituykita kacharipuy* – Set your grandchild free.

Chapter Eleven

NORWAY

At the end of February when I was feeling stronger, we went over to Norway, to introduce Elizabeth to her distant Norwegian relations, and tell them at first-hand what we knew about her father's death.

'Long way, Danny?' Elizabeth's voice kept asking from the back of the car as we travelled to Aberdeen Airport, 220 miles from Ardmore. Eventually we were on the plane heading across the North Sea. 'Big bird!' Elizabeth was very excited. Then as we dipped to land at Oslo she remarked, 'Bird tired carga me, me heaby.' Her understanding of English was coming on, and the words she used to speak to us were a wonderfully enterprising mixture.

Elizabeth was much bonnier now, with glossy hair, bright boot-black eyes, and rounded rosy cheeks which matched her smartly tailored woollen coat. I remembered the fuss as we trailed round the shops in Inverness trying to find something she liked. We had ended up in the most expensive shop where she found the very coat she wanted, double the price of anything else we had looked at. 'Me like dis one.' It was pillar-box red and trimmed with a black velvet collar. This Inca Princess was making up for her years of rags in the jungle.

As we walked towards the passport immigration desk, a Viking of a man in pilot's uniform came up and introduced himself in singsong English. 'How do you do. I'm Rolf Storm. I am married to a Berg. This must be Elizabeth.' He extended a large hand covered in golden hairs and shook ours warmly. Then he was gone as suddenly as he had come.

'Well, they know we're coming, then,' John muttered rather nervously. We had not had an answer to the letter we had written to say we were coming, and were just a bit doubtful. The Bergs, we assumed, were anxious because our trip was being sponsored by a magazine. We had worried over this, but we probably would not have made the trip if it had not been suggested by the magazine. In weighing it up we felt we could not miss such an opportunity for Elizabeth to meet her father's relations. The cost of living in Norway is extremely high; its small population of four million people enjoying extraordinary prosperity from North Sea oil. They say a Norwegian's dream is to own a German Mercedes with a Swedish chauffeur.

The customs official stamped the green passport which Elizabeth had been clutching possessively, she had named it her 'fusspot'. The Norwegian looked up from his stamp to check on this Elizabeth Berg, but, as the photo showed, in front of him stood not a seven-year-old blonde Nordic girl, but a dark exotic creature from another continent.

Once through the customs we were met by Lars Hveem, a slight quietly spoken writer who had made the arrangements for the meeting that was to take place between ourselves and Elizabeth's relations the next day. Outside, Elizabeth tentatively tried out the snow-slippery pavement, sliding in her black patent leather shoes and chortling with delight. Snow was still a new game. The little that had fallen at Ardmore had had her rushing out to taste it, '*Miski?*' – a Quechua word for sweet – she asked.

Meanwhile Lars told us what he had planned. Tomorrow we were to be taken to a hotel in the mountains outside Oslo, where we would meet Elizabeth's great-uncle and great-aunts. He then drove us through the darkening streets of Oslo to a small hotel. It was warm and smelt of cinnamon. At the reception desk there was coffee percolating and a bowl of sweets. When we were shown to our bedroom, Elizabeth rushed to her single bed by the curtained window and proceeded to unpack her dollies and put them to bed. As we flopped down on to ours, it wobbled and slurped. John and I stared at each other in amazement. Here we were in Norway, on a waterbed. Our shock at this surprise made me realise all the more what Elizabeth had to adjust to. Every day for her there were waterbed situations, and she just took them all in her stride.

The phone rang. 'Can you answer it, John?' I called from the adjoining bathroom, where Elizabeth and I were inspecting other enthralling items like a hairdrier attached to the wall and weighing scales. I was worried it would be the Bergs, and I knew they did not speak much English. We were nervous, as if it mattered. But it did matter for Elizabeth.

It was strange for us to worry about the impression she would make on the Bergs. Instinctively I wanted our child to be loved by everyone who met her, yet at the same time I tried to push to the back of my mind the thought that they might want to adopt her and bring her up in Norway amongst her own family. It was a fear that had haunted me ever since Elizabeth came to Ardmore, and if we felt she would be happy here, of course we would have to relinquish her to her own family.

John put down the remote control – there was not much of interest on Norwegian television – and stretched over the wobbling warm waterbed for the phone.

'This is Lars. I will come and pick you up at seven. I will take you to one of the best restaurants in Oslo.'

What a treat it was all turning out to be. Ardmore seemed light years away from this cosseted luxury. Elizabeth and I put on our best frocks for the occasion and went down to wait in the cinnamon lobby for Lars. At Bloms, where crystal chandeliers illuminated a *fin de siècle* elegance, we were led to our table beside a fountain. Worthy artists and writers from another age gazed down from their gilt frames, and Elizabeth gazed in wonderment at the scene before her. Here, in the land of her fathers, she sat where her ancestors might have come to celebrate a birthday or special occasion. It was hard to believe that not even twelve months ago this child was sitting cross-legged on the dirt floor, in raggedy clothes, frightened for her life, eating what meagre food there was from a chipped enamel bowl.

Lars turned out to be a charming host, and we eagerly bent to hear the story he told us in his soft lilting voice. He had managed to find out from records in the Norwegian Maritime Museum that the Bergs had been an important shipping family. Rasmus Berg, a merchant of Stavanger, established a shipping company in 1814, and his wife carried on the company when Rasmus died in 1837 until 1848, when the company was taken over by two of their sons, Gabriel and Alexander. The name of the shipping line was G. & A. Berg, and by the end of the nineteenth century seven of their ships were circling the globe. He seemed to think the family were not involved in shipping any more but were probably quite well-to-do. We were intrigued but even more worried now. They must have been grateful to us for finding out the truth behind Elvin's silence in 1985, but what would they say about Elizabeth? Tomorrow would tell us.

Lars invited us to eat some of the more unusual dishes on the menu. I wondered how I would feel in the morning after the delicious platter of raw marinated fish followed by reindeer. Elizabeth asked for her very favourite 'snake', which John translated for the slightly shocked Lars as 'steak'. Whatever the outcome over the next few days, we all had enjoyed a wonderful evening.

Lars called for us the next morning early, to take us to watch some ski-jumping. John had been intrigued by his descriptions of this sport for which Oslo was famous. The highest ski jump in the world was situated a short way out of the city. The day was crisp and bright; the blue sky and warm sun helped to banish the doubts we had been feeling. It was unreal to be waiting for a meeting that was of such importance to us, while watching death-defying young braves shoot down the steepest longest slope and then catapult into the air like giant birds. We sat high up to the side of the run in a seated area like an amphitheatre. John was exhilarated, but I felt very unsafe just sitting so high, and held tightly on to Elizabeth in case she tumbled forward. What a mouse I felt – fearing we might fall or see someone hurt! Our feet soon got numb sitting in the icy shade, so we killed some more time looking around a museum of skiing since early times.

I had spent six months in Switzerland when I was seventeen. We would ski every afternoon and I had become quite good. Shortly after we married when we returned from Scotland, we decided to take a skiing holiday in Austria to cheer ourselves up. Inevitably in the early stages of marriage couples find out a lot about each other which never comes to light in the courtship. John, keenly competitive in all sports, had thrashed me at tennis with a viciously hard backhand stroke; he was much tougher and faster than me at swimming and most athletic events – but skiing was one of the few things I could actually do better than him. We never took another skiing holiday. John always said he could not afford to hurt his legs – but I wondered.

'It's time to go.' Lars shepherded us along the snowy access road to his car. John sat in front, so he could stretch out his long legs, and Elizabeth and I in the back. She kept on peeping at Lars and catching his eye in the front mirror: she had fallen for our kind escort. We laughed our way to the hotel high up in the snowy mountains, but all the time there was a terrible tightness of apprehension in my stomach, for it was there we were to meet the Bergs.

It was a large old wooden hotel. It being Sunday, there were many families out skiing, and lots of people had propped up their skis outside the hotel and were sitting at tables enjoying the late February sunshine. We went inside, first into a large completely wooden panelled hall rather like a First World War drill hall. Here the skiers could come in in their ski clothes and have coffee and a snack. We followed Lars across the room and up a short staircase, through a panelled glass door and into an elegant dining room with many tables laid with sparkling silver and glass. The white damask tablecloths reflected the brilliant light shining in from the long line of windows. The view looked out on to a gentle snow slope and beyond to dark bands of forest and then snow-covered mountains. It was a dazzling sight. Elizabeth narrowed her almond-shaped eyes adjusting to the brilliance and we looked to see if there was any sign of Mr Berg and his sisters. We did not know them, but they would know us. Elizabeth caused people to turn and look again.

We chose a central table near the windows, so that we would be seen by the Bergs as soon as they arrived. A tall glass of her favourite Coca-Cola was ordered for Elizabeth, and we had lemonade: we wanted to keep our heads clear. We nibbled at dark rye bread covered liberally with delicious creamy pale butter. By one-thirty we decided to order our food, again the unusual, this time moose. Another hour passed and then another. Maybe they were not coming. What were we to do? Lars looked worried. He had arranged the meeting, and as well as being concerned for our feelings, he had a story to write. It would not please his editor if the meeting did not take place.

From our table we had plenty of time to look around the dining room. The hotel must have been built in this remote setting in the last century: the pine panelling had darkened with age. It was a popular place, and many Norwegian families were enjoying a good Sunday lunch.

Low shafts of sun illuminated motes of suspended dust, foreign conversation buzzed in the background, and we waited. I felt circumstances had completely taken over my life, that I was just a speck of dust floating, with no will to take charge of events which were assuming monumental importance. There had been other times: stuck in the pack-ice off the South Pole, the last mile of a marathon, in Peru – a total relinquishing of responsibility and allowing a higher order to take over.

My reverie ended sharply as Elizabeth tugged at my sleeve and pointed to three people coming through the glass-panelled doors: a distinguished silver-haired man in a grey suit, and two smart ladies, one with bright red hair, the other dark. They walked to our table. We all stood up. We all looked at Elizabeth. We all smiled.

Nervously we all spoke at once. John and I introduced ourselves and of course Elizabeth. She stood close to me and looked gravely at her family: Alexander Berg and his two sisters Anne-Marie and Annette. They in turn looked at this child Elizabeth Berg: daughter of Elvin, descended directly as they were from Rasmus Berg. They saw before them a child of seven, with thick shiny dark hair, oriental features, dark almond-shaped eyes set in a pale face. She wore her best dress of indigo blue with red spots; a sash tied in a bow round her waist pushed out the full skirt, and a snowy white collar of lace circled her throat.

After more coffee and much halting conversation, for we spoke no Norwegian and Alexander Berg not much English, they suggested we should go and meet more of the family. Daylight was fading as we left the hotel and followed the car taking the two sisters and brother. We drew up at a comfortable-looking house in a residential area on the outskirts of Oslo. As we walked towards the house, the bright light from the curtained windows illuminated the path and the snow heaped high on either side.

'Come in, come in,' people called, and to our astonishment we found there was a large gathering of people – men, women, children, young, middle-aged and very old. I knew John would be wondering, as I certainly was, how Elizabeth would cope with such attention and interest. However she stood her ground, said nothing above a whisper, held up her head and looked as though she was used to being centre-stage every day of her life.

We were in a large room, a drawing room with a dining room to one side. Both rooms were filled with fine old dark furniture, heirlooms of another age when the shipping line had prospered and relics were brought back from faraway places. We were invited to help ourselves to food laid out on an old mahogany dining table and then introduced to the family. They asked us many questions about our expedition to Peru, and of what little we knew about the attack on Osambre and of Elvin's death. Of course, they also wanted to know all about Elizabeth, were clearly delighted with her, and kept on saying how grateful they were to us for giving her a home.

It dawned then on John and me that perhaps some of the Bergs' initial apprehension had come from their thinking that we wished them to adopt Elizabeth, that we had rescued her from a life of misery and were expecting to hand her over to them. Now we all seemed to have reached an unspoken understanding, each side sensing that the other did not in any way wish to upset the present arrangement.

With one of the knots of worry in the tangled thread I had carried for so long now untied, I could enjoy the gathering of this unusual family who were welcoming us so warmly.

We were taken over to meet a very old lady who told us, while holding Elizabeth's small hand, that she was the niece of Elizabeth's great-grandfather Elvin. She handed Elizabeth a small packet which she opened to reveal a cameo brooch. With it was a photograph of a young woman wearing it: Alida Berg, wife of Olaf, Elizabeth's great-grandfather's brother. The studio portrait had been taken in 1889 in Stavanger, where the family came from. The story that Lars had told us the night before was retold with more detail. Again we listened intently. This story would mean so much to Elizabeth and her children in the future.

In perfect English, the old lady told us that those gathered to meet Elizabeth were descended from Gabriel Berg, born 1826, died 1901; he and his wife Bertha Christine had had twelve children. Bertha Christine, Elizabeth's great-great-grandmother, was much loved and had a street named after her in Stavanger. After her death, one of her sons set up a well-endowed trust to honour her name, the interest from which was spent on embellishments for Stavanger such as the music pavilion.

On the now-cleared long mahogany table, Alexander unrolled a wrinkled chart of the Berg family tree. Pointing his finger to Elizabeth's branch he read, '*Elvin Berg*, born 4 February 1865, died 9 July 1916.' Turning to us he added, in his slow studied English, 'We know he sailed out to Buenos Aires in 1887, when he was twenty-two; he went with his father Gabriel, on one of the family's barques, named after our home town, the *Stavanger*. Elvin took the job as stationmaster for a while, on the railway in Tandil; then he went on to Bolivia in 1891, and he stayed there until the time of the

1903 revolution; then he crossed the Andes into Peru, where he stayed, supervising rubber and cocoa plantations. He married a "girl from the woods" and had two children, Victoria and Abel.

'Elvin never came back to Norway,' Alexander smiled. 'He was too much of an adventurer.' Perhaps there were too many brothers in the family for them all to hold key positions in the family company. Maybe he had just gone to South America to seek his fortune. They did not know much about his 'girl from the woods'. Together, the old lady and Alexander told us how Olaf, Elvin's brother back in Norway, had sent money to help with the education of the two children, Abel and Victoria. Abel had been sent to a strict naval academy in Lima, but he had hated it so much that he had eventually run away, and he had lost contact with his sister. Victoria, whom we had met in Lima in 1985, had also received help with her education. She was trained as a nurse, and had worked in California for thirty-five years. She had kept in touch with her Norwegian relations and had even been to visit them.

We were able to tell the Bergs that Victoria was well, was in her late seventies, had sold her home in Lima and was now living permanently back in California. I thought back to her with great fondness. She had reminded me of Granny Ross – she had displayed that same instant warmth and friendliness towards us. On her special visit to say goodbye on the morning of our departure from Lima, she had held us close as we hugged farewell, the time ticking away fast. I knew we had her blessing and she knew we would do our best for the daughter of her favourite nephew.

We were able to tell them too what we knew of Abel. We had just received a long letter from an English Protestant missionary, Ken Case. He and his wife Frances had spent many years living in an area several days' walk from the Bergs at Osambre. He had counted Abel and his wife Rosa as good friends. He wrote, 'Abel and Rosa were married legally and were entirely faithful to one another (a lot of people there cannot claim these two qualities, or even one of them!). Abel obviously loved the semi-jungle area and preferred to make his life there. Probably he took after his father as an adventurer. Victoria didn't and the difference obviously separated them. I think they had very little contact. Rosa was a noble companion to him and went gladly with him into this isolation.

Elizabeth in Scotland, 1989, aged ten – bonny and brave

John, Rebecca, me and Elizabeth together at Ardmore, 1986

'He told me several yarns about catching a marauding jaguar that had killed some of his livestock; about how he cut a trail out from Osambre to the distant old Inca trail that he wanted to reach to export his produce to Cuzco and bring in livestock; and about discovering exactly where the old Inca treasure was lying buried – he asked me about the Peruvian laws on treasure-trove, and wanted to organise a small expedition to reach it avoiding the dreaded Mascos (a tribe of forest Indians who kill on sight anyone not of their tribe – other Indians and all).'

The Norwegian Bergs listened intently. Apart from the odd letter and one or two visits from Victoria, who had lost touch with her brother, they knew only the bare outline of the story of their cousin Abel and his four children.

We discovered that red-haired Anne-Marie, whom we had met earlier at the hotel, was married to the Viking pilot with the strong handshake, Rolf Storm. 'I could have gone to Peru to visit my relations,' she said, and then added rather regretfully, 'but, you see, I am frightened of flying.'

'And what of the others,' she went on, 'now that poor Elvin is murdered?' We told her that we had heard that Bertha his sister was a frightened recluse. No one knew if the other two, Virgil and Olaf, were alive or dead.

'I will go and find out what has happened to Olaf and Virgil,' John said quietly, but it was a promise that everyone in the room heard. His search for his friend Elvin had turned into an obsession. I knew he would not rest until he had unravelled the whole story.

I glanced across at the old lady. She was smiling fondly down at Elizabeth playing with a young cousin on the old carpet: the Bergs of the next generation, one dark, one fair. She remembered meeting her grandfather, Gabriel Berg, who, exactly a hundred years before, had sailed off to South America on one of the family ships, leaving there, for ever, his twenty-two-year-old son, the original Elvin.

> Time present and time past
> Are both perhaps present in time future
> And time future contained in time past.

I was reminded of Eliot's *Four Quartets*. 'Footfalls echo in the memory'. Each of us was lost with his thoughts.

What we call the beginning is often the end
And to make an end is to make a beginning.
The end is where we start from.

Was this to be yet another beginning?

Chapter Twelve

TOGETHER

'Why no picture? Where picture gone?' Elizabeth imperiously questioned John and me. We were driving the two hundred miles back from Aberdeen Airport after our trip to Norway in my red motor car. Entranced by the passing scenes, she was dismayed when we hit a patch of mist when crossing the high peaty moorland on Struie Hill. It completely blotted out the scene she had been enjoying watching. We did not often go out in the car – our whole universe was Ardmore – but she was well used to the television, and I wondered if she thought that we were sitting in a more sophisticated vision-box with moving pictures being shown on all sides. Elizabeth had been suddenly uprooted from a mediaeval life, and now the twentieth century hurtled bewilderingly all around her. Moreover, her grasp of English was still fairly basic, so she was effectively gagged, unable to ask the questions which would help her to make sense of the strange new world in which she found herself.

It had been a successful four days away in Norway meeting her new family, although I did think the customs officials at Aberdeen had been over zealous in their search of us as we returned to Britain. Perhaps it was because Elizabeth still carried her green Peruvian passport. Did they expect to find South American cocaine as they turned our suitcases inside out? They had their job to do, but we had never undergone a search like this before, and we had, quite rightly, gone through the green Nothing to Declare channel.

I was feeling stronger each day after my operation, and Elizabeth responded accordingly. She was delighted to get home, to find all her dolls and clothes just as she had left them. Each day there was a bit of progress: another word, a braver action, and now always much love. She had been frightened when I was ill that I might not come back from the hospital, and now I was looking stronger, she never stopped hugging me for reassurance.

We had been led to believe that she would be talking English fluently after a year. After six months it was clear to us that this was most unlikely. It was a pity we had had such high expectations. I think it made us worry unnecessarily, and I hope it was not obvious to Elizabeth, because she had so much to cope with and it would have put more pressure on her. I suppose we just wanted to get to know her.

Our life had changed so much with this small girl coming into our family, and we could not imagine life without her. But she was not yet ours. The case for the adoption would not be heard until the winter, and it was possible it would not go in our favour. I could not bear the thought of such an outcome. She was so nearly ours. I longed for her to be able to understand what I wanted to tell her, and read her stories that I knew she would love, and include her in everything strange and wonderful that went on at Ardmore.

People who did not understand the situation inflicted further pressure by their well-meaning questions. Can she talk? How is her English? Can she read? How is she getting on at school? How intelligent is she? I could feel myself becoming the proverbial mother hen and I protected and stood up for her at every turn. She hated being talked about, and her hands would clench my skirt as she hid behind me. Worst of all to her was to hear us talking about her background. She wanted to shut it out, and would pull a face and turn away. I would sometimes put on Peruvian music: the thin wail of the *qena*, the Quechua flute, which we had heard drifting on a light wind high up on the Altiplano. But it was not what Elizabeth wanted to hear. She wanted the pop music her new friends listened to; so we respected her feelings, and it was put away.

More and more snow fell that spring. Sometimes we could not get out to school and the day would be devoted to sliding down the hill on the toboggans with Bec. I could only watch, as I was not yet strong enough to join in. I longed to be whooshing down the slope, for it seemed like only weeks since Bec was eight and we used to toboggan by torchlight when she got back from school. The level of excitement depended on how far up the hundred-foot steep hill you started. Elizabeth, muffled up in her red coat, scarf, gloves and hat which sat on her thick black hair like a lid, was loving it until, on one descent, she momentarily forgot how to stop and shot over the short cliff at the bottom of the hill, became airborne and landed with a thump in the kelp seaweed, mercifully just up from the icy low tide and below the big tumbled rocks at the top of the beach beneath the cliff. She was fine, though very, very cross. 'Me cutta your neck,' she muttered at us all as we collapsed into helpless mirth, our laughter prompted by relief more than anything else.

So now we made snowmen instead. I think she expected them to walk into the house or fly, as we had all watched the cartoon film, *The Snowman*, over Christmas and had shed a tear at our own memories of lost childhood innocence. The one who wept most of all was iron-man, John, who could never watch anything remotely romantic or sad without mopping his eyes and blowing his nose like a foghorn. When John's father, Reg, took John and me to see the West End musical of Victor Hugo's *Les Misérables*, John was in tears almost from the moment the curtain went up and the orchestra struck the first notes. It was very moving, defiant and brave, and we were both like limp soggy rags by the end of the performance. Needless to say, it was a wonderful evening.

Elizabeth's Latin temperament lit up our home, although it hadn't been exactly quiet and tranquil before her arrival. Bec and I were particularly good at sticking up for ourselves when confronted by John's military orders – we had to be or go under. I have often noticed a tendency in Sandhurst-trained men to take over the situation, and boss, or as it is flatteringly termed, 'lead'. It did not always go down well in our house and would usually result in a revolt, with Bec or me screaming at our 'leader' in outrage, and would be followed by the humiliating tears of anger.

Elizabeth loved the drama. She really came alive at these times: 'You cross Danny?' she would screech at me, and then report to John: 'Danny, Mummy cross you,' waiting in a state of high excitement for the next scene in the melodrama. The Quechua women, particularly, are pretty fierce, and I think she felt very much at home in these outbursts. I think also it helped her express her own feelings, for she knew that in this house the emotion would blow over as quickly as it had come.

She now frequently gave vent to her rage at minor slights. Whereas Bec and I stuttered out mild forms of abuse, Elizabeth could summon up and spit out strings of wonderful gutteral dark-sounding words the meaning of which we could only guess at – '*Caiachota*' was a favourite. Then there was 'Me cutta your neck, me knock your head, me cutta your legs,' or any other part of the body she could think of. It was good for increasing the vocabulary! One of her main threats was 'Me big, me wallopy *you.*'

I think she had been 'walloped' a lot back in Peru, certainly judging by the way she destroyed her dolls. Reg had given her two lovely rag dolls, but they did not last looking good for long. She biffed and bashed them mercilessly, ticking them off in a most severe fashion, particularly when she did not think any of us was listening. 'Pappy wallopy me,' she told me in a rather wistful voice one day pointing to the leather belt I was threading through the loops of my jeans. And I felt for the sad family, worn down by hunger and fear and misery, and how easy it would be to hit out at a child for some minor misdemeanour.

There was much laughter too. 'Escapee' continued to delight, and Elizabeth would shriek with laughter as she and John shot around the old kitchen table, bought for ten shillings at an auction twenty years before. She laughed as she rode around on John's or Lance's obliging 'horsey' backs; she chortled as she had us pulling faces and making silly noises.

With us, her personality was emerging strongly but at school she was quite different. The teachers and forty pupils could not have been kinder, but every day was an immense challenge: Elizabeth was almost pathologically frightened of other children. She might be bossy, noisy, flamboyant at home but at school she would sit meekly, not daring to speak out.

'If only we could get her to ask questions, or be a bit naughty,' the teachers would say to me. A fear of authority, which she obviously did not link with me or John at home, coupled with a fear of children, froze her. At the end of the day when she was met off the bus, there was a rush to spend a penny. I think she never went at school.

I received a letter from the school doctor suggesting that Elizabeth should have tests on her hearing. I was intrigued and somewhat worried, as her mother was deaf – perhaps it was hereditary – but also I wondered why we had never noticed. So I did some home-made tests. I filed my finger nails in our bedroom next to hers. She did not know I was there, but as soon as she heard the light rasping sound, she called out to ask who it was. She could hear the cat's faint miaow outside the door before any of us. She could hear the far-off deep boom of the Cape Wrath lighthouse on misty days. I reckoned she was not hard of hearing, just too terrified to respond at school.

As if making up for all her subdued behaviour at school, as soon as she got off the bus she would start winding us up. If I had gone to meet her, as soon as the white bus turned and headed back to Kinlochbervie, Elizabeth would darkly mutter, 'Where's Rebeeka? Why Rebeeka no meet me?' which had exactly the desired effect of making me feel at once both cross and disappointed. So too, if Bec was there to meet her, a similar imperious question would be put: 'Where's Mama?' Then would start the walk home, with Elizabeth either several paces ahead, her black-rubber-booted legs going fast, her shoulders hunched forward in the style of her Inca ancestors, who knew not the wheel and carried everything on their backs, or just far enough behind to make us stop every so often to check she was still coming along. It was a shocking transition for her, between two different worlds which she had to adjust to. Usually by the end of the hilly walk the bad mood had evaporated, and she was bubbling over with good humour and fun.

The teachers at Kinlochbervie, Miss Mackay, Mrs Rookes and Mrs Massie, were endlessly patient with her and very kind. I doubt she could have received better attention anywhere else. For much of her first year she was tutored on her own, although they were careful to integrate her with the other children in all the non-academic activities.

For Elizabeth it must all have seemed entirely strange. There were times, as with any child, when she did not want to go to school, and it sometimes took us a little while to understand what was bothering her. One of these problems was gym. On gym days there was reluctance to get up, gloom at breakfast, no spring in the step walking to the bus – it was as though we were leading a lamb to the slaughter – until we realised what was troubling her. Nudity in any form is unacceptable to the Quechua people, so having to put on little white shorts was abhorrent to Elizabeth. Once we had worked out what was the problem, we agreed she should wear her skirt, and in time she wore shorts just like the others. We had to strike a careful balance between not giving in to her strong will, and respecting her sensibilities.

One of her delights was brightly coloured felt-tip pencils. She would spend hours filling page after page of her books with lettering, in effect developing hand-control, making patterns which had an affinity with the weaving that was her heritage. Sometimes the lined page was covered in black lettering, and sometimes it was coloured. Page after page she would fill, never looking up until a great deal was done.

Her early efforts had started when Nick Asheshov brought her out of the jungle. Sitting next to him in the plane from Cuzco to Lima she tried to copy his scribblings – being a writer he was always reaching for his notebook. Any child will copy an adult, but what was remarkable to us was the precision of her efforts to capture the impression of writing, and the long painstaking hours she spent on filling so many pages with such neatness and such a feel for pattern. She loved drawing and particularly colouring. Everything had to be a riot of colour: red trees, blue cats, houses with purple roofs – the whole page would be filled and very often she would draw a frame around it to finish the masterpiece off.

We heard from a friend that they had seen one of her pictures framed and exhibited at an art show at a Dundee swimming pool. We were amazed – Elizabeth had forgotten to tell us. Another time she won first prize for a competition in the north. The subject the children had to paint was a bird-table. Elizabeth painted the bird-table with birds of course, but then put it in a brilliantly coloured garden; it caught the judges' eye. They sent a letter and cheque. A few days later she showed me the letter which had languished in her school bag, but to my dismay she had thrown away the envelope containing the cheque!

At the Speech Day at the end of the summer term, my heart swelled with pride as she shyly came forward to accept a prize. She was given a book, and Mrs Rookes read the dedication slowly and deliberately so she would understand:

'Elizabeth Ridgway. For Great Endeavour.'

Whenever we could, Elizabeth and I would go 'up top'. This meant getting together our bathing things and a picnic. We would dart down to my little shop on the shore to pick up a sweetie and a drink to have as a treat with our sandwiches. Here I sell our visitors anything from a whistle to an oiled jacket, with varying delights in between, like the Aran-style jumpers which Bec gets knitted locally, waterproofs, walking sticks, whisky, wine, sweets, plasters, and John's books – he has written eleven.

Up the steep hill we would climb, zigzagging our way past pockets of bright heather, the scent reminding me of winter toast dripping with heather honey; past canary yellow St John's wort nestling amidst the deer grass and dark cushions of beaver-like moss; on up past blue scabious, nodding in the breeze. Below us the houses are just patchy roofs, and the sheep-dotted green fields cover the hill like curtseying maids' aprons hemmed by the blue loch's edge. Breathing deeply at the top of the rocky cliff, we gaze beyond to the amphitheatre of those ancient sentinels Foinaven, Arkle and Ben Stack. 'I will lift up mine eyes unto the hills from whence cometh my help.' These mountains have stood over me now for more than half my life. The winters and summers have marked us both.

There is a point at the top of the hill on the Ardmore Peninsula where we can see a small strip of road on the other side of Loch Laxford. It is far in the distance, but I feel a sense of invasion and outrage if I can see a car passing on this narrow stretch. We treasure our isolation; some might not care for it, but for me it turns our home into a sanctuary and I dread unexpected intruders. In the summer we tend to get more strangers arriving by yacht than along the hilly track. Sometimes if we see them coming ashore Elizabeth and I will sneak out of the house and run and hide up on the hill. We both cherish the solitude.

When going swimming we continue on to the peaty saddle, sinking into the thick rose-red Sphagnum moss, white drifts of bog cotton, the yellow green butterwort, a circle of low leaves offering to the sun tender stems topped with purple-lipped flowers, and masses of pale- to deep-lilac orchids. One of the three cats follows us, complaining piteously with every leap over the deep heather.

Eventually, after fifteen minutes of fast climbing and walking through leg-scratchy heather, our nostrils tickling with the pungent smell of bruised bog myrtle, we arrive at our loch, the further of two that are just kept apart by a springy green plug of bog. The first is the water supply; it is sacrosanct – only the red-throated divers are allowed to swim there. Our own swimming pool is deep black, bordered by two steep short hills which shelter it from cool winds and hide it from a bigger world. The summer sun is high enough to shine into it, but it is so black it gives back no secrets. On its skin water-boatman beetles paddle about in a frenzy of activity, as if they know their span is brief. In contrast I lie utterly still on its edge, my fragile body resting on this ancient Lewisian rock formed more than two thousand million years ago. The small yellow northern bog asphodel grows abundantly here by the peaty water's edge and all about is the sticky cadaverous sundew; my giant's eye peers to see its victims held fast, their struggle over.

'Mamalita,' Elizabeth calls impatiently to me. She is struggling to get into her 'peruana' and wants help. Her soft square feet are out of the gym shoes as she gingerly steps over the sharp rocks towards me. Rising out of my stupor, I reach to help. We pull on the dark blue-and-yellow striped bathing costume – insect colours – she could be a small plump wasp. Her body is firm and solid now, but her arms are still thin and her knee joints seem too big for her legs.

Hardly over a year ago she was measured and weighed by Padre Santiago against the church door in the jungle town of Quillabamba. Her body was infested with parasites – she got rid of a thick one-foot tapeworm in Lima – and her black stumpy teeth covered abscesses, which had to be extracted under anaesthetic as she refused to open her mouth. Her head was scabbed and her hair crawling with lice. Now I watched her closely as she squatted, Indian-style, resting on her heels, inspecting the goodies we had brought up with us for our picnic. She had filled out deliciously, her ivory skin glowed, and her dark hair gleamed showing strands of russet in the bright sun. The black teeth lost had been her baby teeth. The new ones growing through looked strong enough; time would tell. Above all she was lively and bright and happy. Our doctor had found on examining her that her liver had been enlarged by the chronic malnutrition; we noticed she could not eat anything creamy without being sick and did not care for fried food or butter, but that was easy to cope with.

The first time she was ill, it started as a cold. She lay on the sofa downstairs surrounded by her battered dollies, gradually getting fainter and fainter, until we feared she was in a coma. Our doctor came, and he explained she had picked up a virus, which abound in places like schools where there are many children, and manifested itself in the respiratory tract causing the wheeziness, coughing and sneezing that we call a 'cold'. She recovered quickly and was soon dashing around, but her barrel chest was frequently wheezy and John feared she would be prone to bronchitis, something that has stalked him all his life.

We put our drinks into the water to cool them and greedily ate our sandwiches watching the iridescent blue dragonflies courting as they whirled across the loch's silky smooth surface. Toes tested the temperature, and then either it was a brave leap or a gradual sliding. I alternated my water entry depending on my mood.

'It's lovely,' I would call out, fooling no one, gasping for air as the icy water shocked me breathless.

Elizabeth was cautious. She preferred to inch in slowly where the peaty amber water lapped the gently shelving shore. Her memories still vivid with jungle fears, how could I persuade her there were no crocodiles or other lurking horrors, except by my own splashing and swimming? She had been with us for three quarters of a year, but recently we noticed she had entered into a period of varied and intense fears which we must help her overcome with the utmost patience and understanding. The fact that I did not fear the water was of no consequence to her, except that she could see my enjoyment and perhaps draw strength from that. The fright extended even to getting into the bath or taking a shower. She was passionately keen to grow her thick dark hair long again, so Bec and I resorted to trickery and told her that washing her hair in the bath or the shower would help to make it grow quickly. We would sing loudly to make her feel brave, and it was not long before the fear evaporated like wet footprints on the sun-hot rocks surrounding our mountain pool.

For Elizabeth another horror was flies of any description. This surprised us as they were far worse where she had come from; if she had felt this way back in Peru, she would have been in a permanent frenzy. Again it was a terror which froze her to the point where she would not, could not, move. Descending the cliff after our swim, we would sometimes have to pass through a cloud of harmless buzzing insects filling the twisted birch and hazel trees with a great hum. Elizabeth would stop and refuse to proceed. Glancing at my watch and realising I had probably not left myself sufficient time for the preparation of supper, I would, in a frantic pantomime, walk right in amongst the trees which had the most insects and would call out to Elizabeth how beautiful they were with their gossamer wings and many-hued glistening bodies, giving them names and telling her stories about particular ones. She unwittingly opened my eyes to their beauty, and in time we both looked out for different types of flies and insects, just as we admired the caterpillars, the butterflies, the moths. We even marvelled at the giant black slugs that left their trail of slippering slime everywhere, although secretly I hated these beasts. They crept out at night and munched through the tender plants I tried to grow in my herbaceous border, a square patch of garden separated from our house by the path that leads to the last house at Ardmore. With my part Indian, part Norwegian helper I would stalk at dusk through tall lupins and dizzying sweet lilies to spear the omnivorous licorice slug.

Our northern summer is quickly over. Once we pass the longest day, 21 June – when it is so light that, should we wish, we can go out and read a newspaper at midnight – the daylight shrinks away fast. The midges come and plague us for the months of July, August and September until the first frost when they are destroyed. Elizabeth coped well with her first summer of midges; expecting everything to have a sting, she probably felt justified when these tiny brutes really did bite.

Autumn meant school for Elizabeth, and more complicated cooking for me. We employed cooks during the summer school in July and August to cater for the children's simple, wholesome needs. For the more discerning adults, I would be involved in the serious business of setting and trying to maintain a higher standard of cooking. I was determined that everything must be home-made, home-baked and as fresh as we could provide here at Ardmore, one hundred miles distant from our nearest suppliers in Inverness. Sometimes I work with a helper, usually without, but with the assistance of the young instructors, some of whom are not happy at all in my cramped steamingly hot kitchen, but others who are 'stars'. Nightly we would aim to turn out a delicious feast for those who were spending a week at Ardmore.

I love to surprise them. The long pine table is carefully laid and decorated with fresh flowers, the candles lit as the first weary guests arrive after their day of mortification of the flesh. Wine is poured and then baskets of warm, freshly baked bread brought in with bowls brimming with home-made soup – sacrament and balm to the shattered nerves and bruised body. As confidence slowly flows back into their veins we follow with delicately cooked fish fresh from Kinlochbervie, perhaps, or our own hand-polished salmon. The lightest of subtle sauces are garnished with surprising delights at great expense from my greengrocer – star fruits flown in from Israel, bunches of crisp watercress, herbs gathered by Ada and me from our Ardmore gardens – some have said that if I was a stick of rock, 'parsley' would be written through my very core. Salads delight the eye and contrast every nuance of flavour and crunch. Only the freshest of vegetables are permitted, cooked at the very last moment and causing almost a third world war nightly as tension mounts in the kitchen towards countdown. Then John will appear 'deus ex machina' at the kitchen door, to do his part as chief waiter, amazing clients who cannot believe that this is the same man who has just delivered them out of the jaws of hell, skippering the yacht off the cliffs of Handa.

Nightly the drama is re-enacted: we have been going through this scenario for twenty-two years and we are both stubborn in our conflicting aims. John wants the plates to be hot and put out quickly. I also want the plates hot and for them to be put out quickly, but get cross if the plates are whipped away before I have finished with them. Good presentation takes a fraction of a second longer than sometimes John, in his impatience, is pre-pared to give. Meanwhile, my team of two chaps swallow in horror as they are caught in the crossfire of abuse between me and John.

Tempers have usually eased by the time it comes to pudding, as we balance twenty or so plates around the kitchen, even extending to the bunker outside the kitchen door, though here we run the risk of inviting an extra guest, a wily greedy old seagull who swoops down and takes food when he gets the chance. I have seen him with stolen chicken legs bulging from his neck as he sits smugly on top of the nearby clothes-line post. Nor are the ducks ever far away. They are always greedy, but mercifully too heavy to fly up and take what we have laid out on the bunker. Some-times it is lightest Pavlova meringue covered in luscious cream with bright fresh berries and dark green mint leaves, or the smoothest of rich chocolate concoctions with crisp freshly baked almond biscuits, or profiteroles piled high and spun into a nest with golden sugar, or brandy snap baskets offering up voluptuous creams, or pastry tarts glistening with their crowning of fruit. Sometimes it is a comforting hot pudding reminiscent of long forgotten nursery suppers: queen of puddings, bread and butter pudding, sticky toffee pudding, castle pudding, warm apple pie, or lemon pudding. Out it goes to the troops now mellow and reassured before the finale of the cheese. John the waiter is easy now, another production over . . . until tomorrow night when it all starts up again.

Meanwhile Elizabeth, who until a year ago had only eaten the simplest of food and very little of that, is thrust into this heady epicurean atmosphere. She sits on a high stool wedged between the draining board and the covered work top. We eat our supper at high speed. Sometimes the quantities have all gone wrong and I am frying eggs for the disappointed instructors because we dished out too much and nothing is left; sometimes it works the other way.

'No, Marie Christine, I can't eat any more profiteroles. I finished up the last of the grilled monkfish and all the mangetout. I'm pogged.'

Elizabeth laughs, she loves all the fun and excitement, and the boys. 'Mama, who's on duty today?' is the question she fires at me first thing each morning when I go in to wake her.

She archly flirts, and the boys are sweet to her. 'How was school? That's a pretty dress.' She glows with delight and casts her dark almond eyes down in utter shyness. Then she hurries on with her job of putting away the ramekin dishes in the very lowest cupboard before placing a bright nasturtium on each of the twenty leaves we have gathered to garnish the pudding.

Lots of adjustments had to be made that autumn. We were all learning to live together, learning to make time for each other. Kay Allinson, the social worker, had wondered how I would cope. She knew I was busy with the courses; making room for another child in my life might mean changes. In reality it was not really possible; we just had to stretch ourselves that little bit more.

In a funny way I think it suited Elizabeth. She was caught up with us in our common cause, very much one of the team, and helped where she could, which is just what she would have been expected to do in Peru. If I had given up my jobs of cooking and the office, and just concentrated on Elizabeth, I think the hot-house atmosphere of magnified attention might have produced behavioural problems.

Certainly, she was wilful; testing how far she could go with us – did we only love her when she was good? Not being a child psychiatrist, I could only follow my instincts, and sometimes when I was exhausted after a tough day and she would play up in a minor way, like refusing to go to bed or deciding she wanted to watch something on the television which we considered unsuitable, I would end up getting very cross, a situation which I felt she was stage-managing. It was partly a bid for attention and partly a clash of wills. If she could not join me in reaching a compromise with both sides saving face, Elizabeth would cry with tears pouring down her luscious cheeks wailing, 'Me want Mummy Lima.' Of course at this point my heart would go out to this child who must be so emotionally muddled, and I would hug her to me, wipe her tears and the storm would pass. What had been at issue was forgotten in the much bigger matter of whether we really loved her, even when she was maddeningly stubborn and awkward, which of course we did.

This phase of testing us gradually passed; she got a bad shock one night when she locked herself in the bathroom and wouldn't come out. I could have just left her there, but I wondered what she might find and do to herself in her despair. John and Bec were both in bed asleep whilst I was trying to persuade her to come out. Entreaties, threats, nothing would work; I could just hear her dark mutterings on the other side of the door. Finally something inside me snapped. I punched the door and caught my wrist on a piece of protruding timber. The intense pain made me cry out, and I crept back upstairs in agony, nursing my throbbing wrist. Very soon afterwards, Elizabeth came back upstairs, quite mortified. She crept in beside me. 'Me sorry, Mamalita; me sorry you get cross me.' All was well, except for my wrist – I think I cracked the bone. It swelled up, and for weeks I could hardly use it.

At last Elizabeth's defences were breaking down and she was starting to feel compassion for others. To survive what she had in Peru she had had to grow a hard shell, or else suffer greatly. Here at Ardmore with us, she was spared the horrors of death and hunger, but small events cropped up every day which required us to feel and care for each other. If she was to make friends and become a useful member of society, we knew she must learn to feel compassion for her fellows – a difficult thing to teach, because first she had to re-learn to love, re-learn to be vulnerable. My damaged wrist was a big step in that direction, and almost seemed a turning point. Confrontations after that night dwindled away.

The six weeks of autumn adult courses finally came to an end, and with it my intensive cooking; we had survived. The Highland schools have a break in October. The school year is now divided into four terms, and what used to be the 'Tatty Picking Break', in the middle of the winter term, is now a two week holiday between the autumn and the winter term. I thought it would be fun for John,

Elizabeth and me to have a proper holiday. (Bec had gone off with Justin to bicycle in the Atlas mountains in Morocco.)

We had not really been on holiday before; so this was uncharted territory. I found a newspaper in the bunkhouse left by one of the course members, and ran my eyes down the holiday section. 'Turkey, the blue Aegean' – that might be nice. In no time I had phoned the man in London and booked for the three of us, and John's father Reg, to stay in a villa close to the sea with a car thrown in at no extra cost. It was an end-of-season bargain. John came on sufferance – he hates holidays – but I felt we had worked so hard that we now all needed to relax together. Also I wanted to get Elizabeth more confident in the water, and the warm, blue, clear Aegean surely would be perfect.

We soon realised why our charter trip was so cheap! We had to fly from Gatwick in the middle of the night, and then had a six-hour coach trip to our destination, finally reaching the villa in the late afternoon. 'Yes, you will be tired, but just go and jump into the Aegean and then you will feel good again,' the Turkish holiday salesman had advised when I queried the length of travelling time, and this is just what we did, with Elizabeth squawking in delight as the silky waves rippled and broke in a warm dazzle along the shore, only steps from our new home. 'Me *like* dis.'

We had though, nearly failed to get there. On our arrival at Izmir Airport, feeling less than crisp at that no-man's-time in the middle of the night, the passport control had queried Elizabeth's green Peruvian passport. She and I were taken to a back room. A severe portrait of the President stared down at us; an even more severe official sat behind a desk; and by the door stood an expressionless soldier armed with an automatic rifle. At this point I thought the best thing that could happen would be for us to be sent back to Britain on the next plane. Elizabeth, however, sussed out the situation. While I tried to explain in German, the only language we could both speak, that we had planned to stay for two weeks in their beautiful country, she charmingly tilted her head to one side and peeped through her dark eyelashes at the stony official. The official winked at Elizabeth; she smiled coyly at him; a visa was issued.

My mind went back to another customs post, years before on the border between Chile and Argentina. Whilst we had been making our attempt to cross the Gran Campo Nevado, regulations had been enforced obliging all visitors to Chile to exchange a certain amount of money each day into Chilean currency, which could not be changed back. By then we had been away for six weeks, there were four of us, and we were going to have to change a very large sum of money which we did not have. Our only hope was to get out of the country fast. The airport was out of the question – they would probably have our names on some list. We hired a taxi and set off for the border post many miles to the north, not quite knowing how we were to play this one. The Communist regime was hardly going to be lenient towards four capitalist foreigners. If we could not pay, it would probably be jail, and for a long time.

As we drew up outside the lonely windswept dusty frontier post, through one window we could see a swarthy man ferociously exercising with a chest expander. In the other room two younger soldiers were sitting picking their teeth with their bayonets waiting for the time to pass. 'You're going to have to distract him, Marie Christine, while we get the passports stamped,' John said sternly, pointing to the muscle man who was continuing to flex his torso. I quickly brushed my hair, pinched my cheeks and straightening my short skirt hopped out of the taxi. I insinuated myself into his office and I gazed admiringly at his bare chest. He fell for the bait. He puffed up with pride, as we talked about his fine muscles, which I was invited to feel. I wondered how long I would have to distract him: his dark Latin eyes were narrowing with lust as he looked at me, and his hands were already stroking my legs. Then, at last, the taxi horn sounded. I swung off his desk and in a trice I was out of the office shouting, 'Ciao!' In a cloud of dust we roared off across the border into Argentina with the passports stamped.

'You needn't have gone that far, Marie Christine,' John severely reprimanded me.

The holiday in Turkey was a success. We made great progress with conversation: so much was new and exciting that Elizabeth bubbled over with delight and the words tumbled forth. We had brought some schoolwork, and at odd times we would have a go at the sums and reading. Elizabeth was keen, but I felt she was floundering around in a great fog brought on by a lack of understanding. Often she was unable to ask a question, and, even if she could, often we could not help her understand the answer. I knew in time we would win through, but in those early days we also knew we had a very long way to go. She had brought out a school reading book, a Peter and Jane type of reader, which I remembered so well from when I taught Bec on our sailing voyage down to the Cape Verde Islands. This one was called *The Party*. In nice big lettering it told the story of a smug-looking girl and a boy going to the party of a rather spoilt little girl called Susan, and how they played Hunt the Thimble and ate a big tea and then went back home and wrote thank-you letters.

This book filled me with a profound sense of gloom. Had we brought Elizabeth from her vivid jungle life to this kind of mumsy bourgeois existence? She did not like it much either, and pointed out rather scornfully that in the picture the boy actually was wearing shorts when the story said trousers. Still we struggled over and over with it. I was so keen for her to learn to read and be in possession of that most precious key to acquiring knowledge.

A year or so later I would find the book at the bottom of a pile in her bedroom. 'Come and have a look at this,' I called to her. She rattled through the story and we laughed together, remembering how difficult it had seemed. 'Lots of things are like that to start with,' I reassured her. 'You just have to have faith and work away, and then suddenly it all falls into place.' It was difficult for her, having lost at least three years of school, always behind the others in her form, to have much belief in herself; we had to build on every success.

Our two weeks in Turkey went in a flash. We returned home restored and Elizabeth went back to school armed with a bit more self-confidence – but still there was much that frightened her. That autumn, walking through our birch and hazel wood, Elizabeth noticed that the wonderful Fly Agaric mushrooms were flopping over and disintegrating.

'They're dying, Isso,' I explained, as we stooped to examine them cautiously with a stick.

'Why dying, Mama?'

I tried to explain that everything lives for a certain time, and then dies – naturally. That is the order of things.

'Me see dying, me see knives, me no want to die, me no want to hurt.'

Shocked, I realised this eight-year-old only knew of violent, premature death. She would have heard much talk of her father's brutal murder. She would have seen the bloodied trousers of her uncle thrown down before her grandmother, with the words, 'Here is your son,' as explanation. She would have heard the sobbing, and felt the grief, and been frightened – very frightened. Now at last she was able to talk a little of her horror, and I tried to explain that she and I and Danny and Rebeeka would probably live for a very long time and then, when the time came, we would probably die peacefully in our beds. One day we would just not wake up. Her wise eyes looked at me unconvinced.

By now, many of her fears and anxieties in Peru had been replaced by other, alternative terrors that we could not really understand. For example, Elizabeth had decided that to be happy and at ease at school she must force herself to conform to a pattern of behaviour which never deviated nor caused comment.

She was now able to do her journey to the bus almost on her own, while I went for my morning run. I would leave the house a little later, catching up with her along the track, turning to return at the tarmac and meet her again on my homeward trot. Each meeting we could have a quick chat, a kiss, and lots of waving and I would know she was not going to miss the bus. One gloomy Monday morning, I reached the top of the quarter-mile uphill climb. Once on the saddle, hot and with rasping breath, I looked into the distance to try and spot Elizabeth, who must be well on her way to the place where she keeps her smart black button shoes in a plastic bag under one of the cars at the start of the road. I saw her straight away, her black duffle coat showing up against the winter colours of bitter orange and the grey of the rock. What was she doing? She seemed to be standing below the wooden footbridge by the Crocach Burn. My mind raced as I sped towards her down Gentle's Brae. I did not want to alarm her, but we all knew, she included, how important it was not to keep Janelma, the bus lady, waiting.

'What is it, darling?' I called breathlessly as I reached the bridge. The water was rushing through and down the rocks, and I could not hear her answer until I was over and standing beside her.

'I fell, coming down the waterfall. My skirt OK now, but my shorts muddy, Mama. Please wash them, please hurry,' she wailed, anxious about the time and the bus. But most of all she was anxious about her muddy shorts.

It was cold, the snow low on the mountains. I put my gloves on the ground for her to stand on, took off her boots, and from under her grey skirt pulled down the white cotton shorts. I soon rinsed the two muddy patches out of the material in the rushing torrent of the icy stream. 'Could we not put these in your school bag? You could dry them on a radiator, or hang them on your hook where your coat goes.'

'No!' she was adamant. 'I put them on now, no matter, they dry on me.' I did my best wringing them and squeezing them with a dry hanky, but they were wet and so very cold. However horrible and miserable it was to put on these shorts, to Elizabeth it was a hundred times better than arriving at school and doing something different, something that would cause comment. She got to the bus just on time, wearing her cold damp shorts under her grey skirt but feeling happy because she would be ready for gym in the afternoon just like the others in the class already wearing their shorts.

These insecurities would ease in time as her confidence grew; of that I was sure. Were any of us without fears at school? They would pass and we should be patient and not dismiss them, for they were real enough to her.

Fate had set this child a great challenge. First, in three months of coming out of the jungle she had had to learn to adapt to life in the suburbs of Lima. The Asheshovs who looked after her spoke Spanish and English and she spoke only Quechua, so right from that moment she was isolated from conversation and in a sense gagged, but with her natural intuition she observed and copied how she must behave if she was to be like them. Now she was here in Scotland having to behave in yet another way, if she wanted to conform.

Perhaps some of the wish to conform and melt into the crowd springs from how one is treated by one's peers at an early age. Children can be very cruel to one another. Maybe we will never know much about the first six years of Elizabeth's life. But she came to us so bravely with such a positive spirit that I was surprised that often when she first met other children, even small toddlers, Elizabeth was terrified. She would grip my hand and try and hide behind me. To be noticed by an adult was acceptable, in fact sometimes a game, but she did not want to be seen by the child.

I wondered about that initial fear of children. (The children she knows she gets on well with, for she is fun to be with and laughs and is merry.) Perhaps being called 'La Gringita' (the little white girl) in Accobamba might have had something to do with it. Not really having love from her mother and only occasionally seeing her father, who would be like a distant uncle riding through and giving her presents, would not help build her confidence. Anyway, whatever we guessed at, we would never know for certain. It had happened, the scars had formed, and it was for us, for me, to help her forward.

The days were shortening fast, gales and rain lashing us as we sped in and out along the lonely track. Summer and the swimming faded from our thoughts. The geese had flown, great skeins honking across the storm grey sky heading south. Elizabeth had been with us now for over a year. John and I were viewing the impending adoption court hearing with trepidation: what if the sheriff did not find in our favour? I felt sick with dread at the thought of Elizabeth being taken away from us.

We expected the hearing to be scheduled sometime before Christmas, and our solicitors were coping valiantly with one or two anomalies in our case – we could not produce some of the documents required: a death certificate for Elizabeth's father; a medical certificate on Elizabeth's mother's condition. There were absolutely no doctors within tens of miles of the Apurimac Valley now that the terrorists were waging their war. Letters were written, translated into Spanish by a schoolteacher in Inverness, and then sent out to Peru. Miraculously, replies to the questions in our letters started to come back from people, in particular Padre Santiago Echeverria, the saintly Spanish Dominican who was one of the few priests brave enough to venture into this area to administer to his people. He had baptised Elizabeth on 22 September 1984 in Accobamba when she was five years old. He had also measured and weighed her when she was brought out of the jungle with Nick Asheshov a year and a bit later. We hoped that the information held in his letters would satisfy the authorities.

On 8 December we heard that we must present ourselves – John, me, Bec and Elizabeth – at the Sheriff Court House in Dornoch on 15 December at 2.45 p.m. Almost the next day, as if on cue, Elizabeth went down with mumps – 'bumps' she quite logically called it. First on one side, then the other, her face swelled up like a balloon. Mercifully she did not feel too ill. With the case coming up in a week's time, I rang the doctor.

'She should be fine, but you must keep her warm,' he said.

I rang the solicitor to warn him. He agreed we must attend if at all possible. So Elizabeth was wrapped up like a Russian doll with a bright red scarf swathing her neck and cheeks.

The day was freezing. We set off in the Land Rover with the back chock-a-block with 150 boxes of smoked salmon, the last load for Christmas posting. I had warned the obliging postmaster at Lairg post office that we would be dropping them off there, and that we could not delay and be late for our important appointment on the east coast. 'Be careful how you go. The road is like a bottle,' he cautioned me in his lilting voice.

Elizabeth was squeezed in beside me. 'You meaty, Mama,' she admonished me as we tried to make space for John to change gear. We all laughed; this was a different way of being called fat. I held her close, wondering about the unthinkable. What would happen if the adoption did not go in our favour? When would she be taken away? Would she go to a home? Would she be sent back to Peru? Bec was as anxious as we were. She and Justin were following us in her car, and I could see in the side mirror that she was biting her lip, a sure sign of anxiety in Bec.

The postmaster was right: the single-track road was 'like a bottle'. Luckily we did not meet much oncoming traffic. On the approach to Lairg, our nearest railhead and fifty miles from Ardmore, we stopped and bought fish and chips. Elizabeth, never off her food, whether she has mumps or her whole future hangs in the balance, ate hers with her usual gusto, but I removed the fatty batter on the fish; we did not want her being sick. We unloaded the beautiful boxes of salmon which had kept me, Bec and Ada busy smoking all November and December – I was not sorry to see the back of them – and sped onward towards Dornoch, the Royal Burgh and County Town of Sutherland, thirty miles away on the east coast overlooking the North Sea towards Norway.

If it had been cold at Ardmore, here it was Arctic. The wind howled in straight from Siberia, and the wide streets were nearly empty save for a few hardy Christmas shoppers muffled up and hurrying to get their shopping done. We were in good time. John stopped outside an Italian ice-cream shop – he could never resist ice-cream even on a day like today.

'Come on, John,' I urged, thinking that the time might pass more quickly if we were waiting at the court, rather than sitting in this out-of-season parlour.

We parked outside the austerely impressive court; opposite stood the ancient cathedral. Justin hopped into the Land Rover. He was going to the butcher to pick up the eight Ardmore sheep which had been brought here a few days ago. They were now slaughtered and butchered, and we would take them back home in parcels and put them into our ten-ton cold store. I wondered, as we walked into the building, if we would return to Ardmore later that day in the same state as our sheep. Once again I felt caught up in a life-changing experience which was quite out of my control. Usually it is possible to rationalise if events do not turn out right – the passing of an exam, or a driving test – this was far worse. The outcome of this case was now more important to me than life itself.

Our kindly solicitor was waiting in the building. Our steps echoed as we walked up the stairs, and we were ushered into an impersonal waiting room, where there were magazines and a gas stove spluttering out some heat. Elizabeth wanted to pee so we went to find the Ladies, and I was struck by the sight of her little face, lopsided with the swelling. Who would take care of her, love her, comfort her if she was taken now? No, I must not allow myself to think like this.

As we came out there was a commotion: we were being called. The sheriff had arrived, he wanted to see us as a family. I held Elizabeth's hand, painfully aware of the importance of first impressions. He fired a few questions at us and asked Elizabeth if she was happy – she did not know what he was talking about. Then Bec and Elizabeth were sent to wait in the jury room whilst John, myself and our solicitor were led like those Ardmore sheep into the sheriff's chambers off the main court.

The heavy door was shut, and I looked round the room. There were a number of officials there who would be privy to this hearing. This was the last hurdle in our long journey, and I felt oddly upset that strangers should intrude – I hoped they had the integrity not to gossip. Then the sheriff, his thick white hair framing a rather red bucolic face, began to speak.

Half-an-hour later we left the room, and found the two girls, one fair, one dark, sitting close together in the gloomy jury room. Bec's sweet face looked anxiously up at us.

'Well . . .?' she asked.

'Here's your new sister,' I answered, and tears of joy began to flow as we all hugged each other.

Elizabeth Berg Huaman Ridgway was ours for ever and ever. The threads had come at last together, our destinies interwoven.

Epilogue

Hailstones like horses' hooves rattled on the roof sufficiently to disturb John and me from our deep slumber. We had got to bed late after an auspicious evening. For the first time in eleven years we had gone next door and eaten our supper in the kitchen we had known so well in our early years at Ardmore. This time we found no piles of letters to be answered, no heaps of brochures, no envelopes spilling everywhere and covering every flat surface. And the hiss of the Tilley and its scent of paraffin were gone too. Instead there were two electric lights hanging down from the low ceiling, their shades directing circles of bright light down on to the sink and on to the kitchen table in front of the curtained window. The table was set with sparkling glass and chinese rose plates.

'Mum, how should I cook these mussels?' Bec stood before me; she was tall, her soft blonde hair tied loosely at the nape of her neck, and many tiny buttons fastened the front of her white embroidered blouse which was carefully tucked into a short woollen raspberry coloured skirt. Her long slim runner's legs ended not in running shoes, for a change, but in shoes of softest grey suede, extravagantly finished with a bow.

'Some garlic.' I smiled. 'Add a touch of tomato puree and a splash of wine . . . Let's put the lid on and leave them until they start to open.'

I picked up the glass of wine Bec had just poured me – this was a party to celebrate lots of things.

'Come and see the other room. Justin has got a really good fire going.' The door from the kitchen into the hall still squeaked, and the handle held its catch that moment longer than you expected. The tiny hall still felt the same too: the uneven third step up the narrow staircase, and the whirl of a pattern I would absentmindedly trace with my finger whilst on the telephone, was still visible in spite of eleven years of extra paint.

'Mama, Mama, you come sit here.' Elizabeth had made herself quite at home in front of the big fire. She had already spent a night here with her big sister, and she was ready to boss me, as I hesitated at the door before coming into the familiar room to join John and Justin, who were deep in discussion over mussel rafts. Low table lamps shed a soft light on the few decorations that Bec and Justin had arranged to transform this room. They had flung wine-coloured Peruvian ponchos on the worn armchairs and sofa; rugs brought back from distant trips brightened the old tobacco carpet. The carved mantelpiece above Justin's glowing fire held an array of photographs and pictures, a Winslow Homer print of a sailing boat slatting on a tropic calm, matched a stunning photo of *English Rose VI*, the ketch in which we had sailed around the world.

'Come on, Mama.' Elizabeth sounded as imperious as ever. I picked my way over to the young girl, sat close to her and, shaking off my bright red best high heels, tucked my feet under my skirt. While the mussels steamed gently in their juices in the kitchen, the four adults looked at each other sitting in this familiar room and each wondered silently how we had all got to this point. Elizabeth, now aged eleven, was absorbed with yet another brilliantly coloured drawing. She never sat and did nothing – it was as though her ancestors were watching, for Quechua women would never be with idle hands; they would use every moment they could to spin yarn with which to weave their intricate fine cloth.

Bec, now grown up, had moved back to the house where she had spent all her childhood. This was the house she remembered as home; but when she was thirteen, the roof leaked so badly we had to move next door. Like John, she had had to be dragged from it into the rebuilt croft house, and then after it was re-roofed we never moved back.

Part of me too was left in this house. This was the house where Granny Ross had been born a hundred years before; the house where we had entertained so many people over the first few years of the school; the house where we had worried and triumphed; the house where we had wept and laughed. It meant so much to Bec. The memories were strong for me but for Bec they ran right through her being.

'That's where I used to sit and draw pictures when I was even smaller than you,' she told Elizabeth, pointing to the small deep window recess. Getting up, she said, 'Come on, let's go and eat the mussels. They must be ready now.'

John and I were so happy Bec had wanted to stay on at Ardmore.

We tried to give her every opportunity to go after that first few months when Elizabeth had been new to us, and Bec had played such an important role as big sister, but happily for us Bec seemed to love Ardmore as much as we did.

'Well, if you really want to stay here instead of going on to university,' John had told Bec, 'you must start by doing a season as an instructor.' He was determined to set her plenty of challenges to increase her confidence and ability. 'Stretch, don't cruise,' was often muttered. So Bec became one of the boys, and perhaps because her father was John she tried even harder. She is naturally shy and soft-spoken, but it was not long before she developed the confidence to handle groups of all ages in most situations. She did one season, then another and another. She became fit and good at climbing, sailing, canoeing and particularly teaching. She learnt to shear and to cook sheep, to type and to change fish nets. During July and August, she would run the young people's courses with a quiet authoritative manner. During the winter she would turn her hand to anything from smoking fish to canoeing round Cape Horn.

'It's lucky I wasn't a boy, Mum,' she said one day to me, as we were just off to run round the loch. 'If Dad's son hadn't been keen on the outdoors it would have been an awful disappointment. Perhaps, I'm an unexpected bonus.'

Justin had kept in touch since our journey to Peru, and he and Bec together ran in the 1988 New York Marathon – John was thrilled. Justin had a sore leg and doubted if he would complete the course. He did, however, and the following year he and Ed Ley-Wilson completed a mammoth run, two thousand miles across the Himalayas, averaging twenty-three miles per day for eighty-six days. They raised money for Intermediate Technology. Justin had 'won his spurs'.

During the winter of 1989 John returned to Peru to try and trace Olaf and Virgil – he had not forgotten the promise he had made to the Bergs in Norway. He took Bec with him.

This time I stayed at home with Elizabeth. She could not waste one moment of catching up with her precious education, and needed all the love and security I could give her. But it was once more, with the familiar heavy heart, that we said goodbye. I knew only too well the danger and the risks. Bec was every bit as determined to go as I had been all those years before, and once again my mother mounted a campaign with the rest of the family to dissuade her. History repeated itself twenty years on, except it was not me this time: it was my twenty-one-year-old pretty blonde daughter. I knew it was a waste of time. She had made up her mind.

Elizabeth and I waved goodbye from our home at the top of the hill at Ardmore and watched as the boat carrying them disappeared behind the island on the way to where the road begins at the end of the loch. I tried to banish thoughts of what could happen from my mind. It was easy in daytime but I would be woken up at night by vivid dreams of ambushes with Bec calling out to me in terror. We had always been close, and I wondered if these were dreams. Was this really happening? Was she in trouble? Why had I not stopped her from going? Elizabeth's warm little body snuggled beside me in our bed reminded me of why Rebecca had wanted to go with her father: it was so she could help find more pieces of the Berg jigsaw in Peru. In time she knew her Quechua sister would want to know what had befallen her father's family.

It was a long six weeks for Elizabeth and me, hearing nothing. Knowing they would be in a situation of great personal danger made the waiting as hard as it had ever been. Since our time in Peru three years before, the *Senderos* had strengthened their grip on the country and thousands of innocents had perished.

But John and Bec did survive and the story they brought back chilled me. They had taken one of the instructors with them, Malcolm from Buckie, whose gentle voice and smile belied his strength. In Lima they were joined by Igor Asheshov. Being a Peruvian and understanding the customs, Igor was an invaluable ally.

Once across the Andes, they hired guides to take them through a huge area of terrorist-controlled deep jungle. This time they had gone armed – the terrorists were everywhere and once again there was every chance of an ambush. The old paths were overgrown and the jungle too thick for mules, but after several days of cutting their way through the undergrowth they were finally led to Olaf.

He was gaunt, tough and haughtily proud, and appeared totally in charge of the situation. 'I willed you to come. Now you are here. It shows the power of the mind,' he told John. 'I live only to avenge my brothers' deaths. They would expect that of me.' Olaf and his band of dispossessed people were united in their aim to destroy the *Senderos*.

He told John of the attack on Osambre: of Elvin's brutal death; of how the gun the terrorists had held to his own head had not gone off, and how, after shooting two terrorists dead he had escaped; of how his other brother, Virgil, had been dynamited while fighting for his own life; badly wounded, he too had managed to escape into the jungle, where he had wandered half-conscious and without food for two weeks before being found. Olaf and the Indians had cared for him, but he died a few months later from his injuries. He had gone quite mad from the horror. It was a terrible story.

Olaf told John he had no home. For five years he had been sleeping in the trees, a different place each night, so no one on earth would ever know exactly where he was. By day, Olaf and his band panned for gold among the shifting gravel banks in the deep Apurimac Gorge; ever alert for attack they were armed with grenades and rifles. The terrorists left messages in the trees, urging them to join them, but Olaf's only request from John was for a cyanide pill he could take if they ever caught him.

It mattered a lot to Olaf that John had come, and he went to great trouble, explaining the sad history of the Bergs in South America, so John could one day tell Elizabeth.

Looking across the table at my younger daughter, I could not help but think how bonny she looked. Shiny long black plaits hanging over each shoulder which she now insisted on doing herself, made her look very Quechua. She had picked out a bright blue jumper to wear under a smart navy skirt which was held up by two embroidered braces. Her round face glowed as she butted into the conversation. The words still tumbled out a bit mixed up, but she was quick to understand everything. Her reading and sums were coming on apace. It would soon be time for her to go, as Bec had, away to boarding school, for there is no secondary education on the west coast. We had visited a lovely school, a castle, in Midlothian, close to Yvonne, my eldest sister. Elizabeth was excited at the prospect of going. Her fear of other children was fading fast as her confidence increased. But, like any mother, I dreaded the day she would have to go.

My mind went back to her other family in Peru and how they must have felt saying goodbye to Elizabeth. I knew they would be happy if they could see her here now looking so bright, and I thought of the letter John had brought back from his and Bec's visit to Peru. I kept it carefully in the top drawer of our Irish

mahogany chest. Sometimes I would take it from beneath the
folded lavender scented hankies and read the translation:

29 January 1989

Dear Marie Christine
    We are safe and well in Accobamba, and we send you our
greetings. We now live in our own house, unlike before, when
we had to rent one.
    We are very happy that Elizabeth is now under your care.
We thank you for having our grand-daughter, and Josephina
also says she is well and healthy. And Leocadia also sends her
greetings to Marie Christine.
    We should like you to treat Elizabeth as your very child,
for which we will remain forever grateful.
    For this visit which John has made on behalf of you all,
and for the presents he has brought, we are very thankful.
    We are sending a *manta* for you all, so you can carry things
around in it. This was made by Josephina, and it has taken her
a long time to weave this fine thread. The dark colour comes
from a dye made from the leaves of a tree outside the house.
    We also send you a present of some roasted coffee beans
which were grown by Juan. Unfortunately, the coffee season
has long been over, or we would send you much more. The
coffee trees are in flower at this time.
    We are sorry we don't know how to sign this letter.
    Juan Huaman Chavez
    Josephina
    Leocadia

'To the new house, Bec and Justin.' John lifted his glass and we all in
turn clinked ours together, Elizabeth's orange slurping slightly in
her eagerness not to miss drinking the toast.
    Then turning to his dark-haired younger daughter, he said, 'To
the new school, Elizabeth.' She beamed broadly. 'Perhaps they will
teach you to speak Spanish there.'
    'I come on the next trip, Danny?' Elizabeth looked up at her
father. 'I want to go on a horse with Mama and Rebeeka, and you,
Danny – we'll take lots of presents for my real mummy and my
granny.' She looked at me. 'A skirt? A dress? What you think

Mama?' 'Both,' I nodded, thinking of how she used to shut out that part of her life.

'Yes, we'll go, Elizabeth – one day,' John said quietly. 'I promise you.'

The hail soon stopped, and it was quiet again. I could hear John's steady breathing, briefly at peace from his worries. Pictures of my two daughters danced in my head. The struggle to live here would continue – for as long as we all wished. Elizabeth. Rebecca. What would they do? Would they stay on here on this remote and beautiful peninsula on the outer edge of the world? Over the years we had been able to breath life into Ardmore – perhaps now at last it was: a place for a woman.